I0815122

THE AMERICAN REVOLUTION AT 250

The Revolutionary Age

Francis D. Cogliano, Christa Breault Dierksheide, Eliga H. Gould, and Patrick Griffin, Editors

The American Revolution at 250

Twenty-Four Historians Reflect on the Founding

Edited by Francis D. Cogliano

University of Virginia Press
Charlottesville and London

The University of Virginia Press is situated on the traditional lands of the Monacan Nation, and the Commonwealth of Virginia was and is home to many other Indigenous people. We pay our respect to all of them, past and present. We also honor the enslaved African and African American people who built the University of Virginia, and we recognize their descendants. We commit to fostering voices from these communities through our publications and to deepening our collective understanding of their histories and contributions.

University of Virginia Press

Printed in the United States of America on acid-free paper

First published 2026

3 5 7 9 8 6 4 2

ISBN 978-0-8139-5462-2 (hardback)
ISBN 978-0-8139-5463-9 (ebook)

Library of Congress Cataloging-in-Publication Data is available for this title.

Cover design: David Drummond

For our students

CONTENTS

Introduction: 1776 and All That 1

Part One. Inherent Tensions

1776 13
Brendan McConville

Thomas Jefferson, Optimistic Visionary 23
Annette Gordon-Reed

Slavery and Hypocrisy: How the Founders Talked About America's Original Sin—and Why It Matters 33
Eliga H. Gould

Part Two. Race

Americans Are Beautiful: Race, Immigration, and the American Revolution 47
Christa Dierksheide and Nicholas Guyatt

Race, Fear, and Political Persuasion: The Problem of Slavery on the Eve of Revolution 61
Robert G. Parkinson

What Is the American Declaration of Independence at 250 to Me? 72
Marlene L. Daut

Hidden in Plain Sight: The George Rogers Clark Statue at the University of Virginia, 1921–2021 85
Allison Bigelow and Teresa R. Pollak

Part Three. Political Foundations

Original Intentions, Unintended Consequences 101
Peter S. Onuf

Appeal for a New Revolutionary Narrative: The Curious Tale of *The Crisis* 112
T. H. Breen

The Declaration of Independence, Institution Building, and the Orderly Transfer of Power in Revolutionary America 122
Rosemarie Zagarri

What Does the American Revolution Mean to Me? 137
John A. Ragosta

Embracing the Founders' Legacy 150
Lindsay M. Chervinsky

Part Four. Lived Experiences

The Presence and Absence of Religion in National Unity 163
Katherine Carté

Infectious Disease and the American Revolution 174
Woody Holton

Legacies of the Revolution's Domestic Warfare 183
Lauren Duval

The Citizen-Soldier Is Dead. Long Live the Citizen-Soldier. 194
Ricardo A. Herrera

Part Five. Remembering the Revolution

The Irrelevance of the American Revolution 209
Michael A. McDonnell

The Ethos of Revolution: Past and Present 220
Joanne B. Freeman

The American Revolution in France (1976–2026) 231
Bertrand Van Ruymbeke

Echoes of the Revolutionary Era 241
Andrew M. Davenport

Epilogue: A Case for Redemption 251
PATRICK GRIFFIN

Acknowledgments 257

Notes on Contributors 259

Index 263

THE AMERICAN REVOLUTION AT 250

Introduction

1776 and All That

★

Some of the readers of this book might remember "Bicentennial Minutes," which were broadcast on CBS, sponsored by the Shell Oil Company, during prime time between 1974 and 1976. Others may recall Operation Sail and the visit of the tall ships to the East Coast during the summer of 1976. I went to see the tall ships when they arrived in Boston Harbor on July 10. For me, growing up in eastern Massachusetts in the 1970s, the memory of the American Revolution was ever present. Our next-door neighbor, Mr. Burns, was a Minuteman. Well, actually, he was an airline pilot who participated in reenactments on weekends. It was Mr. Burns who, when I told him that Esther Forbes's *Johnny Tremain* was my favorite book, encouraged me to read the novels of Kenneth Roberts. Overall, the bicentennial was characterized by a lot of what the radical historian Jesse Lemisch described as "bicentennial schlock," patriotic-themed ephemera—I have a distinct memory of McDonald's placemats that illustrated key moments from the War of Independence.[1] Schlock it might have been, but I'm quite certain that exposure to this material stimulated my interest in the period.

I started graduate school at the end of the 1980s, just as a decades-long debate between historians over whether ideas or material interests motivated the American revolutionaries was petering out. Then, in 1992, I went to the United Kingdom and have now spent more than three decades researching and teaching about the American Revolution outside of the United States. My time in the UK coincided with the Atlantic (latter global) turn in early American history. The stories historians tell about the Revolution now include the Caribbean, Europe, West Africa, and

South Asia, as well the whole of the North American continent, not just the Atlantic Coast. As I write this, I can see Edinburgh Castle. In 1780 an American sailor imprisoned in the fortress carved an American flag on one of the castle's inner doors in defiance of his imperial captors.

This introduction's subtitle is a nod to *1066 and All That,* by W. C. Sellar and R. J. Yeatman, which presented an irreverent look at British, especially English, history as indicated by their subtitle, *A Memorable History of England, Comprising All the Parts You Can Remember, Including 103 Good Things, 5 Bad Kings and 2 Genuine Dates.* Originally appearing in the satirical magazine *Punch* and first published as a book in 1930, it challenged traditional patriotic pieties that often characterized accounts of the history of their nation.[2] Almost nine hundred years after the event, Sellar and Yeatman used 1066, a foundational date in the history of England, as jumping-off point to offer a critical (and amusing) view of English history and the rise of the British Empire in the wake of the First World War. My subtitle acknowledges the value of challenging received historical pieties while reminding readers that, in global historical terms, the United States remains, at a mere 250 years, a relatively young nation. Perhaps it's too soon for Americans to feel irreverent about their history, especially at a moment of intense political partisanship, social and ethnic conflict, and international tension. But it is worth marking this significant anniversary by asking what the founding of the nation means. That is the purpose of this volume.

My understanding of the American Revolution has been shaped by my study of the subject as well as my life experience. (After all, outside of the United States the American Revolution appears different than it does within the country. For one thing, non-Americans are not as invested in the meaning of the Revolution as US citizens are.) The same is true for the contributors to this volume. With the 250th anniversary of the adoption of the Declaration of Independence approaching, each of them, all experts on the period, grappled with a simple question: "What does the American Revolution mean to you?" Perhaps it will come as no surprise, given the diverse perspectives represented in this volume, that there is no single view on what the founding of the United States means to the experts who study it.

We historians are trained neither to write in the first person (and certainly not to write about ourselves) nor to explicitly address contemporary concerns. Yet historians are aware that, like all people, we're creatures of particular moments in time. Certain broad themes do emerge, notably uncertainty about whether the principles of the Revolution bind Americans together and whether its legacy speaks to the experiences of all Americans. We are aware that there are numerous local, state, and national efforts—both public and private—to mark the 250th anniversary of the Declaration of Independence. Like the commentary in this volume, there is no single interpretation or message behind these events. We hope that readers will discover that among the people who study the late eighteenth century for a living, there are diverse voices and viewpoints over the founding of the United States, and we also hope that these viewpoints might inform readers' own thinking and discussions about the American Revolution in 2026 and beyond.

It might come as a comfort to know that we've been here before. The historian Michael Hattem has recently shown that the preparations for the celebration of the bicentennial in 1976 were characterized by partisanship, infighting, and confusion over messaging. Multiple agencies, public and private, as well as corporations, often with competing or contradictory aims, sought to lead (and profit from) the national and local efforts to celebrate the 200th anniversary of the Declaration of Independence. Hattem reminds us that while ours is an age of intense conflict at home and abroad, so too were the early 1970s. Racial strife, student unrest, Watergate and Richard Nixon's resignation, and the American defeat in Vietnam provided the important context for the rather chaotic planning for the bicentennial. There are more than a few echoes of 1976 to be found in 2026.[3]

While there are some similarities between our own time and the early 1970s, there are, where the American Revolution is concerned, telling differences as well. Hattem shows that conservatives, conscious of the Cold War struggle between capitalism and Marxism, embraced a patriotic interpretation of the Revolution in the 1970s, ignoring or downplaying internal divisions within the rebellious colonies-cum-states. On the left, by contrast, historically marginalized groups in the United States emphasized their contributions to the American Revolution, challenging the perceived whiteness of the dominant narrative while calling attention to contemporary inequality and injustice[4] What is striking is that, in 1976, both the Left and the Right felt that they had a stake in the American Revolution. Five decades later that no longer seems to be the case.

Since the 1990s, with the end of the Cold War and advent of the Global War on Terrorism, and the rise of new technologies, including potent social media platforms, the American Revolution seems to have become a casualty in the (seemingly) endless "culture wars" that are now a common feature of American life and politics: Today the Right has co-opted a simplistic version of the Revolution, which is much less sophisticated than it was during the bicentennial, and the Left has largely abandoned the Revolution altogether.[5]

Consider the 1619 Project, an initiative conceived and edited by the journalist Nikole Hannah-Jones and published by the *New York Times Magazine* in August 2019 to mark the 400th anniversary of the first documented arrival of enslaved Africans in British America. Hannah-Jones sought to center the African experience in American history. In an introductory essay she paid particular attention to the American Revolution and its origins to argue that the true founding of the country should be 1619 not 1776. Hannah-Jones argued that protecting slavery was one of the main motivations for some white Americans to declare independence from Britain in 1776. Gesturing toward Dunmore's Proclamation (which offered freedom to enslaved persons in Virginia who fled from rebel masters to fight for the British), she wrote, "Conveniently left out of our founding mythology is the fact that one of the primary reasons some of the colonists decided to declare their independence from Britain was because they wanted to protect the institution of slavery."[6]

Hannah-Jones's argument engendered significant discussion within universities, the media, and beyond.[7] Her achievement—and this point seems to have been missed by many of her critics—was not that her argument was original but that she reached a huge audience in making it. She synthesized a rich body of existing scholarship for a general audience. In so doing she helped to refocus the public debate over the Revolution and its legacy. The 1619 Project confirmed and accelerated the rejection of the American Revolution by many on the American left, a rejection that had been under way for a generation.

Meanwhile, on the right, the Revolution has been appropriated for partisan ends. In September 2020 President Donald J. Trump convened a "1776 Commission" partially in response to the 1619 Project, but also to the widespread protests after the murder of George Floyd in May of that year. In announcing the creation of the commission, which included no professional historians, Trump claimed that the unrest was caused by poor history education. "Left-wing rioting and mayhem are the direct result of decades of left-wing indoctrination in our schools," Trump said at the National Archives as he launched the commission.

Two months earlier, Trump had given a Fourth of July address at Mount Rushmore in South Dakota which anticipated the findings of the 1776 Commission. "Our nation is witnessing a merciless campaign to wipe out our history, defame our heroes, erase our values, and indoctrinate our children," Trump declared. "Angry mobs are trying to tear down statues of our Founders, deface our most sacred memorials, and unleash a wave of violent crime in our cities."[8]

According to Trump, those who sought to topple "the heroes of 1776" were enemies of "real" Americans. "Their goal is not a better America," he declared; "their goal is the end of America." Trump called on his supporters to defend the founding fathers: "We will never let them rip America's heroes from our monuments, or from our hearts. By tearing down Washington and Jefferson, these radicals would tear down the very heritage for which men gave their lives." When the commission issued its report in January 2021, it called for "patriotic education," focused on the American Revolution, to counter the radical anti-American version of the nation's history allegedly promulgated in US schools.[9] At the beginning of his second administration President Trump issued an executive order on January 29, 2025, reviving the 1776 Commission (which had been abolished by President Joe Biden). "The purpose of the 1776 Commission is to promote patriotic education," Trump declared, "as well as to advise and promote the work of the White House Task Force on Celebrating America's 250th Birthday ("Task Force 250") and the United States Semiquincentennial Commission in their efforts to provide a grand celebration worthy of the momentous occasion of the 250th anniversary of American Independence on July 4, 2026."[10]

The appropriation of the Revolution for partisan ends, and its reconfiguration along simplistic lines by those on the right that ignores much of the scholarship on the subject, has only accelerated its rejection by the Left. Two broad camps have emerged, summed up by the dates 1619 and 1776: one that is critical of the founding of the United States and skeptical about the motives and ideological claims of the revolutionaries; and another that diminishes or ignores the revolutionaries' faults and seeks to promote a triumphalist, celebratory account of the nation's founding.[11] Neither the 1619 Project nor the 1776 Commission caused the broader divergence between Left and Right over the Revolution. Rather they should be seen as expressions of tendencies that have developed and become increasingly pronounced since the end of the Cold War. They are evidence of the vast gulf between Left and Right over the meaning of the American Revolution. This gulf is different from what we saw in 1976.

ALTHOUGH "1619" and "1776" may be shorthand summaries for different interpretations of the American Revolution, they have deep historiographical roots. For most of the twentieth century historians of the Revolution fell into two broad camps: those who prioritized the ideas that animated the revolutionaries (as well as their imperial and loyalist opponents) viewing the American Revolution in ideological terms; and historians, who, by contrast, sought the motives behind the ideals of the Revolution. The latter built on the insights offered by social history to recover the experiences of marginalized groups and showed how political and economic power shaped the founding of the United States. During the bicentennial, people on the left and right drew on both traditions to shape their versions of the Revolution.

After the Cold War, historians of the United States were less interested in questions of ideology and class struggle (though these concerns never entirely disappeared) and increasingly focused on questions of race, identity, and geography. The result has been an efflorescence in scholarship on the American Revolution. We know much more about enslaved persons, Indigenous people, women, and the poor in the Age of Revolution than ever before. We've also expanded the geographic scope of the Revolution well beyond the thirteen colonies along the Atlantic littoral in North America. The American Revolution can no longer be confined to the stories of a few elite "founding fathers" in Virginia, Pennsylvania, and Massachusetts.[12]

Despite this surge in scholarship, some of the best of which has been produced by the contributors to this volume, the Revolution itself seems to have lost its relevance for many, both scholars within the academy and American citizens in general.[13] We are left with a paradox: We know more about the American Revolution than ever before yet, apart from a few popular studies of well-known figures (and a smash Broadway musical inspired by them), often produced by journalists, interest in the subject seems to be declining. The question our authors address—what does the American Revolution mean to you?—takes on particular urgency in such a context. The essays here largely fall into three categories, although the boundaries between them are not absolute. They emphasize ideas and ideology, questions of class and marginalization, or race and identity.

The American Revolution means different things to the scholars who have shared their thoughts in this volume—which makes it an exciting subject of study. This volume might be read as a primary source, a snapshot of the wide range of views among scholars about the meaning of the American Revolution. This diversity of perspectives offers readers a provocative spectrum of opinion which we hope might stimulate discussion during the semiquincentennial and beyond. For me, the American Revolution means several things. As a bloody and uncertain movement for national self-determination, the Revolution created the United States and "Americans" as a people.[14] The revolutionaries established a republican government: antimonarchical, with sovereignty derived from the people, in the new United States. In so doing they transformed themselves from colonial subjects into self-governing citizens, a truly revolutionary transformation. We know that the revolutionaries had a narrow conception of who merited inclusion in their new political community and that race, class, and gender imposed barriers to citizenship. In 1776 "the people" were a much smaller political community than they are today. Not all of the residents of the new republic enjoyed the fruits of the revolutionary struggle. The subsequent history of the United States might be seen as an imperfect and incomplete struggle to expand and extend rights to all Americans and fulfill the promise of the Declaration of Independence. Nonetheless, the Revolution provides Americans with the language to define themselves and their relationships with each other. Without it, the nation lacks a common identity and a viable political community. This, to me, is its greatest legacy. We, contemporary US citizens, may not be as interested in the American Revolution as at other points in our history, but it continues to define who we are.

Moreover, having lived outside of the United States in the immediate aftermath of the Cold War when the United States (briefly) enjoyed a hegemonic global position, as well as for the 9/11 attacks and the subsequent Global War on Terrorism and the current wars in Europe and the Middle East, I am daily reminded of the degree to which American power continues to shape the modern world. The rhetoric frequently used to justify the deployment or withholding of US force, usually the defense of liberty and democracy, can be traced directly to the American Revolution.[15] From my perspective, the American Revolution matters because it continues to shape the world in which we live.

Just because the Left and Right at the moment seem to have different levels of commitment to the American Revolution—and different conceptions of its meaning and legacy—doesn't mean that these positions will remain fixed. History is a never-ending colloquy between the past and present, shaped by the questions that preoccupy us in our time. Our preoccupations and concerns will change in the future, and we (and our successors) will ask different questions of the past, yielding new insights. Indeed, renewed attention to the era of the American Revolution in 2026 and beyond may be the catalyst for such a change. We may well be on the cusp of a new burst of scholarship and public interest in the founding of the United States, and this volume, in a small way, might be a harbinger of that change. I, for one, am looking forward to seeing what this century's equivalents of "Bicentennial Minutes" and McDonald's placemats might yield among the future historians presently in elementary school.

Notes

1. Michael D. Hattem, *The Memory of '76: The Revolution in American History* (Yale University Press, 2024), 245–46.
2. W. C. Sellar and R. J. Yeatman, *1066 and All That: A Memorable History of England, Comprising All the Parts You Can Remember, Including 103 Good Things, 5 Bad Kings and 2 Genuine Dates* (Methuen, 1930).
3. Hattem, *Memory of '76*, chap. 21.
4. Hattem, *Memory of '76*, 237.
5. See Hattem, *Memory of '76*, chap. 24.
6. Nikole Hannah-Jones, "1619 Project: Introduction," *New York Times Magazine*, August 14, 2019.
7. After several historians, including Gordon Wood, criticized this claim, the *Times* eventually altered the wording. See "We Respond to the Historians Who Critiqued the 1619 Project," *New York Times Magazine*, December 20, 2019; and Jake Silverstein, "An Update to the 1619 Project," *New York Times Magazine*, March 11, 2020. The debate over the wording of that passage justified some critics, especially those on the right of the political spectrum, in dismissing the entire project. The project was published as a book in 2021: Nikole Hannah-Jones, ed., *The 1619 Project: A New American Origin Story* (Viking, 2021).
8. "Remarks by President Trump at South Dakota's 2020 Mount Rushmore Fireworks Celebration Keystone, South Dakota, July 4, 2020," https://trumpwhitehouse.archives.gov/briefings-statements/remarks-president-trump-south-dakotas-2020-mount-rushmore-fireworks-celebration-keystone-south-dakota/.
9. The President's Advisory 1776 Commission, *The 1776 Report*, January 18, 2021, https://trumpwhitehouse.archives.gov/wp-content/uploads/2021/01/The

-Presidents-Advisory-1776-Commission-Final-Report.pdf; Michael Crowley and Jennifer Schuessler, "Trump's 1776 Commission Critiques Liberalism in Report Derided by Historians," *New York Times*, January 18, 2021.

10. Donald J. Trump, "Ending Radical Indoctrination in K-12 Schooling," Executive Order, January 29, 2025, https://www.whitehouse.gov/presidential-actions/2025/01/ending-radical-indoctrination-in-k-12-schooling/.

11. I am not equating the 1619 Project and the 1776 Commission's report. The former was based on (at least) two generations' worth of scholarship, and popularized an interpretation that is widely accepted among historians. The latter was a rather superficial, cursory statement that had little scholarship to support it.

12. See Michael A. McDonnell and David Waldstreicher, "Revolution in the *Quarterly?* A Historiographical Analysis," *William and Mary Quarterly* 74, no. 4 (2017): 633–66; and Trevor Burnard, *Writing Early America: From Empire to Revolution* (University of Virginia Press, 2023).

13. Michael D. Hattem, "Revolution Lost? Vast Early America, National History, and the American Revolution," *William and Mary Quarterly* 78, no. 2 (2021): 269–74.

14. I am aware that "Americans" is used, especially in non-Anglophone countries, to describe the peoples of North America, South America, and the Caribbean. I am using it here to describe the political community created by the American Revolution, that is, citizens of the United States, which is its common usage in the United States and many (but not all) Anglophone places.

15. I explored this in Francis D. Cogliano, *Emperor of Liberty: Thomas Jefferson's Foreign Policy* (Yale University Press, 2014), introduction; and Francis D. Cogliano, "The Lowest of the Diplomatic Tribe: Idealism, Realism, and the Perils of Presentism," *Passport: The Society for Historians and American Foreign Relations Review* 45, no. 3 (2015): 14–16.

PART ONE

Inherent Tensions

1776

BRENDAN MCCONVILLE

I INITIALLY FOUND the prompt for this essay to be something of a shock. Surely everyone knows the relevance of 1776 to the American nation and indeed its relevance to every person on this planet. American independence and the United States' rise to global dominance is one of the greatest stories of the last 250 years. And surely most Americans know something about the drama of the nation's birth. The mobs and the tarrings; Thomas Paine's *Common Sense;* the Declaration of Independence; the struggle of Washington's army to survive in the fall of 1776; the miracle victories at Trenton and Princeton that saved the Revolution; the emergence of new leaders who shaped the great experiment in self-governance that has defined Americans as a people; the mobilization that created a new political consciousness in the general population; and the efforts of tens of thousands of enslaved people to attempt to gain their freedom in one way or another. It seemed impossible to need to explain the importance of these events or justify their place in our civic history. With American independence, self-governance on republican principles became a central aspect of global political theory in a way that it simply was not before.

The relevance of 1776, however, has been largely forgotten in many parts of our society. A significant portion of students arrive at college with at best a vague sense of the American Revolution, early America, or indeed anything that happened before 1929. For those students who do know about the year of independence, indifference or even contempt is not an uncommon view. This is especially true of their views of the revolutionary leadership, who seem to be completely out of synch with the values and needs of our own time, especially as understood in the American academy.

The revolutionary leaders appear to many to have been strange men in strange garb wearing weird wigs who insisted on holding on to disturbing beliefs about society and government even as the Revolution engulfed them. And Jefferson . . . I mean, where to start? The Declaration's primary author is at best a walking set of contradictions, at worst a hypocrite and an exploiter of the cruelest type. Some young people see the founders and indeed the whole revolutionary generation as a burden to be borne rather than the creators of a legacy to be embraced. They make for good musicals but are anachronistic guides to our own troubled times.

Such views might be understood as expressing the fashionable disdain of youth magnified by the fact that we are living in a society undergoing rapid technological change. But these views are not limited to students. Elements within the American intellectual-political community have publicly attacked the values and attitudes born in 1776. They are repudiators of 1776. For progressives of both the neo-Marxist and identity politics types it has become obvious that the Revolution and what came with it are an impediment to what they consider a more perfect and equitable society. Books calling for the abandonment of the revolutionary legacy in part or whole written by pundits and academics are now appearing with regularity and being reviewed in the mainstream press.[1]

What is much more surprising is the intellectual challenge to the legacy of 1776 coming from the right. For Marxists and postmodernists and critical theorists, the American Revolution and the American nation as we have known it has always been a problem, not a solution. Their repudiation of it thus expresses an intellectual and political continuity. But until very recently, to be conservative in America was to be of 1776, and of the Constitution, to embrace the flag and to champion the America experiment that began with independence.

Something has clearly changed. Those now labeled "tradcons" want what they see as a traditional family structure tied to a formalized church-state order that will provide moral and spiritual direction to American society. Others, labeled "postliberal," believe the American Revolution and the liberal individualism it unleashed broke the bond between God and government in a manner that undermines the idea of ultimate truth itself. For those holding these positions, what is necessary is the abandonment of 1776 and its legacy of creative destruction, social atomization, and relentless upheaval. They advocate for replacing the American order that began in 1776 with a new church-state settlement.[2]

It thus seems that a significant percentage of the American intellectual community find that the Spirit of '76 has outlived its usefulness. Passively or actively these thinkers are advocating for a new American order based on new principles of some kind. For them the archaic values inherited from our long-ago Revolution need to be catalogued in the graveyard of failed systems among those other pasts that have run their course.

I BEG to differ. I think perhaps we have collectively been too eager to deny the relevance of 1776 to us today, too sure of our own superiority to listen to the revolutionary leaders' advice about society, human nature, and government, and too quick to disparage or simply ignore the national past that began in those desperate and idealistic days 250 years ago. The relevance of 1776 is wide and varied. It is the origin point of our national civic history. Key concepts in our contemporary political philosophy were first practically applied then. It provides a legacy of a unique type of utopianism whose success has been so wild that it no longer seems utopian at all but rather just normal. And the legacies of the year of independence do not simply come from those who supported independence. Those who resisted the Revolution, or tried to avoid taking sides, or saw it as an opportunity to escape enslavement speak in relevant ways to our tumultuous present.

The political relevance of 1776 is not tied to specific governing institutions. In fact, none of the revolutionary institutions or constitutions from 1776 have survived into our own time. All the state constitutions written at that time have been scrapped and rewritten repeatedly. The Declaration of Independence was of course not a constitution and offered no advice on political practices other than to acknowledge the independence of what had become an archipelago of independent republics on the North American coast. The entire Articles of Confederation government tacitly if not formally accepted in 1777 (it was not formally ratified until 1781) was gone by 1789, replaced by the constitutional order under which we still live. The committees of safety and correspondence, the wounded landscape left by relentless warfare between the British and American armies in New York and New Jersey, and in Georgia, Massachusetts, and the Carolinas, these too are now forgotten shadows in the collective mind of a nation that moves forward relentlessly. That we are in a time of rapid technological change only serves to intensify this historical amnesia.

The relevance of 1776 is conceptual and philosophical. It is about how the drive to independence led the revolutionary generation to think about government and society and themselves. In the United States, public political time begins in 1776. It is the beginning of American history, as opposed to British American or imperial or Anglo-American history. As such it anchors our public life and national self-perception. It is from then that we measure the development of our national values and practices and the American experiment's health. Such statements are seen in some quarters as problematic given the complexities and bitterness of our cultural politics in this moment. The denunciations of nationalism that have become commonplace only make it more so. But to deny this reality shades into irrationality. The historical is central to the fabric of coherence that holds our society together and holds its leaders accountable. Our national past begins then, in 1776, with independence.

Independence also led to the practical application of a host of philosophical concepts whose power extends to today. Popular sovereignty, contract theory, natural right and natural law, fear of arbitrary government, and the rule of law: Independence led Americans to reconfigure these practices and values to serve a regime based on popular sovereignty. Foremost among these was their radical (for that time) proclamations concerning contract theory and natural rights. The use of these concepts had precedent in the English civil wars, and a form of contract theory had been used to legitimate the Glorious Revolution of 1688–89. John Locke, the patron saint of contract theory, supported the winners in that earlier glorious upheaval. But those earlier British revolutionaries had also sought to preserve as much of Britain's monarchical order as was plausible given the circumstances.

Not so many American revolutionaries. They saw the Revolution's outbreak as a sign of a deeper dissolution of what had been and the beginning of something quite new. "Government is dissolved," roared Patrick Henry in September 1774 during an emotional exchange at the First Continental Congress. "Fleets and armies," he continued, "and the present state of things show that government is dissolved. Where are your landmarks, your boundaries of Colonies? We are in a state of nature, sir." Faced with that state as a reality rather than a legal or philosophical abstract, the delegates struggled with its implications. "I go upon," Henry stated, "the supposition that government is at an end. All distinctions are thrown down. All America is thrown into one mass."

Not all the gathered worthies agreed with this. Among these, New Yorker John Jay was the most emphatic. "I can't," he believed in the early fall of 1774, "yet think that government is at an end." He was trying to hold on to what had been. But by 1776 even conservatives like Jay realized that society could be torn up and somehow remade by those who believed themselves empowered to act.[3]

Such thought became the driving force of change in American society. It soon took on universalist meaning as one American leader after another proclaimed their struggle to preserve not only their own rights, but rights common to all humanity. Washington, though often portrayed as a staunchly conservative revolutionary, in 1776 described the imperial army that had occupied Boston as sent to "trample on the rights of humanity," one of the first of many proclamations made by him and others concerning the American Revolution's universal implications. It was as radical a statement as one could make in the monarchical world of the eighteenth century.[4]

Perhaps the deepest political legacy from that generation is the suspicion of power. Legislative representatives voted into office became deeply entrenched as an essential part of the revolutionary liberty they were fighting for. And yet the population remained suspicious of governing institutions, even those which they elected; perhaps especially so.

They knew themselves too well to do otherwise. No one could be trusted with power indefinitely, no matter how committed they were to revolutionary principles. Human nature was too frail for that. They never fully trusted people who served in governing institutions for pay. That tendency in our political belief system is shaping our contemporary politics even as I write this sentence.

Collectively the thought that gained hegemony in 1776 forms a kind of conceptual boundary that restrains as well as liberates. It divides humanity's political past to 1776 from a very different future that began that same year. In 1776 a process began that would fundamentally alter humanity's collective perception of itself, of the roots of sovereign power and the ways individuals could alienate their sovereignty that fundamentally altered the understanding of the nature and role of government in people's lives.

This conceptual heritage helps explain America's political divergence from the rest of the Anglophone world regarding the role of government in society. America has never really had a true conservative party. American conservatives or Republicans are in their own ways radicals, radical capitalists determined on a project that has led to constant reinvention for the entire society, or, more recently, radical populists determined to rewrite the character of political culture.

Nor has America had a party that really equates to the British Labor Party or the social democratic parties of Europe. In America there is no workers' party that stands for capital control and class rights. Rather, America's "left" parties have been dedicated to social mobility within a fluid and malleable order, the creation of institutions to enable that mobility, and more recently the use of identity politics to demand "equity" in the American order.

The tendency to reorganize power and social relationships unleashed in 1776 could not be contained and never fully has been for 250 years. Each of the great internal crises in the United States since independence has involved, to some degree, pressure to further extend equality in the society, especially to African Americans who have been repeatedly and brutally excluded from full rights in the past. These efforts at extension, whether successful or failed, have expressed the unique utopianism unleashed by the American Revolution.

The views of American revolutionaries were radical in the extreme at independence. In different guises they have remained current in American society ever since. Yet the passage of time has obscured a central truth about that particular kind of radicalism. The rupture with Great Britain and that which unfolded in its wake were driven by a quite unique utopianism, one that distinguishes the American Revolution from all other revolutionary upheavals and goes far to explain the remarkable staying power of the American republic.

Simply put, even in the heady days of independence, the revolutionary generation and most of the revolutionary leadership refused to delude themselves about people generally or themselves specifically. While they believed human beings improvable and capable of self-government, they also recognized that darker impulses were constants in human nature. They never believed they could create anyone like the French Revolution's perfect citizen, or the new Soviet man of the Russian Revolution, or the perfect cadre of the Chinese Revolution, and they never really tried.

Their understanding of human nature has been said to be rooted in a strange fusion of Calvinist theology, English Country ideology, and enlightened ideas. Whatever its source, it tempered what the revolutionary leadership asked of its citizens. For certain, there were cries about corruption and calls for republican purity and self-sacrifice throughout the revolutionary period. But these were always limited because those making them knew that human beings can only live their highest ideals fully for short periods. If they were tested too frequently, their revolutionary commitment would soon wane.

Americans had utopic hopes for the transformative power of their revolution from the beginning but knew that power would never completely remake humanity. Someone better? Yes? Someone perfect, a perfect republican citizen free from the darker sides of human nature living in a perfect republic? It was not possible.

What allowed that perception from sinking the society into despair or despotism was the belief in improvement—of self, of soul, of community, and ultimately of nation—that fueled a strong optimistic current in our society. "Improvement" has driven investment and entrepreneurialism, civic voluntarism and civic engagement, and even our desires for physical and mental self-improvement.

Accepting that people were flawed allowed the Revolution to eventually succeed beyond their wildest hopes. In 1776 and forever thereafter Americans understood that the new society would be built by self-interested, often greedy, and even occasionally violent people, and whatever they built would be imperfect. Even in 1776 some among them were shrewd enough, and perceptive enough, to believe that these impulses that were considered negative in classical political and social theory might give great power to a society if properly harnessed.

Part of the secret to their success in this regard was assuming that individuals and groups would have economic failure as well as success. The new society changed how human economic endeavors were understood. A person who failed in business or farming could try again, start a new business or get a new farm. They could do it better the next time, become more proficient, and improve their chances somehow. Debtor laws and debtors' prisons remained, but in the decades after July 4, 1776, debt and even bankruptcy gradually lost the social and economic stigmas they once had. America became the utopia of second chances.

This helps explain why they never advocated for social leveling in the manner of revolutionaries in other societies. There were struggles over control of interior lands between yeomen, squatters, speculators, and Native Americans, bloody and destructive struggles. But from the perspective of the European settlers these were struggles to gain private property and establish oneself in the society in the hope of social mobility. For certain, those hopes came at the expense of Native American societies displaced from their traditional lands, often suffering devastating losses and a sea of death in the process. These Native peoples saw their own cultures undermined and, in places, destroyed as European Americans pursued their own interests and their own utopias.

In institutional politics a losing candidate for election could also hope to eventually change their fortunes. They could stand again, or stand for a different office with some hope of reversing their fortunes, or move to another state and try for office there. There were no bloody purges of these opponents, even when they were vulnerable, and people generally surrendered their offices peacefully if defeated in an election. They accepted loss as well as victory as a product of the system and the price of their utopic freedom. These practices that we now take for granted allowed for the continual release of political pressure in the new system. They were, though, in that moment radically new.

These achievements always contained a central paradox: Race-based chattel slavery continued and indeed expanded in some states after 1776 as the basis of their economic prosperity. Many in the free white population knew slavery was incompatible with the Revolution's highest values and goals, and certainly the enslaved knew that as well. Yet slavery continued in the Southern states and died only slowly in the others.

Some among them came to realize that it could not go on forever in such a manner. But their immediate dreams and problems encouraged them to avoid the reckoning they knew must come. They left the enslaved in bondage and completely excluded from institutional political expression, with flight their only hope. Their exploitation would continue into what had to seem an endless future. Is the failure to fully confront slavery in 1776 still shaping the reality of race relations in our society? I believe it is, very much so.

The states that emerged in 1776 rested conceptually in some measure on base assumptions about human beings and human nature. The revolutionaries believed perfection impossible, though they had hope for improvement. There were ever-present reminders of their imperfections and the gulf that existed in their society between its highest ideals and lived realities. And it is precisely because of the acceptance of humanity's frailties and their understanding of the imperfections of any society created by human hands that the utopian polity created by the American

Revolution survived, thrived, and ultimately has lasted long enough to seem . . . normal.

Making everything about now is at the core of the humanities and social sciences in the twenty-first-century academy. That campaign has been conducted in a way that has robbed the past to make tribute payments to the present. We have been emptying the vault of time for most of my career to make the ever-changing "now" more smugly comfortable with itself than perhaps it should be. An unsavory habit has developed of hauling up a person, event, value, or culture from the past and proclaiming them deficient by contemporary standards, which some assume to be the pinnacle of human development and a new baseline for all human morality. That those in the past didn't think of and adopt our values is seen as only a further indictment of them as human beings. Such instrumentalization has reduced rather than increased interest in the Revolution and distorted our understanding of change over time in that central period in our national history.

This is tragic precisely because it does not nor cannot diminish the centrality of 1776 or the American Revolution to our society. Whether we acknowledge it or not, and whether we like it or not, we live in a political world that began in 1776. We live with the political values and languages that were restructured, rethought, and given public legitimacy in that year of independence and revolution. That the Revolution contributed to the flawed reality we live in and created an imperfect nation is undeniable. There never has been a perfect reality or a perfect nation, and there never will be. That it took Americans centuries to allow everyone in our society to live the Revolution's promises is without doubt true. But we are in no less need of knowledge about 1776 than any previous generation of Americans. In some ways we may need it more.

The revolutionaries of 1776 began a transformation in the human condition when they unleashed the idea of the rule of the people on a hierarchical, monarchical world. Their heirs would go on in the decades and centuries that followed to offer at least one kind of liberation to an oppressed and suffering humanity. That so many have grasped at this unique utopian experiment over the last 250 years stands as real testament to the enduring power of its message of hope.

Notes

1. See the review of Erwin Chemerinsky, *No Democracy Lasts Forever: How the Constitution Threatens the United States* (Liveright, 2024), by Samuel Goldman in the *Wall Street Journal,* June 28, 2024. Professor Chemerinsky of the University of California, Berkeley, apparently feels that the revolutionary heritage has become such a burden that doing away with it is far less dangerous than living with its imperfections. One imagines he sees himself in the role of future lawgiver, a prospect which is perhaps not as appealing to others—many others—as it is to him.
2. For a recent public discussion of some of the views of the postliberals and the roots of their thought, see the *Wall Street Journal,* July 17, 2024, A17.
3. Edmund C. Burnett, *Letters of Members of the Continental Congress* (Washington, DC, 1921), 14–15.
4. *Constitutional Gazette* (New York), April 10, 1776, 2.

Thomas Jefferson, Optimistic Visionary

ANNETTE GORDON-REED

> I steer my bark with Hope in the head, leaving Fear astern. My hopes indeed sometimes fail; but not oftener than the forebodings of the gloomy.
>
> —Thomas Jefferson

The Notion of Progress

In 1760, sixteen-year-old Thomas Jefferson wrote to John Harvie, one of the five men who had become his guardians upon the death of his father, Peter Jefferson, just about three years before the teenager's missive. In the letter, young Thomas expressed his desire "to go to the College" (William & Mary). Impatient with the press of "Company"[1] at his boyhood home Shadwell that took up too much of his time, "the College" appeared the perfect escape to a world where he could meet new people and have different experiences even in ways that would not leave him at the mercy of others.

In addition to the expressed irritation at being put upon by visitors, one hears the expectation in Jefferson's tone. He sounds quite certain that William & Mary would be his entrée into a new world, one that would help him take his rightful place in society and would allow him to continue his engagement with his already strong relationship with and devotion to books. In this earliest extant letter from Jefferson, one gets a glimpse of the approach to life that would become familiar to all who study him—the appeal to industry, the methodical approach to problem solving that he employed in almost every aspect of his life, from politics, to music, to architecture, to running his farms with enslaved labor. One also detects the optimism that would come to be seen, by both his admirers and detractors, as a characteristic feature of his personality. Jefferson had a vision of college as a vehicle, a transformative space that would help make him the kind of person who could move forward in life.

It shouldn't surprise that one who had such a deep belief in the power of self-improvement would think this way. Throughout his entire life, Jefferson appears to have been on an endless, in some ways seemingly frantic, drive to create a progressively better version himself. This was in perfect keeping with his early adherence to an Enlightenment-based philosophy that pushed him to view the world through the lens of science. The scientific method required posing rational questions and providing rational answers, even if that often resulted in discarding received wisdom and set-in-stone verities. A society that wanted to advance had to accept this reality or remain mired in a backward past.

What was true for society as a whole could be true of individuals. As societies escaped the sway of religious dogma and rigid hierarchies, communities could fashion new ways of ordering themselves that would make life better and better, with discoveries that would improve life for mankind. If individual people, unencumbered by superstition and prejudice, opened their minds to the possibilities placed before them, they could make decisions and take actions to reach the correct results. With a proper degree of curiosity, with the right methodology and work ethic, self-improvement was available.

For Jefferson, the process was inexorable. Progress throughout the world was all but inevitable. There would be those who might try to hold it back—reactionaries, or, in his terms, "Tories" and "Monocrats," but most human beings would want to move forward. Events in his lifetime bore this out. Benjamin Franklin, who later would become one of his valued colleagues, had done his famous experiments with electricity that opened up a new world when Jefferson was a nine-year-old boy. And then there were mechanical devices that made copying letters easier, ploughs that worked more efficiently, inoculation, which saved people from the scourge of smallpox, with the promise that the technique might be applied to other illnesses. All these things, and more, had appeared during his lifetime, and there was no reason for Jefferson to think that innovation would not continue. Nor was there reason to doubt that these advancements in the fields of science and technology had implications beyond just science and technology. They contained lessons for the day-to-day existences of human beings, how they ordered their individual lives, how they interacted with members of their community, and, very importantly, how they constituted the government under which they lived.

At a critical period in his life Jefferson participated in the disruption of the society he had lived under for his thirty-three years of existence. In all respects, it had been a world in which he had thrived. There could hardly have been a more fortunate individual born during his time. A member of the Virginia gentry, he had received the best education that a young person could obtain in his region. And just as he had anticipated as a teenager, William & Mary put him in contact with people who helped set him further along the road to influence within the Virginia Colony that his privileged birth had afforded him. His teachers and associates at Williamsburg, most notably George Wythe, with whom he studied law for nearly five years, bolstered his view of himself as a forward-thinking individual, and their favor verified the rightness of his chosen course of self-improvement. He became a member of the bar and, like his father before him, a member of the House of Burgesses. This gave him an opportunity to write and help enact rules in keeping with his understanding of the road the Virginia Colony should take. He was able to make an advantageous marriage, and when his wife's father died ten years later, he inherited thousands of acres of land and control over 135 enslaved people. There was every reason to believe that Jefferson, as a subject of the British Empire, could have expected to deploy his optimism and his implacable will to the fullest extent possible within the confines of that monarchical system. Even without the American Revolution, he would have had a good and productive life at the top of his society.

Changed Circumstances

The conflict during the 1770s between the Great Britain and the thirteen North American colonies created a very different context for Jefferson, one that he could not have foreseen as he began the process of fitting himself to be a leading light in his community. As many scholars have noted, it was not his initial intention, nor that of his revolutionary cohort, to break away from the British Empire. He, and they, saw themselves as Englishmen. It was in that spirit that he wrote, in 1774, *A Summary View of the Rights of British America,* the pamphlet that so impressed leading lights of the growing resistance to Great Britain that he was asked to write the American Declaration of Independence. He and other American revolutionaries were, instead, seeking to vindicate what they took to be their rights under their understanding of the British constitution. It was only when it became clear that British authorities, who were well into the process of re-forming the British Empire after the victory over France in the Seven Years' War, had no intention of listening to Americans' complaints that they decided to declare their independence and begin the process of creating a new country. In these new circumstances, Jefferson's imagination, his conception of himself, and his particular brand of Enlightenment-infused optimism and energy took flight.

This situation was perfectly suited to one who had such enormous self-confidence and a basically optimistic nature. He had deployed these traits in service of attempting to improve Virginia, as a legislator and would-be constitution-maker. The American Revolution, in which one form of government—a monarchy—would be replaced with a republic, opened the door for experimentation on a large scale. Even if there was no thought of throwing out every law, rule, or custom, the creation of a new country, new constitutions, and new laws excited Jefferson. It was a part of the progress that he believed the Enlightenment foretold. Americans had the chance to be right in the center of it, making the world. Even more importantly, *he* had the opportunity to shape the new edifice of government that would be erected.

The political circumstances in which Jefferson the revolutionary turned statesman found himself after the successful separation from Great Britain played so much to his inclinations, self-image, and way of approaching the world. Not everyone who supported the Revolution would necessarily see it as an opportunity to make wide-ranging changes in society. Dissolving the connection to Great Britain would be enough. People could go about their business in pretty much the same way as they had before. Of course, some changes would necessarily have to take place because the basic structure of a republic differs from that of a monarchy. Subjects become citizens with new responsibilities that would alter the contours of society. Men, though certainly not all of them, would have to get used to voting. In the American context, there would be no established national church, so people could arrange themselves in a potentially ever-expanding list of religious groupings, a process that continues to this day in the United States. But there would really be no need to think of, and certainly not to speak of, making a whole new type of man, or a new type of woman.

From both his rhetoric and his actions over the years, Jefferson thought otherwise. Upending a monarchy, the predominant form of government in the world, was proof indeed that a new day was dawning. It was part of a larger evolution of society in which monarchs and established religion would be cast aside. Of course, he could not speak too freely about what he really thought of the possible transformation of the role of religion as he knew it was too touchy a subject to be broached with the same enthusiasm he brought to criticizing monarchy. That issue had to be handled more delicately. If the Americans were not really operating with a tabula rasa after breaking from the British Empire, there was substantial opportunity to write a different story for the newly created United States, one that would help transform the world. Jefferson sounded this theme throughout his political career and until his death.

What was happening in American society in the aftermath of the Revolution spoke in particular ways to Jefferson's manner of moving through the world, not just in terms of his intellectual beliefs, theories, and philosophy, but in the way he approached life in general. The most obvious way was in his penchant for working with structures: Jefferson was an architect and a builder. He very famously said to a visitor to Monticello, Margaret Bayard Smith, "Architecture is my delight and putting up and pulling down" was "one of [his] favorite amusements."[2] In whatever house he lived, even for a short time, Jefferson took the trouble to remodel the place to his specifications. This was not typical behavior, even for people who had the resources to invest in such endeavors. Many people may *think* about remodeling a temporary shelter or building a house on a mountain—and really want to do those things—but never take the step to bring the dream to reality. Having a vision of an outcome and being willing to do what is necessary to carry it out are two different things. We will likely never know what quirk of personality makes one person take the action and another refrain from doing so.

During the very beginning of Jefferson's time in Paris, while living in a residence on which he had just a year's lease and did not plan to live in beyond that time, he remodeled the place. He did the same thing after he returned to the United States and moved to New York to serve in Washington's cabinet. In his first residence there, he installed bookcases and redid rooms in a house that he knew was not to be his permanent residence.[3] Of course, the most famous example of Jefferson's determination to realize a long-held vision, often at great expense and with a huge dose of impracticality, was his multidecade project of building and rebuilding

Monticello. He had first thought of constructing a house on top of the mountain when he was a young boy. The preparation for the building was a herculean task. The top of the mountain had to be leveled. Wells had to be dug, and, often, water had to be transported up the mountain. And as picturesque as it was, people had to venture up the mountain at great effort to get to the house.

A word about the impracticality of building a house atop a mountain: Living in a time of slavery, Jefferson had no reason to consider that aspect of the vision, as he did not bear the direct cost of the impracticality. He could compel the work of enslaved people, a group of men and women hired from a neighbor, to complete the arduous task of flattening out the mountain to prepare for the house he would build. As is very often the case, we admire the end vision without thinking of the costs paid for it by those who are invisible to us.

In *Notes on the State of Virginia*, Jefferson portrayed slavery as a school for despotism: "The parent storms, the child looks on, catches the lineaments of wrath, puts on the same airs in the circle of smaller slaves, gives a loose to his worst of passions, and thus nursed, educated, and daily exercised in tyranny cannot but be stamped by it with odious peculiarities."[4] One wonders how much self-knowledge Jefferson had about these particular points. He captures so much of the injustice of slavery in the language in this passage—the ever-present threat of violence, of sexual abuse, and the inevitability of developing the personality of a tyrant. There is every reason to believe that having grown up in a slave society helped nurture Jefferson's capacity and willingness to carry forward visions without having to think too much about the cost of doing so. Indeed, his political opponents chided him for what they characterized as his utopian visions that imposed costs that they felt he did not see. Again, we may admire the end result of some of his endeavors, but the ruthlessness with which they were sometimes pursued can be a bit frightening.

The 1790s

Jefferson's propensity for having visions of desired end results and his willingness to develop plans—sometimes extreme ones—to bring those visions alive showed itself during the bruising political battles of the 1790s. He had strong beliefs about what the American Revolution meant. It was evidence of the march of progress that required a break with Great Britain and the creation of a republican society in which "the people," rather than elites, ruled. It soon became clear to him that some of his fellow revolutionaries did not see things as he did. That these same people also expressed skepticism about the French Revolution, which was occurring at the same time, heightened his alarm. Jefferson fervently believed that he and the rest of the world had a stake in what was taking place in France. He was convinced that American politicians who were hostile to the French Revolution were obstacles to building the kind of society that he hoped would emerge in the United States and around the world.

Jefferson, recently arrived from France not long after the fall of the Bastille, was full into the idea of the transformative power of the "age of revolution." He had been supportive of the storming of the Bastille and the mobs of Paris, seeing "the legitimacy" of their actions.[5] He remained supportive of the Revolution long past the point that many came to see that things were going too far in France. He made his views clear in a letter to William Short in 1793: "My own affections have been deeply wounded by some of the martyrs to the cause, but rather than it should have failed, I would have seen half the earth desolated. Were there but an Adam and an Eve left in every country, and left free, it would be better than as it now is."[6]

This is one of Jefferson's most famous (infamous) letters. Even for one who often expressed himself with hyperbole—about things from the deliciousness of a slice of cherry pie to the utility of an action of government—his language in this letter goes far beyond usual. People familiar with what was going on in France at the time he wrote these words (namely, the Terror) and familiar with the correspondence between Jefferson and Short in which Short grows increasingly desperate about the unfolding violence appear shocked by Jefferson's seeming indifference to the suffering of those who had been killed or were under the threat of violence. Indeed, Jefferson's overall attitude about the French Revolution was given book-length treatment by the Irish journalist and statesman Conor Cruise O'Brien in *The Long Affair: Thomas Jefferson and the French Revolution.*

O'Brien was positively scathing in his condemnation of Jefferson's response to the French revolutionaries' excesses, calling him a "visionary fanatic."[7] And the so-called "Adam and Eve" letter was O'Brien's central piece of evidence against the Virginian. Here was a case in which Jefferson's propensity for visions that encapsulated his notion of an idealized end, coupled with his preternatural tolerance for almost any means that might be employed to have that vision realized, was a decidedly negative combination. The idealized end was a world in which common people—the people—rather than elites were the true leaders of society. Significantly to Jefferson, the world that was being destroyed was one in which thousands had perished through poverty, famine, and wars of adventure prosecuted by kings, religious figures, and members of the elite. No one counted those deaths and that destruction in the balance, as that was taken simply to be normal life. Of course, Jefferson didn't say eggs had to be broken in order to make an omelet, but he may as well have.

The Revolution of 1800 and Beyond

We get a clear picture of the possibilities that Jefferson saw in the Revolution in his response to his election as president in 1800. The radically different views about what was and was not possible in the wake of the American Revolution had been exposed during the 1790s, and Jefferson saw his victory as putting things back on track. That is why he referred to his election as the Revolution of 1800. Republican forces had beaten back the counterrevolution and restored the Spirit of '76. Although he affected a posture of bipartisanism in his First Inaugural Address—"We are all Republicans. We are all Federalists"—he also wrote that he intended to "sink federalism into an abyss from which there shall be no resurrection."[8] Given what he believed was something akin to a mandate to revive revolutionary ideals, the quote about sinking the opposition into an abyss expressed Jefferson's true position on the matter. He went about remaking American politics, during both of his terms and afterward in retirement through his acolytes and surrogates, with the alacrity with which he knocked down walls and rebuilt sections of his house.

All of this was in service of Jefferson's vision of the ideal American republic, and his belief that he could drive the process. Not long after his inauguration, he wrote to Joseph Priestly noting the momentous circumstances the country and the world faced:

> As the storm is now subsiding & the hori[z]on becoming serene . . . *we can no longer say there is nothing new under the sun. for this whole chapter in the history of man is new.* the great extent of our republic is new. . . . the mighty wave of public opinion which has rolled over it is new. . . . the order & good sense displayed in this recovery from delusion and in the momentous crisis which lately arouse, really bespeak a strength of character in our nation which augurs well for the duration of our republic.[9] (emphasis added)

The sense of excitement and *newness* was heightened by the later purchase of Louisiana and the doubling of the size of the country, or at least giving the United States the right to contend for the land with the people who were already living in large swaths of the territory. The Jeffersonian juggernaut stalled a bit in his second term with the hostility to his championing of the Embargo Act of 1807. Here was an instance in which Jefferson could not, through the sheer force of his will, successfully bring his vision—of a peaceful alternative to war—to reality by means of an economic sanction. He moved into retirement, however, confident that he could continue to shape the new republic from Monticello.

Jefferson's confidence, in part, grew out of his faith in the American experiment. As streams of visitors climbed the mountain to pay homage to him in retirement, he continued his efforts to shape that experiment through the men he had mentored, like James Madison and James Monroe. He also began work on a very public effort to influence the course of American society by developing a plan to build a university for Virginia, one that would put the state in the forefront of higher education, and it would be just a few miles from Monticello. This also must count as another somewhat improbable vision that Jefferson saw through despite some very daunting odds. He designed the structure, planned the curriculum, drove the first markers for the first building, picked the faculty, and even consulted on the food that would be served to students. Again, dreaming of building a university in an out-of-the-way place, planning every detail of it, and actually doing it are vastly different things.

Jefferson embarked on another project—this was in near total secrecy—designed to help American society along to his vision of a progressive end: He once again took up his plan to create a version of the Bible shorn of what he considered every supernatural element. Once these, in his view, fantastical items (the Trinity, the Resurrection, and other described miracles) were removed, republican citizens could unite around the pure teachings of Jesus of Nazareth, the gospel of love and brotherhood. This certainly appealed to his idea of progress toward a "new man" and a "new woman," and it would all begin in America and then, hopefully, move across the globe.

In sum, Jefferson was the quintessential American "exceptionalist" because he saw himself as exceptional. He moved through the world as if he were and managed to achieve a great deal in many different endeavors. In the end, of course, by many serious measures, the exceptional man failed in his personal life. But the ideas about the country he helped found, for better and worse, have guided many toward the spirit of aspiration, a thing absolutely vital to any republic.

> We are destined to be a barrier against the return of ignorance and barbarism. old Europe will have to lean on our shoulders, and hobble along by our side, under the monkish trammels of priests & kings, as she can. what a Colossus shall we be when the Southern continent comes up to our mark! What a stand will it secure as a ralliance for the reason & freedom of the globe! I like the dreams of the future better than the history of the past. so good night! I will dream on, always fancying mrs. Adams and yourself are by my side marking the progress of ages and countries.[10]

We should measure ourselves against these words, today.

Notes

1. TJ to John Harvie, January 14, 1760, in *Papers of Thomas Jefferson*, ed. Julian P. Boyd et al., 49 vols. to date (Princeton University Press, 1950–) (hereafter *PTJ*), 1:3.
2. Margaret Bayard Smith, *A Winter in Washington, Or, Memoirs of the Seymour Family* (New York, 1824), 2:261.
3. Dumas Malone, *Jefferson and His Time*, 6 vols. (Little Brown, 1948–81), 2:5, 8, 257.
4. Thomas Jefferson, *Notes on the State of Virginia*, ed. Robert Pierce Forbes (Yale University Press, 2022), Query XVIII.
5. TJ to Diodati, August 3, 1789, in *PTJ*, 15:326.
6. TJ to William Short, January 3, 1793, in *PTJ*, 25:14.
7. Conor Cruise O' Brien, *The Long Affair: Thomas Jefferson and the French Revolution* (University of Chicago Press, 1996).
8. TJ to Levi Lincoln, October 25, 1802, in *PTJ*, 38:566.
9. TJ to Joseph Priestly, March 21, 1801, in *PTJ*, 33:394
10. Jefferson to Adams, August 1, 1816, in *Papers of Thomas Jefferson: Retirement Series*, ed. J. Jefferson Looney, 22 vols. to date (Princeton University Press, 2005–), 10:2.

Slavery and Hypocrisy

How the Founders Talked About America's Original Sin—and Why It Matters

ELIGA H. GOULD

MARY MIDDLETON BUTLER knew what her rights were. During the fall of 1782, she sat down at her desk to make sure General Sir Guy Carleton understood too. For the last year, Mrs. Butler and her Irish-born husband, Major Pierce Butler, had been living with their six children as patriot refugees in Philadelphia. Her home, however, was South Carolina, where her family were among the wealthiest owners of enslaved African Americans in the state. Like many Low Country patriarchs, her father had taken advantage of South Carolina's liberal women's property law to settle a plantation and several hundred slaves on her when she married.[1] Under the law of coverture, which exempted married women's property from confiscation for the transgressions of their husbands, that inheritance should have been safe when Charleston fell to the king's forces, but the garrison's engineer, Colonel James Moncrief, had commandeered two hundred of her enslaved laborers anyway.[2] They were all, as Butler informed the commander in chief of the king's land forces in America, "my absolute property (if you will allow me to make use of the expression with respect to a fellow creature) by marriage settlement." Appealing to the general's humanity and sense of justice, she asked to have them "restored to me" as expeditiously as possible.[3]

Mary Butler was obviously a hypocrite. Although the Revolutionary War imposed terrible costs on the people whom she enslaved, her letter's focus was on the "cruel injustice" of Colonel Moncrief's actions, his disregard for her own property rights, and the harm to her children, all of whom, it scarcely needed to be said, were "innocent of any offence." Now, according to friends in Charleston, Moncrief intended to remove her slaves when the British evacuated the city and put them to work on land that he owned in East Florida. His misdeeds practically spoke for themselves. "I need not trouble you with another syllable on the subject," she told the British general. "A Savage might blush to be accused" of such things.[4]

If the double standard in Mary Butler's thinking was remarkable, so was her willingness to acknowledge it. Butler readily admitted that the people whom she claimed as her property were "fellow creatures." She also recognized—at least for public consumption—how morally indefensible the claim was. Most striking of all, as Butler may or may not have realized, was the number of South Carolinians who shared her point of view. One of the best known was Henry Laurens, whose son John, as anyone who has seen Lin-Manuel Miranda's Broadway musical will know, shared the antislavery views of his friend Alexander Hamilton. During the summer of 1776, Henry told his outspoken son, "You know, my dear son, I abhor slavery." Before the war, Henry Laurens had been one of the largest importers of enslaved Africans in Charleston. (His main competitor was Mary Butler's father, Thomas Middleton.) Nonetheless, he wanted John to know that were it not for "the laws and customs of my country," as well as his own avarice "and the avarice of my countrymen," he would never have become involved in the institution in the first place. If it were possible to extricate himself from its clutches now, he would happily do so.[5]

Whether the topic is slavery's enduring legacy of racism and inequality or the burgeoning climate crisis or any of today's countless other problems, hypocrisy is something that most of us have encountered in our own lives. At one point or another, if we are honest, we have all been hypocrites ourselves. But what, exactly, does it mean to be a hypocrite, and what did it mean to Mary Butler and the founding generation? One answer, it seems to me, is to recognize that hypocrisy is a double-edged sword.[6] Accusations of hypocrisy, including self-accusations, can be a powerful incentive to action, but they can also be excuses for inaction. And that insight helps explain two apparently incompatible facts about slavery and the American Revolution. First, the Revolution produced the first cracks in slavery's formidable legal, moral, and political edifice, opening the way for Black Americans to claim rights in ways that weren't possible before 1776. Second, the Revolution left slavery firmly, if unevenly, ensconced in all thirteen colonies that became the United States, nowhere more so than in Mary Butler's South Carolina. Although hypocrisy was a driving force behind the first reality, it helps explain why Butler and her contemporaries, no matter who they were or where they lived, felt so little compunction about the second.

To understand the challenge that the Revolution posed to slavery, it is important to realize that in 1776 there was nothing new about the hypocrisy of a free people subjecting other people to chattel servitude. For Henry Laurens, his misgivings had nothing to do with the principles in the recently adopted Declaration of Independence. What troubled him was enslavers' religious hypocrisy and the fact that slavery and Christianity had developed "under the same authority and cultivation." For critics who did think in terms of the Declaration's ideals, it is worth noting that neither Thomas Jefferson nor the other authors seem to have discerned any conflict with chattel servitude. Although Congress proclaimed the self-evident truth that "all men are created equal," that equal condition occurred in the state of nature, not civil society, where men and women were self-evidently not equal—and, according to most writers on the law of nature, could be held in bondage to other men and women. The self-evident truth about humanity's equal creation appears in the second paragraph. As the first paragraph made clear, the Declaration's primary goal was to secure the former colonies' place "among the powers of the earth." Most of the powers whose ranks the founding generation hoped to join were colonial, slave-based empires, hardly a democratic club.[7]

The meaning that an author intends, however, is rarely the meaning that a text retains after it is published. That is especially true when the values in the text, regardless of what the author intended, are so obviously at odds with the author's actions.[8] Within months of the Declaration's publication, Lemuel Haynes, a free Black Continental soldier from Massachusetts, seized on the words "all men are created equal" and set the phrase on the path to becoming what a modern historian has called a "universal declaration of human rights." Significantly, Haynes titled his essay "Liberty Further Extended."[9] By the end of the Revolutionary War, this sense of expanding liberty was sufficiently pervasive for Boston's African American poet Phillis Wheatley to cast the newly independent United States in her poem "Liberty and Peace," written to mark the ratification of the Treaty of Paris, as a "new-born Rome"—meaning a Rome without slaves—that would someday "give Britannia law." To do otherwise would have been to abandon the ideals upon which the union had been founded.[10]

Although she may have been thinking of the African slave trade, which several states had already banned, Wheatley could just as easily have meant the abolition of slavery. In 1778, her home state of Massachusetts had rejected a constitution that denied the franchise to "negroes, Indians and mulattoes."[11] While saying nothing, pro or con, about chattel servitude, the document that replaced it in 1780 dropped the racial restrictions on voting while adding a Declaration of Rights that proclaimed the natural equality of all men. As towns approved the new charter, African Americans began leaving "the service of those who had been their owners." In some places, acts of emancipation and self-emancipation were already under way; in others, they gained new energy.[12] Among the self-emancipators was Elizabeth Freeman, or Mum Bett. In 1773, her enslaver, Colonel John Ashley, chaired the committee that drafted the Sheffield Declaration.[13] As a maid in Ashley's household, Freeman could have overheard the text's affirmation of a popular right to "the undisturbed enjoyment of their lives, their liberty and property," though she credited a reading of the Declaration of Independence at the town meetinghouse as the reason for her suit. A violent encounter with the colonel's wife, who struck Freeman with a hot shovel while trying to hit her sister, was a factor too. What allowed Freeman's suit to go forward and ultimately succeed, though, was the bill of rights in the state's constitution.[14]

Although Massachusetts was unusual in ending slavery outright, it was not the only state to take steps in that direction. In Pennsylvania, the initiative came from the legislature, which enacted a gradual emancipation law in 1780. Because it was a "post nati" measure that only liberated children born after its adoption—and because it indentured children whose parents were enslaved until they turned twenty-one—the law did not immediately free anyone, but it emboldened African Americans to push for more. When a proslavery faction in the State House tried in 1781 to exempt slave-owning Southern refugees from the new law—a group that included Mary Butler and her family—free Blacks in Philadelphia drew up a petition and forced the legislature to limit the exemption to six months. Emancipated African Americans also thwarted a legislative attempt to reenslave people whose masters had failed to register them (as required under the 1780 act). "To make a law to hang us all, would be *merciful*" by comparison, wrote a Black correspondent in the *Freeman's Journal*. "What must we think . . . of the [emancipation] law" and the words that heralded a new "creed regarding slavery?"[15] Words mattered, including words that implied more than the law's authors intended.

For property-owning Blacks, mitigating and, in some places, rejecting slavery's hypocrisy also created openings for the right to vote. Although Georgia, South Carolina, and Virginia limited the franchise to white men, suffrage laws in most states, including Maryland and North Carolina, said nothing at all about race.[16] Some of this may have been the result of sloppy legislation or failure to anticipate that African Americans might try to vote, but that was not true everywhere. In Massachusetts, where the clause disfranchising people of color was among the reasons that towns mentioned for rejecting the draft constitution in 1778, the omission was deliberate. At Westminster, voters made clear that they objected to depriving any "part of the human Race of their Natural Rights, mearly on account of their Couler—Which in our opinion no power on Earth has a Just Right to Doe." Citizenship, the town of Upton agreed, should be available to all "without regard to Nation or Colour."[17] Today, Massachusetts has the oldest constitution in continuous use in the world. The article affirming its citizens' right to vote, regardless of race, is part of the original text.

Affirming a right in the abstract was one thing, of course. Making that right a reality was another. In 1780, Paul Cuffe and his brother John, mixed-race Black Wampanoag mariners from Dartmouth on Massachusetts's south coast, petitioned the legislature for relief from taxation because they and the petition's other five signatories had "no vote or influence in the election of those that tax us." Dartmouth had unanimously rejected the draft constitution in 1778, noting "the inconsistency of excluding the negroes, &c.," but it also made clear that "no Negro, Indian or Molatto" participated in the vote. Although the sentiments in the motion may have been sincere, the statement about who voted was accurate too. After the legislature failed to act on the Cuffe brothers' petition, the town briefly jailed them for nonpayment of taxes. The brothers responded by asking the selectmen to clarify whether "free negroes and mulattoes" were entitled to the same rights as "white people," especially the right to vote. The record of the case's outcome is vague, but John Cuffe ultimately agreed to pay eight pounds, twelve shillings, in back taxes for himself and his brother.[18] Paul Cuffe, who was twenty-one in 1780, went on to become a prosperous ship captain and forceful advocate for African American rights. Late in life, he was reported to be the wealthiest Black man in the United States, wealthier, certainly, than most of the white townsmen who had tried to tax him without representation. Given this history, it seems unlikely, though it is impossible to say for sure, that either brother would have accepted a deal that did not recognize their rights as citizens.[19]

Despite this consensus over slavery's hypocrisy, there was considerable variation in how people responded. As the multiple paths to Black emancipation above the Mason-Dixon Line showed, that was certainly true of the so-called "free states" of the North. It was equally true of the response in Virginia, the Carolinas, and Georgia. For the Low Country's planter elite, it often seemed as though acknowledging slavery's hypocrisy, invariably followed by a stated desire to free the people enslaved on their own plantations, was concession enough. Writing in 1788 to a friend in England, Mary Butler's husband, Major Pierce Butler, went to great lengths to emphasize his own discomfort with the institution.

> If America should be the means of opening the Eyes of the Enslaved, so as to make them cast off their Chains, I shall be better reconciled to my suffering & losses [from enslaved workers who escaped during the recent war]. You may naturally ask me Why, with these Sentiments, do you hold so many in Bondage. I answer You, that I would free every one of them tomorrow if I could do it. That is if the Legislature would permit it. I ardently wish I never had anything to do with such property.[20]

Although Butler's hypocrisy was hard to miss, so was his willingness to acknowledge it—and in that acknowledgment to excuse himself for an evil that he claimed to be powerless to do anything about.

Significantly, Butler's confession appeared in a letter to an Anglican churchman in London. Written at a moment of growing support for antislavery in England, Butler's double standard allowed him to remove a stumbling block to a friendship that he valued, while excusing him from doing anything about it. The same tension was evident in Mary Butler's letter to General Carleton and in Carleton's response. As is well known, the commander in chief refused to return men and women who had earned their freedom by serving in the British army. Nearly three thousand Black loyalists left New York with the British army in 1783, initially for Nova Scotia but many of them eventually for Sierra Leone, where they founded the so-called Province of Freedom. But not everyone was allowed to leave. In the face of Washington's objections, Carleton agreed to appoint a joint commission with the power to hand over Blacks in the New York garrison whose emancipations were judged to be irregular. A week after the general received Butler's letter, one of his aides forwarded it to General Alexander Leslie, commandant of the Charleston garrison, asking him to look into the matter. When Pierce Butler returned to South Carolina the following spring, he reported that he had "receiv'd more of my Negroes than I expected."[21] Although his use of the first-person possessive raises questions about whose property he was talking about, it seems likely that at least some were part of Mary Butler's estate. If that is correct, her use of hypocrisy worked.

Not surprisingly, the rhetoric of hypocrisy—and the different purposes that it could serve—proved especially fraught in the states' relations with each other. History has not been kind to the Articles of Confederation, which served as the union's first federal constitution, but the Confederation's loose-knit structure, which to its critics was its chief failing, was also one of its main virtues. When South Carolina attempted in 1778 to revise the fourth article, which guaranteed the "free inhabitants" of each state all the privileges of "free citizens in the several States," and to insert the word "white" before "inhabitants," only two delegations voted in favor, while eight voted against and one divided.[22] An attempt to count enslaved African Americans as three-fifths of a free person, which James Madison added to a proposed revenue measure during the spring of 1783—and which he would later write into the Constitution—also went down to defeat.[23] In a union of free and independent states, the citizens of each state were free to abolish slavery and to allow people of color and women to vote, all without having to worry about what Congress or the citizens of any other state thought. They were also free, of course, to do none of those things.

One did not need especially good vision to see trouble on the horizon. In Massachusetts, the failure of South Carolina's attempt to limit the fourth article's guarantee of citizenship rights to whites was a victory for Black and Indigenous mariners like the Cuffe brothers, who regularly crossed state lines.[24] In the Palmetto State, on the other hand, the unrevised article threatened the rights of South Carolinians whose property included human property. During the summer of 1783, the governments of the two states found themselves at loggerheads over a cargo of thirty-four enslaved men, women, and children from Waccamaw Neck, sixty miles north of Charleston, that the Massachusetts brig *Tyrannicide* had seized in 1779 from a British privateer and brought to Boston. Although most captives returned to South Carolina, allegedly on their own volition, fourteen remained in Massachusetts under an agreement between Anthony and Percival Pawley, Low Country planters who were in no apparent hurry to retrieve them, and a Boston merchant named John Winthrop with business interests in the Carolinas. Over the next four years, the former captives settled into the city's Black community, marrying, changing their names, and, in several cases, simply disappearing.[25]

In 1783, the Pawleys belatedly decided to act. Whether the impetus was the cessation of hostilities with Britain or Judge Cushing's jury declaration in the case of Quock Walker, the brothers hired a South Carolina lawyer named Samuel Hasford and sent him to Boston to retrieve their property. As Hasford discovered, what until recently would have been a straightforward case had become problematic. Massachusetts courts no longer recognized Blacks enslaved under the laws of other states as their enslavers' property. To do otherwise would be the ultimate act of hypocrisy. After a magistrate refused Hasford's request—the state constitution, he said, did not allow him "to apprehend and secure this kind of property"—Hasford petitioned Governor John Hancock, who proceeded to imprison eight people whom the attorney had located. Within days, Judge Cushing ruled that whatever the merits of the Pawleys' civil claims, there were insufficient criminal grounds to keep the former captives in jail. While the brothers were free to continue their pursuit, they must have decided the uncertain outcome was not worth their time and expense. In 1790, Jack Phillips, George Pauley, and Jack Pauley, men of color who had arrived with the *Tyrannicide*, were living as heads of household in Boston, according to the census. All were free.[26]

South Carolina's defeat, of course, was short-lived. When news of Cushing's decision reached Governor Benjamin Guerard, he was furious. Massachusetts, he said, was using slavery to assume "dominion" over another state, which—in a veiled reference to the hypocrisy that religiously moderate Southerners associated with New England's well-known history of religious enthusiasm—Guerard attributed to "Puritanism."[27] During the Federal Convention in 1787, South Carolina's delegation, led by none other than Mary Butler's husband, Pierce Butler, made sure that the new Constitution protected the rights of enslavers in ways that the Articles of Confederation did not.[28] In setting the size of delegations in the House of Representatives and the Electoral College, states were allowed to count three-fifths of their enslaved population as part of their total; courts where slavery was no longer legal had to return bound laborers who self-emancipated by crossing state lines; and Congress was barred from abolishing the slave trade until 1808. If we had to choose a moment when slavery engrafted itself into the American union, March 4, 1789, the day that the new Congress assembled in New York, would be a strong candidate. Nowhere, however, did the Constitution make use of the word "slave" or "negro" or any other term specific to Black slavery. According to a letter in the *Connecticut Journal*, the omission was by "design" and reflected embarrassment over the new charter's implicit sanction of the institution.[29] Even in slavery's moment of triumph, the hypocrisy of a free people holding another in bondage was impossible to avoid.

Obviously, the struggle between slavery and freedom was only just beginning. It was already clear that hypocrisy, often used hypocritically by enslavers like Henry Laurens and the Butlers, would be part of slavery's survival and expansion, enabling enslavers to honor the Declaration's second paragraph while continuing to profit from practices directly opposed to its ideals. There were limits, however, to how far hypocrisy could be used to defend the indefensible. As free-soil jurisdictions spread, from Pennsylvania and Massachusetts to Sierra Leone and Haiti, and from the western and southern Atlantic to England, Scotland, Denmark, and France, chattel servitude, which in 1776 had been the legal norm just about everywhere, started to look like an exception. To be sure, the cracks that opened in slavery's once formidable edifice did nothing to diminish the racism and white supremacy that were destined to become ever more important to its survival. But the institution relied as never before on special laws that were disparaged as "odious," in the words of Chief Justice Mansfield's famous 1772 *Somerset* opinion, or used euphemistic language to avoid scrutiny.[30] Even when deployed by hypocrites, hypocrisy in such a world had the potential to be a double-edged sword.

For the truth of that statement, let us close with the publication history of the letter that John Laurens, modern star of stage and screen, received from his father in 1776. Unlike Jefferson and Adams, whose correspondence often seems to have been written for posterity, Henry Laurens's letter was a private communication meant only for his son. So it might have remained had it not been discovered by a member of New York City's Zenger Club, which included it in a published volume of Laurens's letters in 1861. That, of course, was the first year of the American Civil War. Sensing an opportunity to rally Northern opinion—and determined to show that "it is the South which has changed, not the North"—the publisher G. P. Putnam printed the letter as a pamphlet under the title *A South Carolina Protest Against Slavery*. As a description of Southern attitudes in 1776, Putnam missed the mark, but he did not miss by as much as historians have sometimes suggested. Although Henry Laurens, Mary Butler, and the other members of the planter elite had no intention of freeing their slaves, they knew that slavery was wrong. And however self-serving their use of that knowledge was, the acknowledgment helped ensure that the founders' misgivings would be available to people who really did want to end the institution and overcome its legacy.[31] Hypocrisy, to make an obvious point, is not the only part of slavery's history during the American Revolution that mattered, but it did matter—and still does.

Notes

1. Malcolm Bell, *Major Butler's Legacy: Five Generations of a Slaveholding Family* (University of Georgia Press, 1987), 6–7.
2. Lauren Duval, "Mastering Charleston: Property and Patriarchy in British-Occupied Charleston, 1780–82," *William and Mary Quarterly*, 3rd ser., 75, no. 4 (2018): 605–8.
3. Mrs. Mary Butler to Sir Guy Carleton, Philadelphia, September 16, 1782, British National Archives, PRO 30/55, no. 5604 (1–2).
4. Mrs. Mary Butler to Sir Guy Carleton, Philadelphia, September 16, 1782, British National Archives, PRO 30/55, no. 5604 (1–2).
5. Henry Laurens to John Laurens, August 14, 1776, in *The Papers of Henry Laurens*, ed. Philip M. Hamer, 12 vols. (University of South Carolina Press for the South Carolina Historical Society, 1968), 11:224–25; Bell, *Major Butler's Legacy*, 7–14.
6. Karoline Gamma, Robert Mai, and Moritz Loock, "The Double-Edged Sword of Ethical Nudges: Does Inducing Hypocrisy Help or Hinder the Adoption of Pro-Environmental Behaviors?," *Journal of Business Ethics* 161, no. 2 (2020): 351–73.
7. See Eliga H. Gould, *Among the Powers of the Earth: The American Revolution and the Making of a New World Empire* (Harvard University Press, 2012); and Steven Sarson, *The Course of Human Events: The Declaration of Independence and the Historical Origins of the United States* (University of Virginia Press, 2025).
8. J. G. A. Pocock, "Introduction: The State of the Art," in *Virtue, Commerce, and History: Essays on Political Thought and History, Chiefly in the Eighteenth Century* (Cambridge University Press, 1985), 1–35.
9. Woody Holton, *Liberty Is Sweet: The Hidden History of the American Revolution* (Simon & Schuster, 2021), 248.
10. Phillis Wheatley, *Complete Writings*, ed. Vincent Carretta (Penguin Random House, 2001), 101.

11. Oscar Handlin and Mary Flug Handlin, eds., *The Popular Sources of Political Authority: Documents on the Massachusetts Constitution of 1780* (Harvard University Press, 1966), 202, 231, 249, 769.
12. Manisha Sinha, *The Slave's Cause: A History of Abolition* (Yale University Press, 2016), 68; Gloria McCahon Whiting, "Emancipation Without the Courts or Constitution: The Case of Revolutionary Massachusetts," *Slavery and Abolition* 41, no. 3 (2020): 458–78.
13. Bethany K. Dumas, "Freeman, Elizabeth (1742–1829), slave, nurse, and slavery lawsuit plaintiff," American National Biography.
14. Dumas, "Freeman, Elizabeth (1742–1829), slave, nurse, and slavery lawsuit plaintiff"; Arthur Zilversmit, "Quok Walker, Mumbet, and the Abolition of Slavery in Massachusetts," *William and Mary Quarterly*, 3rd ser., 25, no. 4 (1968): 618–19; Handlin and Handlin, *Popular Sources of Political Authority*, 442.
15. Sinha, *Slave's Cause*, 72–73.
16. Alexander Keyssar, *The Right to Vote: The Contested History of Democracy in the United States* (Basic, 2000), 328–29, table A.1, "Suffrage Requirements, 1776–1790."
17. Douglas Bradburn, *The Citizenship Revolution: Politics and the Creation of the American Union, 1774–1804* (University of Virginia Press, 2009), 245.
18. George H. Moore, *Notes on the History of Slavery in Massachusetts* (New York, 1866), 196–98; Henry Noble Sherwood, "Problems of Citizenship," *Journal of Negro History* 8, no. 2 (1923): 162–66.
19. Charles H. Wesley, "The Negro's Struggle for Freedom in Its Birthplace," *Journal of Negro History* 30, no. 1 (1945): 65.
20. Quoted in Bell, *Major Butler's Legacy*, 48.
21. Maj. Frederick Mackenzie to General Alexander Leslie, New York, October 5, 1782, in Royal Commission on Historical Manuscripts [Great Britain], *Report on American Manuscripts in the Royal Institution of Great Britain*, 4 vols. (London, 1904–9), 152; Bell, *Major Butler's Legacy*, 40.
22. Bradburn, *Citizenship Revolution*, 246.
23. David Waldstreicher, "The Beardian Legacy, the Madisonian Moment, and the Politics of Slavery," *American Political Thought* 2, no. 2 (2013): 275–76.
24. W. Jeffrey Bolster, *Black Jacks: African American Seamen in the Age of Sail* (Harvard University Press, 1997), 160–76.
25. Emily Blanck, *Tyrannicide: Forging an American Law of Slavery in Revolutionary South Carolina and Massachusetts* (University of Georgia Press, 2014), 2–3, 99–112.
26. Blanck, *Tyrannicide*, 115–45.
27. Blanck, *Tyrannicide*, 133.
28. Bell, *Major Butler's Legacy*, xx, 69–79.

29. "Letter from Massachusetts," *Connecticut Journal,* October 17 and 24, 1787, in *The Documentary History of the Ratification of the Constitution,* ed. Merrill Jensen (State Historical Society of Wisconsin, 1976), 3:375.
30. Gould, *Among the Powers,* chaps. 2 and 5. For the countervailing power of racism and white supremacy, see Robert G. Parkinson, *The Common Cause: Creating Race and Nation in the American Revolution* (University of North Carolina Press, 2016).
31. Joseph P. Kelly, "Henry Laurens: The Southern Man of Conscience in History," *South Carolina Historical Magazine* 107, no. 2 (2006): 82–123.

PART TWO

Race

Americans Are Beautiful

Race, Immigration, and the American Revolution

CHRISTA DIERKSHEIDE AND NICHOLAS GUYATT

A DAY AFTER making speeches at Valley Forge and Philadelphia, President Gerald R. Ford flew south on the morning of July 5, 1976, to the final event of the bicentennial weekend: a naturalization ceremony for a hundred immigrants at Thomas Jefferson's magnificent Virginia home, Monticello. Franklin D. Roosevelt and Harry Truman had made the same pilgrimage, but Ford was the first US president to do so since 1963, when the Thomas Jefferson Foundation had begun to include the ceremony as part of independence celebrations. When Supreme Court Justice Lewis Powell finished swearing in these newest citizens, President Ford addressed the crowd on the west lawn. The title of his speech was "Americans Are Beautiful."[1]

A half century later, the idea of an American president rhapsodizing about immigration seems hard to imagine. During the 1970s, however, commentators and officials routinely presented immigrants as a wellspring of national purpose. Ford's advisors sent an early draft of his Monticello speech to Irving Kristol, the neoconservative journalist and intellectual, who urged the president to play up the exceptionalism of American immigration: "The United States is, to my knowledge, the *only* nation in history which, for most of its existence, permitted unrestricted immigration," Kristol noted. "We gambled that we could take in anyone, from anywhere . . . and the gambles worked." Kristol's claims about "unrestricted" immigration stretch credulity, but the direction of his advice was clear: Americans often called themselves a nation of immigrants, and Ford should emphasize the enduring radicalism of that fact.[2] The final speech followed Kristol's prompts. Immigration had made Americans "a new kind of people," Ford told the crowd. Thomas Jefferson, in particular, had "very deliberately and very daringly set out to construct a new kind of nation." The meaning of the Revolution resided not only in the unprecedented act of creating a new nation and a new people, but in the extraordinary commitment to keep open the nation's doors and to "absorb anyone, from anywhere"—Kristol's exact words.

It was easier for visitors to overlook slavery on a visit to Monticello in the 1970s than it is in the 2020s, but President Ford nonetheless recognized the need to locate African Americans within this soaring framework. The founders were free from "ancient hates," but "we admit they had stubborn blind spots in their lofty vision." Were Black people a part of Ford's nation of immigrants? He suggested, awkwardly, that they were. "Their forbears had been Americans almost as long as [the founders']," he reminded the crowd, before embarking on a curious tangent which gave him the title of his speech: "'Black is beautiful' was a motto of genius which uplifted us far above its intention," the president declared, recognizing the 1960s movement which had celebrated Black identity and culture. "Once Americans had thought about it and perceived its truth, we began to realize that so are brown, white, red, and yellow beautiful." Ford's advisors had recommended that he drop this part of the speech: "'Black is beautiful' . . . seems out of place and should be cut," wrote one. But Ford kept the line because it did so much work in the story he wanted to tell. If diversity and the conscious affirmation of American nationality were the Revolution's greatest legacy, the president could hardly exile African Americans from those achievements.[3]

The Revolution was a pivotal moment in the forging of American ideas about race, nationality, and immigration, and Thomas Jefferson was at the heart of these debates and innovations. Gerald Ford's attempt to align Black belonging with the story of immigration would have been unrecognizable to Jefferson, however, and to most of the founding generation. The future of Black people—most pressingly, of the 750,000 enslaved people in the thirteen colonies on the eve of the Declaration of Independence—became entangled with broader questions of rights, identity, and demography that were electrified by the revolutionary struggle. But Ford's claim that Americans had "been willing to absorb anyone from anywhere" was wildly misleading. In fact, the Revolution inaugurated three interlinked developments which would make the new nation's promise of rights highly selective: the promotion of further settlement from Europe; the undermining of slavery as an institution of paramount economic importance; and an insistence on the need to remove Black people from the new United States. For Thomas Jefferson in particular, immigration was presented not only as a boon for white people but also as a necessary counterpoint to another population movement: the expatriation of African Americans. In Jefferson's vision of American independence, Black banishment was integral to creating a stable and durable United States.

THE NOTION that North America represented a different kind of space from the Caribbean islands became a commonplace in eighteenth-century colonial discourse, even as enslavers like George Washington and Thomas Jefferson built their fortunes on the labor of enslaved people. From at least the 1670s, when Bacon's Rebellion brought chaos to Virginia, Western settlers characterized slavery as an instrument of a coastal elite rather than a prerequisite for the conquest of the continent. Benjamin Franklin vividly captured this position in his 1751 "Observations Concerning the Increase of Mankind." "The number of purely white people in the world is proportionably very small," he noted. "Why increase the Sons of Africa, by Planting them in America, where we have so fair an Opportunity, by excluding all Blacks and Tawneys, of increasing the lovely White and Red?" (Franklin's reference to "White and Red" referred to the emotional expressiveness of white people's faces, not to Native Americans.) Franklin's vision of empire—which he projected energetically until almost the eve of the Revolution—envisioned the North American colonies as a natural outgrowth of Britain, with the Western Hemisphere providing the land upon which British liberty could be perfected for millions of white inhabitants.[4]

Enslaved people were corrosive to this vision in two respects. First, they complicated the efforts of white colonists to insist that North America was an integral part of the British nation, which in turn made it harder for Franklin and his fellow colonists to insist on their equal rights within that expanded political community. Second, enslaved people occupied land that could otherwise be worked by new (white) immigrants: Slavery artificially constrained the population of the British colonies, and the enslaved people who worked the land were denied any of its benefits. During the first phase of the imperial crisis, when American colonists challenged London to recognize their rights as Britons rather than as colonial inferiors, radicals like the Massachusetts lawyer James Otis complained that ordinary Britons regarded the North American mainland as a mere extension of the Caribbean—"a parcel of little insignificant conquered islands," as he put it in a 1764 pamphlet protesting the Sugar Act. It was hardly surprising, then, that "the common people of England" assumed that mainland colonists were "a compound mixture of *English, Indian,* and *Negro*" rather than "freeborn *British white subjects,* whose loyalty has never yet been suspected."[5]

Slavery's tendency to tarnish the identity of mainland colonists—to make them seem both tyrannical and "mongrel"—nudged even enslavers to consider whether the institution had a future in North America. This was particularly the case in the aftermath of the Seven Years' War, when the Crown's prohibition on Western settlement created new alliances between poorer Western settlers and wealthy coastal enslavers who saw huge profits in land speculation and the management of Western tracts. George Washington was one of many elite Virginians who hoped to seize this moment: In the mid-1760s he worked to secure huge landholdings in western Pennsylvania and Ohio, reasoning that the Proclamation Line of 1763—the king's attempt to halt settlement at the Appalachians and placate Native Americans—was merely a "temporary expedient." Crucially, Washington and his fellow speculators did not expect these new lands to be settled by enslaved people. Instead, they envisaged white tenant farmers who would (to paraphrase the historian Bruce Ragsdale) establish the political order of the new Western region at the same time that they made Eastern elites even richer.[6]

When it became clear that the Crown was stubbornly disinclined to view the Proclamation Line as temporary, Virginia enslavers like Arthur Lee and George Mason took a different approach. In 1767 Lee crafted a bill in the Virginia legislature to restrict the importation of any more enslaved people, with the explicit rationale that this would increase the immigration of European settlers and ratchet up the pressure on London to push back (or even erase) the Proclamation Line. "Encouraging the Importation of free People & discouraging that of Slaves has never been duly considered in this Colony," wrote George Mason, "or we shou'd not at this Day see one Half our best Lands in most Parts of the Country remain unsettled, and the other cultivated with Slaves."[7]

Prohibitions on the slave trade were debated across the eighteenth century before Britain and the United States introduced national bans in the first decade of the nineteenth. Supporters of slave-trade restriction were driven by a variety of motives. In the 1790s, for example, even South Carolina and Georgia accepted the need to restrict the influx of enslaved people as the Haitian Revolution raged. At other junctures, enslavers supported bans for more mundane reasons; to buttress the value of the enslaved people they already owned, for example.[8]

Whatever their motive, advocates of a ban faced the same problem: Before the American Revolution, their efforts could be easily undone by the refusal of the king to give assent to legislative proposals from the colonies. Given the grip of the Caribbean sugar interest over London politics—and especially over any measure which appeared to undermine the rights of enslavers—it was unsurprising that George III rejected the Virginia Assembly's proposal for prohibitive import taxes on enslaved people in 1767, 1769, and 1772. In the context of the deteriorating relations between the colonies and the metropole, these serial refusals by London to accommodate American antislavery measures were to assume an outsized infamy in the years that followed.[9]

As MANY historians have noted, colonial protests against British repression after 1763 were suffused with the language of enslavement. This is usually—and persuasively—read as evidence of the hypocrisy of those patriots who continued to buy and sell human beings while styling themselves as slaves of Britain. The language was crucial, however, in staking a claim for American rights which Britain seemed determined to deny. As the protests against Britain took shape in the 1760s, patriot writers began to develop new arguments about nationhood and belonging to counter the outrages and indignities emanating from Westminster. As early as 1764, James Otis made the striking claim that colonists were "entitled to as *ample* rights, liberties, and privileges as the subjects of the mother country are, and in some respects *to more*." The insistence that the active work of settler colonialism conferred political equality upon white Americans was made by Benjamin Franklin, Alexander Hamilton, Thomas Paine, Thomas Jefferson, and many others. American colonists were freeborn and white; they were not the tyrannical, "mongrelized" oppressors who presided over wealth extraction in the Caribbean. They had undertaken the novel task of settling a new continent, and they had a right to expect at least an equal share in its management and rewards.[10]

For Thomas Jefferson, whose 1774 *Summary View of British America* represented the summation of these claims, George III's repeated veto of the Virginia legislature's anti-slave-trade measures was a perfect illustration of the corruption at the heart of the empire: "For the most trifling reasons, and sometimes for no conceivable reason at all, his majesty has rejected laws of the most salutary tendency." Following a logic that would structure the first draft of the Declaration of Independence, Jefferson insisted that "the abolition of domestic slavery is the great object of desire in those colonies, where it was unhappily introduced in their infant state." Nonimportation was the first step in the "enfranchisement" of slaves—a term Jefferson understood to mean freeing enslaved people rather than giving them citizenship. But "our repeated efforts to effect this by prohibitions, and by imposing duties which might amount to a prohibition, have been hitherto defeated by his majesty's negative." Jefferson was surely right to blame "a few African corsairs"—slave traders and their Caribbean customers—for the king's veto. He was on shakier ground in insisting that Virginia had already experienced an antislavery epiphany, though at least some of his compatriots were stirred by "the rights of human nature," and still more had begun to imagine a future in which white rather than Black people would farm the continent's vast interior.[11]

The notion that American colonists had begun to address the problem of slavery but had been knocked back by Britain was irresistible to Jefferson, who like many of the founders was adjusting to a new universe in which the colonists' claims to equal rights (or more!) had metamorphosed into a luminous separatism. Breaking from Britain allowed patriot writers fully to own the novelty of their colonizing achievements; instead of rebutting the lazy condescension of London's ruling class, the founders now presented the entire colonial era as preparation for independence. It is ironic that, when Jefferson came to supercharge his 1774 reflections on the royal negative in the first draft of the Declaration of Independence, his words were cut from the text by Congress precisely because of the sensitivities of patriot enslavers. By then, though, the chaos in Virginia occasioned by Lord Dunmore's 1775 proclamation had presented yet another reason to doubt slavery's long-term future in an independent United States. If Dunmore—who as the last royal governor of Virginia had previously been sympathetic to anti-slave-trade legislation—could suddenly destabilize the entire system by offering freedom to the slaves of patriots who would fight for the king, it seemed obvious that the institution of slavery represented a threat to American independence.[12]

To those patriots who saw this threat clearly, the question remained: How could slavery actually be ended? Patrick Henry, writing in 1773, candidly confessed to the antislavery Quaker Robert Pleasants that he continued to enslave people mostly from "the general inconveniency of living without them. I will not, I cannot justify it." Granville Sharp, the London radical who had become a fervent opponent of slavery in the 1770s, wrote to Benjamin Rush in the summer of 1775 with a practical suggestion: "Slavery might be changed into a condition more nearly resembling that of Hired Servants." It was typically British of Sharp to imagine a solution which reaffirmed inequality: Freed people would be "a new and useful order of men," he insisted, "a hardy body of *Free Peasants*, serving either as trust Tenants or Farmers, to improve the Estates of Landed Gentlemen." To be fair to Sharp, this wasn't far removed from Washington's schemes for settling his new Western lands, save for one vital detail: In the 1760s Washington had expected to leave African Americans at Mount Vernon, and to entrust the settlement of the West to white people.[13]

Sharp's proposal to structure a mixed-race society around a permanent Black peasantry seems disconcertingly visionary if we look at slavery's eventual collapse a century later. In the 1770s, though, the combination of British military emancipation and racially charged American propaganda made the prospect of Sharp's "scheme of general enfranchisement" seem impossibly distant. As the historian Robert Parkinson has shown, patriot propagandists ruthlessly presented Black loyalists and Native Americans as the bogeymen of American independence, and in turn rooted a new American national identity in an embattled whiteness.[14]

A more representative idea for how slavery might end came from another of Benjamin Rush's correspondents, the historian and physician David Ramsay of South Carolina. As the British army occupied swaths of the South in 1779, Ramsay lamented the folly of "rich planters who engross much land & many negroes." With only a "very few white men" in the state's coastal regions, the British met little resistance in their advance. Ramsay himself favored the arming of enslaved people, though when this proposal came to the state legislature that same year it was roundly voted down by enslavers unwilling to part with their lucrative property. No matter, Ramsay told Rush, because the British monopoly on military emancipation would soon shake planters from their complacency and greed. "King George, for once in his life, is promoting the grand cause of American liberty and republicanism," Ramsay wrote. The British "will teach people experimentally the folly of accumulating negroes and will point out the superior policy of encouraging the settlement of poor white people." It was ironic that the enemy, Britain, was pointing out the "true interest" of the new republic: By increasing the number of white people and decreasing the number of Black people, Americans could complete their revolution.[15]

THOMAS JEFFERSON'S views closely followed this trajectory. His draft of the new Virginia state constitution in June 1776 introduced the abolition of the slave trade and the encouragement of European migration in adjoining articles: No new enslaved people could be brought to Virginia, and any white migrants arriving in the state could claim "all the rights of a person natural born" after a qualifying period. In 1779, as part of the general revision of Virginia's laws he undertook with George Wythe and Edmund Pendleton, Jefferson helped craft a plan which clarified the limits of his thinking. The plan promised not only to free any enslaved people brought into Virginia (including from other US states) within a year but also to banish enslaved people who were manumitted by their owners—again, with the threat that if they remained in Virginia more than a year after their manumission, they would be placed "out of the protection of the laws." In a nod to Virginia's long history of legislating against the prospect of mixed-race equality, the plan also banished any white women who had mixed-race children—along with those children, of course. And it prohibited Black sailors visiting Virginia ports from spending more than twenty-four hours on shore—an idea which would be revived by South Carolina and seven other Southern states in the controversial Negro Seamen's Acts of the antebellum years.[16]

Despite the plan's meticulous commitment to banishing freed people from Virginia, it was not presented to the legislature and would only become widely known after the Revolutionary War. Jefferson became state governor in June 1779, and instead of advancing his antislavery proposals, he found himself presiding over Virginia during some of the most trying moments of the war. In the first half of 1781 Jefferson was chased from Richmond and then from Monticello during Benedict Arnold's invasion, and the proximity of British troops prompted enslaved people to flee from the estates of Jefferson, Washington, and the Revolution's other liberty-loving enslavers.[17]

While the fall of 1781 would bring the climactic victory at Yorktown, Jefferson's experience of the war's final years was freighted with despair. His daughter Lucy Elizabeth died that spring, in the midst of the British invasion. After standing down as governor in June, Jefferson faced uncomfortable questions about his management of the state's defense. And in September 1782 his wife, Martha, died at Monticello. Jefferson initially retreated from public life, though he was soon prevailed upon to join the Confederation Congress and, before long, to serve as American minister to France. He also began writing what would become his only book, the *Notes on the State of Virginia,* which was privately published in Paris in 1785.[18]

The *Notes* would serve as Jefferson's lasting contribution to debates over race, slavery, and belonging. They were, however, deeply shaped by the trauma of the Revolutionary War's final phase. Jefferson first learned in 1780 that François Marbois, a member of the French diplomatic mission in Philadelphia, had requested information about the progress of the newly independent states. He began sketching responses for Virginia almost immediately, and continued to expand on the manuscript through the British invasion. Jefferson sent his first draft to Marbois in December 1781. He tinkered with and expanded the manuscript across the next two years, before finally sending it to the printer in 1785 after his move to Paris.[19]

Jefferson was well aware that French readers saw slavery as the Revolution's elephant in the room. (He and other patriot enslavers had heard as much from the Marquis de Lafayette and other French volunteers during the war.) In the *Notes,* he rehearsed the familiar line that George III had blocked the colonists' attempts to end the slave trade, and that the newly independent state of Virginia had confirmed its antislavery bona fides by passing a ban at the earliest opportunity. He alluded to his abortive 1779 antislavery plan but added a twist: He claimed that if the bill had been brought forward, it would have been accompanied by an amendment which would clarify how the existing enslaved population would be brought to freedom.

The amendment shared some features with the blueprint of gradual emancipation which became law in Pennsylvania in 1780. African Americans would be freed, but only when they reached a specified age (twenty-eight in Pennsylvania; eighteen [for women] and twenty-one [for men] in Virginia). But it also outlined a series of new ideas. First, enslaved children would receive some form of state education "at the public expence" in "tillage, arts, or sciences, according to their geniuses." Second, it pledged that when they reached the specified age, they "should be colonized to such place as the circumstances of the time should render most proper." Third, it provided for a simple population swap: The state should "send vessels at the same time to other parts of the world for an equal number of white inhabitants, to induce whom to migrate hither, proper encouragements were to be proposed." In Jefferson's characterization, the Virginia antislavery amendment would help to secure the outcome envisaged by Benjamin Franklin in 1751: the settlement of the North American continent by an exclusively white populace.[20]

The 1779 amendment's extraordinary proposal for population transfer was the pretext for Jefferson's infamous discussion of Black racial debility in the *Notes on the State of Virginia*. Jefferson's protracted racism in this section made him an outlier even in his own historical moment: He drew rebukes from the race theorist Samuel Stanhope Smith, South Carolina historian David Ramsay, and the French revolutionary leader Henri Grégoire, among others. It is crucial to note, however, that Jefferson's determined effort to assail Black ability was driven by the need to answer a pressing question he himself posed: "It will probably be asked, Why not retain and incorporate the blacks into the state, and thus save the expence of supplying by importation of white settlers, the vacancies they will leave?"[21]

It was the commonsensical power of this question which drew from Jefferson his most overtly racist theorizing, but which also pulled him back into the recent memory of slavery's dangers to white people in a time of war. Like George Washington, Jefferson responded to the flight of his own enslaved people with a stunned sense of betrayal. Washington and Jefferson had imagined Mount Vernon and Monticello to be redoubts of "benevolent" slaveholding. Both fancied that their enslaved people were cognizant of—even grateful for—their paternalism. Both were shocked that the proximity of the British army could undo a social order they had imagined to be both liberal and durable. The Revolution's sustained military mobilization illustrated an old truth: Slavery was rarely a source of strength during times of war. Jefferson in particular juggled fear, suspicion, and bitterness in the war's last months. If his antislavery came into sharper focus during this period, so did his belief that Black people could not be trusted to play a role in an independent United States.

JEFFERSON'S NEWLY refined view of antislavery exclusion set the tone for decades of theorizing about colonization in and beyond Virginia. The broader circumstances of American slavery changed enormously over the half century that followed the Declaration of Independence, but the banishment of Black people (and their replacement by white people) remained Jefferson's North Star from Monticello to the White House and back. When the Virginia legislature passed a new manumission bill in 1782—to enable enslavers to reward wartime service by enslaved people rather than to encourage gradual emancipation—the increase of the state's free Black population only reinforced calls for Black freedom to be made conditional on expatriation. In 1806, Virginians finally embraced the principle Jefferson had outlined back in 1779: Any enslaver who manumitted a Black person would be responsible for ensuring that that freed person left the state within a year. With colonization advocates struggling to mobilize the enormous resources required to transport Black people beyond the United States, the 1806 manumission law was intended to ensure that freed people would at least be transported out of Virginia.[22]

As for Jefferson's fantastical suggestion in the *Notes* that Virginia might send Black people across the Atlantic and bring back an equivalent number of white people from Europe, we need to recall again the historical context of his thinking. The Atlantic slave trade reached its peak in the 1780s: Around eighty thousand Africans endured the Middle Passage every year in that decade. Virginia had the largest enslaved population in the nation—more than two hundred thousand people—but Jefferson was confident that its growth might be speedily arrested while the state made provisions for a mass deportation.[23]

Despite placing his hopes for the removal of slavery on an influx of white Europeans, Jefferson was careful in the *Notes* to disavow unlimited immigration. "The present desire of America, is to produce rapid population by as great importations of foreigners as possible," he observed. But "are there no inconveniences to be thrown into the scale against the advantage expected from a multiplication of numbers by the importation of foreigners?" American assemblies had been legislating against the arrival (and continued residence) of paupers since the colonial era, and with the onset of republican government Jefferson believed that the moral and political quality of immigrants was especially important. The American populace would need to manifest "common consent" and an appreciation of political principles "more peculiar than those of any other [government] in the universe." Since Jefferson expected most immigrants to come from European monarchies, he feared the contamination of America's fledgling political system: "They will infuse into it their spirit, warp and bias its directions, and render it a heterogeneous, incoherent, distracted mass." Jefferson allowed himself the luxury of looking beyond the immediate problem of slavery and of regulating the expanding *white* population of Virginia on the other side of a wholesale removal of Black people. In doing so, he betrayed an early unease with the idea of a "nation of immigrants" even if those new arrivals were uniformly white.[24]

President Ford's 1976 address, like many later invocations of the founding era, retooled the facts of early American state building to suit the tastes of a contemporary audience. Our own historical moment's hostility to immigration cannot be entirely aligned with the founding era: For all of Jefferson's caution about the need for a "more homogeneous" government, both the federal government and state governments adopted relatively liberal naturalization laws in the years after the Revolution, and America's borders remained mostly open—in part because they were so hard to police. Crucially, however, these first naturalization laws featured the earliest appearances of the word "white" in the statute books of the new republic. The insistence on whiteness as a qualification for citizenship didn't only reflect a burgeoning racism in the new United States but also a broader project of population replacement by which the (enslaved) Black inhabitants of the United States would be supplanted by free white arrivals. Whereas today's advocates of "replacement theory" present immigration as a conspiracy against whiteness, Thomas Jefferson and other revolutionary-era antislavery proponents saw new white arrivals as the best hope both for ending slavery and for securing a white America.[25]

Notes

1. "Schedule of the President's Visit to Monticello," Box 68, "Fourth of July (1976)—Monticello," John Marsh Files, Gerald R. Ford Presidential Library.
2. Irving Kristol to Robert T. Hartman, memorandum, Box 5, "Monticello Drafts (1)," Robert T. Hartmann Files, Gerald R. Ford Presidential Library.
3. Gerald R. Ford, *The American Adventure: The Bicentennial Messages of Gerald R. Ford* (The White House, 1976), 25–28; Stephanie M. H. Camp, "Black Is Beautiful: An American History," *Journal of Southern History* 81, no. 3 (2015): 675–90.
4. Benjamin Franklin, "Observations Concerning the Increase of Mankind," in *The Papers of Benjamin Franklin*, ed. Leonard W. Labaree, vol. 4 (Yale University Press, 1959), 225–34.
5. James Otis, *The Rights of the British Colonies Asserted and Proved* (London, 1764), 36–37; Jack P. Greene, *Evaluating Empire and Confronting Colonialism in Eighteenth-Century Britain* (Cambridge University Press, 2013), 156–57.
6. Bruce Ragsdale, *Washington at the Plow: The Founding Farmer and the Question of Slavery* (Harvard University Press, 2021), 68–72; Michael A.

Blaakman, *Speculation Nation: Land Mania in the Revolutionary American Republic* (University of Pennsylvania Press, 2023), 35–57.

7. Arthur Lee, "Address," *Virginia Gazette*, March 19, 1767; Richard K. MacMaster, "Arthur Lee's 'Address on Slavery': An Aspect of Virginia's Struggle to End the Slave Trade, 1765–1774," *Virginia Magazine of History and Biography* 80 (1972): 141–57.
8. W. E. Burghardt Du Bois, *The Suppression of the African Slave Trade to the United States of America, 1638–1870* (New York, 1896), 7–15; Leonardo Marques, *The United States and the Transatlantic Slave Trade to the Americas, 1776–1867* (Yale University Press, 2016), 23–24, 44–46.
9. Woody Holton, *Forced Founders: Indians, Debtors, Slaves, and the Making of the American Revolution in Virginia* (University of North Carolina Press, 1999), 66–73.
10. Otis, *Rights of the British Colonies*, 38; Holton, *Forced Founders*, 72. Eva Sheppard Wolf, *Race and Liberty in the New Nation: Emancipation in Virginia from the Revolution to Nat Turner's Rebellion* (Louisiana State University Press, 2006), 13–14.
11. Thomas Jefferson, *A Summary View of the Rights of British America* (London, 1774), 14.
12. Alan Taylor, *The Internal Enemy: Slavery and War in Virginia, 1772–1832* (W. W. Norton, 2013), 23–27.
13. Patrick Henry to Robert Pleasants, January 18, 1773, Allinson Family Papers, HC.MC-968, Box 6, Haverford College Quaker and Special Collections; Granville Sharp to Benjamin Rush, July 18, 1775, Rush Family Papers, Library Company of Philadelphia; Ragsdale, *Washington at the Plow*, 71.
14. Robert Parkinson, *The Common Cause: Creating Race and Nation in the American Revolution* (University of North Carolina Press, 2016).
15. David Ramsay to Benjamin Rush, June 3, 1779, in *David Ramsay, 1749–1815, Selections from His Writings, Transactions of the American Philosophical Society*, ed. Robert L. Brunhouse, n.s., vol. 55, pt. 4 (1965), 59–60; Edward Pearson, *The Enslaved and Their Enslavers: Power, Resistance, and Culture in South Carolina, 1670–1825* (University of Pennsylvania Press, 2023), 276.
16. "Bill Concerning Slavery" (1779), Founders Online; Michael A. Shoeppner, *Moral Contagion: Black Atlantic Sailors, Citizenship, and Diplomacy in Antebellum America* (Cambridge University Press, 2019).
17. Wolf, *Race and Liberty in the New Nation*, 102–3; Taylor, *Internal Enemy*, 27–29.
18. Lorri Glover, *Founders as Fathers: The Private Lives and Politics of the American Revolutionaries* (Yale University Press, 2014), 83–88.
19. Thomas Jefferson, *Notes on the State of Virginia*, ed. Robert Pierce Forbes (Yale University Press, 2022), xxix–xxxvi.

20. Thomas Jefferson, *Notes on the State of Virginia* (Paris, 1785), 251–52.
21. Nicholas Guyatt, *Bind Us Apart: How Enlightened Americans Invented Racial Segregation* (Basic, 2016), 26, 62.
22. Alejandro de la Fuente and Ariela J. Gross, *Becoming Free, Becoming Black: Race, Freedom, and Law in Cuba, Virginia and Louisiana* (Cambridge University Press, 2020), 87–89.
23. Herbert S. Klein, *The Atlantic Slave Trade* (Cambridge University Press, 1999), 71.
24. Jefferson, *Notes*, 154–58; Hidetaka Hirota, *Expelling the Poor: Atlantic Seaboard States & the Nineteenth-Century Origins of American Immigration Policy* (Oxford University Press, 2017), 17–19; Kristin O'Brassill-Kulfan, *Vagrants and Vagabonds: Poverty and Mobility in the Early Republic* (New York University Press, 2019), 17–25.
25. Kunal M. Parker, *Making Foreigners: Immigration and Citizenship Law in America, 1600–2000* (Cambridge University Press, 2015), 60–70. On the determination of states to make naturalization law into the nineteenth century, despite the apparent federal monopoly on this power, see Parker, "Citizenship and Immigration Law, 1800–1924: Resolutions of Membership and Territory," in *The Cambridge History of Law in America*, vol. 2: *The Long Nineteenth Century (1789–1920)*, ed. Michael Grossberg and Christopher Tomlins (Cambridge University Press, 2008), 172–76.

Race, Fear, and Political Persuasion

The Problem of Slavery on the Eve of Revolution

ROBERT G. PARKINSON

In 2001 I started working on a project about how patriot leaders like John Adams, Benjamin Franklin, and Thomas Jefferson convinced enough of their fellow countrymen that *their* definitions of liberty, rights, and justice were the proper ones, and that the American public needed to follow them, even if it meant suffering tremendous losses to their bodies, families, or fortunes. Those leaders had to make the Revolution's cause common enough to get a majority of people to rally around them. In searching for how they made a "common cause," an ever-increasing mound of evidence suggested to me that, once the shooting started, those leaders focused their campaign on how the British were trying to use enslaved people, Native people, and foreign mercenaries to quell the rebellion. In other words, the "common cause" quickly evolved into scaring the American public into believing that the Crown would stop at nothing to destroy their liberties, including using African Americans and Indigenous people to kill them.

Sound familiar? It certainly did to a number of people I discussed my findings with over the first two decades of the twenty-first century. For years, when I talked about revolutionary leaders using race and fear to secure political goals, the responses often revolved around present issues: Oh, that's really about 9/11, or the Patriot Act, or terror threat levels, or the Iraq War, or the Tea Party backlash, or immigrants, or Barack Obama's birth certificate. It wasn't, but I found it very interesting just how easy it was to reach such conclusions. That so many American politicians had used race and fear to secure political goals in the fifteen years I was writing what turned out to be *The Common Cause: Creating Race and Nation in the American Revolution* (2016) was hardly surprising. It was, indeed, prevalent during those years, but not just those years. Race, fear, and politics have been inextricably intertwined throughout the history of the United States; after all, as I found, they were from the start, during the very movement that produced independence. This set the stage. So why would we assume that later such instances in our history would be any different?

This essay explores just how entangled race, fear, and politics were from 1773 to 1776, especially in the case of African Americans and the future of enslavement in what would become the United States. The consequences of that campaign and the use of race and fear to achieve political goals would have devastating effects for generations of African Americans. The start of the Revolution was, in fact, complicated when it came to the problem of slavery. There was far more contingency about it than we often think. There *was* a brief moment when it looked as if the thirteen colonies might divest themselves from slavery. How that moment was squandered by the use of race and fear is an important and contingent one that we should pay a good deal of attention to.

SLAVERY WAS as important to the British colonies in North America as it ever was in the 1770s. British merchants dominated the transatlantic slave trade by 1770, and the percentage of African Americans as a proportion of the total population of the thirteen colonies was greater than it had ever been before (21.4 percent), a level it would not again reach until the eve of the Civil War. The economic and commercial reliance on slavery penetrated deeper than ever into British American society and culture. In fact, the importance of the slave trade had reached such a degree that a backlash was also brewing in London about just how dependent the empire was on selling captured African people into New World slavery.

In the spring of 1772, testimony began on what would become known in England and the empire as the "Great Negro Cause." The trial, *Somerset v. Steuart*, was before the Court of the King's Bench, presided over by Britain's chief justice, Lord Mansfield. James Somerset was an enslaved person and brought from Virginia to London by his enslaver, Charles Steuart. When Steuart tried to force Somerset to return across the Atlantic with him, he resisted, saying that by carrying him to England, Steuart had broken his bondage. England was a land without slavery, the abolitionists who were supporting and representing Somerset argued. Mansfield found for Somerset, arguing that since England had no slave code, no positive law defining the status of slaves, Steuart did indeed free him by bringing him to England—the opposite of how the US Supreme Court would decide *Dred Scott v. Sanford* eighty years later.[1]

Granville Sharp, the leading British abolitionist, claimed that the *Somerset* decision automatically freed all of the fourteen thousand bonded men and women who then lived in Britain—and hinted that perhaps the decision might also apply out in the empire as well. There was wide speculation about Britain's legal and political commitment to slavery in the 1770s, therefore, even as commercially it was growing ever more involved.

"This Cause seems pregnant with consequences," stated one account of the *Somerset* decision that appeared in several colonial newspapers. As abolitionists tried to maximize the public response to *Somerset,* slaveholders in the Western Hemisphere were concerned. In Britain, it was the "much talked of cause of Somerset," and enslavers in North America and the West Indies wondered where that conversation might lead.[2] One newspaper report worried that *Somerset* "will occasion a greater ferment in America . . . than the Stamp Act itself."[3]

For those who benefited from the profits and prosperity that the upswell in British engagement in the transatlantic slave trade had reached by the middle of the eighteenth century, *Somerset* was concerning. Surely the Crown would not turn its back on them—or the riches that were to be gained from this commercial opportunity—would it? Even though they had nothing to worry about (Mansfield's decision explicitly reassured them of this), abolitionists worked hard to *imply* the case might undermine Britain's commitment to slavery in the Atlantic. So, planters did in fact worry. In the years since 1763, there were many in North America who were wondering who the empire was really for, if it taxed them without their consent, tried to prevent them from speculating on Western lands, or sent troops to patrol their cities. Was slavery to be added to the list of "rights" that the Crown might in fact take away?

THUS, "ENSLAVEMENT" was one of the ways writers framed the resistance movement to British imperial reform. They argued that British attempts to strip them of their liberties constituted a form of slavery. "*We* are therefore—SLAVES," John Dickinson memorably wrote in his *Letters from a Farmer in Pennsylvania* (1769). This political metaphor of slavery, however, was detached from the actual plight of enslaved people.[4] Ironically, after *Somerset,* it was more often applied to *slaveholders* than the enslaved.

Some connected the two issues, however. James Otis, in a 1764 pamphlet, wrote, "It is a clear truth that those who every day barter away other men's liberty will soon care little for their own."[5] In 1773, Benjamin Rush, the Philadelphia physician turned patriot political leader, implored his colleagues to include enslaved peoples in their calls for liberty: "Where is the difference between the British Senator who attempts to enslave his fellow subjects in America, by imposing Taxes upon them contrary to Law and Justice; and the American Patriot who reduces his African Brethren to slavery, contrary to Justice and Humanity?"[6]

All this talk of liberty encouraged African Americans to test patriot fidelity. Seventeen enslaved people in Massachusetts appeared in court to sue for their freedom between 1764 and 1774, a substantial increase from earlier in the century.[7] When, in 1795, one of the lawyers who was often involved in these cases, John Adams, was asked about these prerevolutionary suits, he said, "I never knew a Jury by a Verdict, to determine a Negro to be a Slave. They always found them free."[8]

Criticism of slavery in the 1770s often turned more on the transatlantic slave trade than on the legal holding of enslaved people in America. In 1771, the Massachusetts General Court approved a bill prohibiting the African trade, but Governor Thomas Hutchinson did not sign it. A year later, the Virginia House of Burgesses also passed a heavy import tax on enslaved peoples in an effort to slow the trade there. This was pitched as a humanitarian measure, but by the 1770s, slave importations had been so successful, natural increase had begun to satisfy the labor need, and tobacco had so worn out the soil that Virginia enslavers now began to see incoming slave ships as a problem not a solution. This attempt, too, failed when the king refused to give his assent. The following year, Quakers in New York successfully maneuvered the legislature to pass a significant tax on bringing slaves into the colony, but it too failed. And, in 1773, the New Jersey Assembly amended the slave code to allow enslavers to manumit their slaves and also attempted to abolish the slave trade.[9]

By the summer of 1774, therefore, there was enough political action connecting American liberty and antislavery that Jefferson was able to write in *A Summary View of the Rights of British America* that August, "The abolition of domestic slavery is the great object of desire in those colonies where it was unhappily introduced in their infant state."[10] When they met in October, the First Continental Congress capitalized on what was thought to be a universal feeling when they included enslaved people on the list of items that were not to be imported under the Continental Association boycott. When the Association passed, Congress delegate Benjamin Rush was thrilled. "We have now turned from our wickedness," he wrote to Granville Sharp. "I venture to predict there will not be a Negro slave in North America in 40 years." Rush gushed that with this realization of antislavery, he now felt "a new attachment to my native country."[11] At this moment, slavery and politics coincided with American proclamations of freedom and liberty. Here comes the contingency, for that situation would soon—very soon—change.

THE TIME would be measured in weeks, not years. Even before news arrived in Williamsburg of the Battles of Lexington and Concord, the prospect of slave insurrections gripped Virginia. In the third week of April 1775, colonists all along the James River heard rumors of potential revolts. With the colony roiling with unrest, Virginia Governor Lord Dunmore ordered nearby Royal Navy marines to confiscate all of the gunpowder barrels stored in the public magazine in Williamsburg, which they did in the middle of the night. The town awoke with feelings ranging from fear to fury. When Williamsburg officials confronted Dunmore about the town being left defenseless, he roared back that if they continued to protest, he would "declare freedom to the slaves and reduce the City of Williamsburg to ashes."[12]

This was how Virginia's Revolutionary War began, with an explicit threat to draft enslaved people into Britain's war effort. The town officials did concede to Dunmore's threat in April, but by June, his political reputation was such that, to protect himself and his family from being taken hostage by patriot militias, he fled Williamsburg for the safety of a British warship. He would never return to the capital. He would, however, return to his April threat.

Over the following summer, as George Washington took command of the thousands of New England militia who had fought the British at a climactic battle at Bunker Hill and tried to form that group into a "Continental Army," patriot leaders accused a host of other imperial officials in the Southern colonies of "instigating" insurrections. North Carolina Governor Josiah Martin and Navy Captain John Collett were thought to be sheltering and protecting runaway slaves at Fort Johnston in Newbern, which lay in ashes by the end of July. When he arrived at his new posting as the governor of South Carolina in midsummer, Sir William Campbell quickly found himself wrapped up in the messiness of the trial of Thomas Jeremiah, an African American harbor pilot whom patriot leaders had arrested for boasting that he would assist in a potential British invasion of Charleston.

Then, in the fall, Dunmore made good on his spring threat to free and arm Virginia's slaves. In September, a hurricane swept over the lower Chesapeake, exacerbating tensions that had recently arisen over another Black pilot, Joseph Harris, having run to British protection. The storm grounded a British boat, and Virginians set it on fire. That act, which the colonists justified because of British obstinance in returning Harris to his enslaver, escalated hostility in the region. In late October, Dunmore had his marines seize a printing press in Norfolk, and within a few weeks, he used that device to issue a proclamation declaring that any able-bodied, male slaves whose enslavers resisted the Crown were free if they could reach his lines, where they would be armed and put into the king's service. The stipulations and limitations of Dunmore's Proclamation would be ignored by hundreds of enslaved people—men, women, and children—who responded to this offer of emancipation. Although patriot leaders did their best to stem the tide of enslaved people going to the governor by ordering militia to shoot runaways on sight and vastly expanding slave patrols, the best estimate is that about one thousand people did take the risk and rallied around Dunmore's forces around Norfolk and the lower Chesapeake Bay.

By year's end, British Indian Superintendent John Stuart—who himself had to flee Charleston after being accused of trying to get Native peoples to aid the Crown—wrote from exile in Florida that "massacres and intended insurrections were Words in the mouth of every child."[13] Stuart was right: Those phrases weren't there by accident. Patriot leaders worked very hard to make sure that even children knew British officers were behind all this threatening unrest with the enslaved population. They used every opportunity they could to publicize how imperial officials tried to use the enslaved to assist in putting down the rebellion. Washington worried from Massachusetts that if Dunmore's actions were not checked in Virginia, the situation with enslaved people would become a "snow Ball in rolling."[14] Patriot publicity leaders all over North America—political and military officers working in tandem with sympathetic newspaper printers—were essential in trying not only to neutralize that out-of-control snowball but also to turn it to the Revolution's advantage by capitalizing on the public's outrage. They used race and fear to convince Americans to support the Revolution. In fact, the sentence before Stuart described how colonial children were all talking about slave insurrections in 1775, he noted how that phenomenon was happening: "The newspapers were full of publications calculated to excite the fears of the people." Those calculations were being done by patriot leaders in assembly houses, army camps, and print shops all over America.[15]

In short, once the resistance movement tipped over into war, the problem of slavery didn't become any less vital to the Revolution, but it did change momentously. Now, as British leaders became more associated with enslaved peoples working together to halt the rebellion—an association broadcast loudly by patriots—the voices who called for an end to American slavery began to fade. In June 1775, John Adams received a letter from an anonymous stranger in Fredericksburg, Virginia. Inside were "hints" for him to consider if they wanted to win. Only "bold, daring, and strenuous exertions of Force" would "effectively preserve [American] liberty," he wrote. And what would be more daring than "to proclaim instant Freedom to all the Servants that will join in the Defence of America?" The letter continued: "Is it not incompatible with the glorious Struggle America is making for her own Liberty, to hold in absolute Slavery a Number of Wretches?"[16] Adams was not among those loud voices for liberty, but he did oppose slavery. What might he have done with that letter had he received it even six months earlier? Perhaps he would have discussed it and even showed it to some of his colleagues. It's likely he would have done more with it than he did when he received it a few days before the Battle of Bunker Hill, which was nothing. Evidence suggests he folded it up and put it in his papers, for nothing remains to prove that he mentioned these "hints" to anyone.

This change in how patriot leaders began to grapple with the slavery problem after the war began is most evident in the Declaration of Independence. There were twenty-seven reasons listed in the Declaration for why the American colonies were justified in leaving the British Empire. Jefferson and the Congress did not assemble them randomly, but with much purpose. The Declaration was primarily a political propaganda document. Congress wanted to project unity and inclusion, so they wanted the grievances to include as many colonies among the thirteen as possible. And they wanted the list to persuade audiences at home and abroad, so the list was intended to build toward a dramatic climax.

The final grievance in Jefferson's rough draft reflects both of these impulses, union and drama. It was by far the longest accusation lobbed at King George, referring to the empire's engagement with the transatlantic slave trade as waging "cruel war against human nature itself." Jefferson used thunderous words, some of them in all capital letters, to describe the slave trade: "piratical warfare, the opprobrium of INFIDEL powers, is the warfare of the CHRISTIAN king of Great Britain." King George, Jefferson raged, was "determined to keep open a market where MEN should be bought and sold; he has prostituted his negative for suppressing every legislated attempt to prohibit or to restrain this execrable commerce." Americans, Jefferson's Virginians included, had tried in the 1770s to put an end to this "assemblage of horrors," but had been stymied at every turn by corrupt imperial interests.

Thus, in the Declaration's rough draft surfaced the "great object of desire" that Jefferson had described twenty-three months before. Jefferson resuscitated those claims from the time before the shooting started and featured them at what he hoped would be at the very heart of the Declaration.

But Jefferson wasn't finished. Although the first half of this impassioned, shouting grievance was about 1774's "desire," the second half reflected the changes that had occurred since Lexington and Concord. Jefferson pivoted away from antislavery to then implicate Lord Dunmore and his colleagues for taking advantage of enslavement to destroy American liberty. "He is now," Jefferson continued, "exciting those very people to rise in arms among us, and to purchase that liberty of which he has deprived them, by murdering the people on whom he also obtruded them: thus paying off former crimes committed against the LIBERTIES of one people, with crimes which he urges them to commit against the LIVES of another."

None of this grievance would survive Congress's editing sessions of July 2–3. If it had, the Declaration of American Independence would have indeed contained the most antislavery statement of any of the documents that would follow in the generational "Age of Revolutions" that was to follow. But that would have cut against the central impulse of American unity that was a critical factor in July 1776. Congress cut the whole thing.

But not exactly the whole thing. The first half vanished forever, but the second half, the accusation about British agents working with enslaved people, was saved. Congress turned Jefferson's emotion-laden sentences into five words and merged them with the other accusation of people acting in concert with the king's forces, Native peoples. Now the final grievance would read: "He has excited domestic insurrections among us, and has endeavoured to bring on the inhabitants of our frontiers the merciless Indian savages, whose known rule of warfare is an undistinguished destruction of all ages, sexes and conditions." In so doing, the "great object of desire" vanished while the outrage over Dunmore's Proclamation survived, and was featured, even, at what would actually be the Declaration's climax. Abolition disappeared; fear remained.

For the remainder of the Revolutionary War, this preference for defending slavery by excoriating British emancipators continued. When General Henry Clinton issued a similar emancipation proclamation in 1779 or when Sir Guy Carleton defended African Americans who took shelter in Manhattan from their masters when they tried to come into the city to reenslave them, patriot leaders again called them tyrants and destroyers of American households. The "great object of desire" of 1774 didn't vanish completely, but it was overwhelmed by shouts to defend American slaveholders from British attempts to "steal" or "tamper with" their slaves.

THUS, THE complications and, especially, contingency about slavery at the start of the Revolution. Abolition of at least the Atlantic slave trade was near the center of what patriot leaders believed they should have the authority to legislate in the fall of 1774. Twelve months later, it had all but vanished, overwhelmed by an avalanche of stories about British agents working with enslaved peoples to subvert the freedom of white colonists.

Several generations of historians have now uncovered how central African Americans were to the experience of Revolution, and they have highlighted how the specter of slavery as a metaphor consistently informed colonial definitions of liberty. But there is even more to it. There was indeed a possibility that as patriot leaders approached the precipice of revolution they may have embraced antislavery.

It was, however, a moment lost. It was the appearance of a different monster—one made of the three faces of race, fear, and politics—that destroyed it. The need to achieve a common purpose, to mobilize the American people to take up arms together and defend *their* freedom, meant that it had to vanish, or so patriot leaders calculated. Jefferson explained later just how much pain he felt when Congress cut all of his remarkable, impassioned phrases about the evils of the slave trade (a pain that was hardly equivalent to what generations of African Americans would experience), but he did not protest loudly. He calculated, like the rest of his colleagues, that the larger point, the shoring up of a political movement, was irresistible. Publicizing the fear over British-sponsored domestic insurrectionists won out over the "assemblage of horrors."

The use of race to frighten the public to get them to support a particular political goal, in this case independence, has been central to American history. In every generation, including ours, when American politicians want to secure their agendas and achieve victory, it is this device they have turned to time and again. It is a strategy as old as the United States itself.

Notes

1. George Van Cleve, "Somerset's Case and Its Antecedents in Imperial Perspective," *Law and History Review* 24 (2006): 601–45; David Waldstreicher, *The Odyssey of Phillis Wheatley: A Poet's Journey Through American Slavery and Independence* (Macmillan, 2023), 151–64.
2. "Pregnant," *Boston News-Letter*, July 23, 1772; "Much talked," *Virginia Gazette* (Purdie & Dixon) July 23, 1772.
3. *New York Journal*, August 27, 1772.
4. John Dickinson, *Letters from a Farmer in Pennsylvania* (1769), in *The American Revolution: Writings from the Pamphlet Debate, 1764–1772*, ed. Gordon S. Wood (Library of America, 2015), 450.
5. James Otis Jr., *The Rights of the British Colonies Asserted and Proved* (1764), in *American Revolution: Writings from the Pamphlet Debate*, ed. Wood, 70.
6. Benjamin Rush, *An Address to the Inhabitants of the British Settlements, on the Slavery of the Negroes in America* (Philadelphia, 1773), 30.
7. Emily Blanck, *Tyrannicide: Forging an American Law of Slavery in Revolutionary South Carolina and Massachusetts* (University of Georgia Press, 2014), 37.
8. John Adams to Jeremy Belknap, Quincy, March 21, 1795, Founders Online.
9. Arthur Zilversmit, *The First Emancipation: The First Emancipation of Slavery in the North* (University of Chicago Press, 1967), 91–93.
10. Jefferson, Summary View, in *The Papers of Thomas* Jefferson, ed. Julian P. Boyd et al., 49 vols. to date (Princeton University Press, 1950–), 1:130.
11. Benjamin Rush to Granville Sharp, November 1, 1774, in "The Correspondence of Benjamin Rush and Granville Sharp, 1773–1809," ed. John A. Woods, *Journal of American Studies* 1 (1967): 13, 14.
12. "Deposition of Dr. William Pasteur, in regard to the Removal of Powder from the Williamsburg Magazine," 1774, *Virginia Magazine of History & Biography* 13 (1905): 49.

13. John Richard Alden, "John Stuart Accuses William Bull," *William & Mary Quarterly* 3rd ser., 2 (1945): 320.
14. George Washington to Richard Henry Lee, December 27, 1775, in *Papers of George Washington: Revolutionary War Series*, ed. W. W. Abbot et al. (University Press of Virginia, 1985), 2:611.
15. Alden, "Stuart Accuses Bull," 320.
16. Letter to John Adams, Fredericksburg, VA, June 9, 1775, in *Papers of John Adams*, ed. Robert J. Taylor (Harvard University Press, 1977), 3:18–20.

What Is the American Declaration of Independence at 250 to Me?

MARLENE L. DAUT

I WAS A professor of Black studies at the University of Virginia during the August 11 and 12, 2017, white supremacist rallies, locally dubbed the "Summer of Hate."[1] Before taking up an appointment at the storied Carter G. Woodson Institute, I had taught for seven years at the Claremont Graduate University in Claremont, California. When I told family and friends that I was contemplating taking a new job at UVA, reactions seemed mixed. My mother worried that her grandsons, then aged six and four, might encounter more racism in a Southern state like Virginia than they would in Southern California. "It's not like the KKK just walk down the street every day," I quipped, reminding her that Orange County, where I was partly raised, is home to multiple and equally menacing neo-Nazi skinhead gangs.

Then, in July, shortly after we moved to Charlottesville, a small KKK rally occurred in the middle of the city. The event was sparsely attended, with more counterprotesters than white supremacists present, but it marked the second visit to the city by a white supremacist group in as many months (a white supremacist tiki torch rally took place in May, just before we moved). Around this time, I had a conversation with another new faculty member who had yet to move to town. "I am not really impressed with the place that will be my future residence," she said. I wasn't either, but lost in the commotion of my own big move across the country, which took me far from my family and most of my friends, I tried to put out of my mind the fact that the KKK did in fact periodically march down the street of my new hometown.

Eventually, Friday, August 11, arrived. We had family visiting from France and Vermont. I happened to be away at a conference in Denmark. The third of the white supremacist rallies had been planned for months. I feared leaving my family in such potentially perilous circumstances—at the July KKK rally, the police had pepper-sprayed the counterprotesters, creating a violent scene—but away I went at my husband's urging. That night I watched in horror from thousands of miles away as hundreds of white men wearing white polo shirts and khaki pants (instead of white robes and pointed masks) marched through the University of Virginia's famous lawn carrying lighted tiki torches. Many of the men were carrying signs that said things like, "You will not replace us." Others repeated the Nazi chant "blood and soil," while still more waved Confederate flags and other inveterate symbols of antisemitism, anti-Blackness, and general white supremacy, some of them repurposed, as in the case of the Detroit Red Wings logo.[2] Although this event was highly publicized before it occurred, with its organizers citing the right to free speech and peaceful assembly, neither the university nor the City of Charlottesville took steps to prevent such a threatening display of white power.

As if August 11 were not an appalling enough display of brazen racism, August 12 saw more racists calling themselves "white nationalists" descend upon the city. This time, they marched down Market Street, all the way to a park housing a statue of the military leader of the Confederacy, General Robert E. Lee, where they met yet more counterprotesters. After the rally had finished, the counterprotesters and white supremacists alike dispersed. Many of them found their way to a large outdoor retail center known colloquially around town as "the mall." While the mall is mostly a pedestrian environment, there are two streets that cars can use to pass through. On one of them, counterprotester Heather Heyer (a white woman) met her death when "avowed white supremacist" James Alex Fields decided to plow his car into the crowd that had gathered on that street. His car struck Heather, killing her, while he injured nearly two dozen more. Some of the other white supremacists began to attack and beat the counterprotesters, many of whom were permanently maimed.[3] Two Virginia state troopers also lost their lives when their helicopter crashed after they had completed surveillance of the protests.[4]

Before the deadly days of August 11 and 12, most people in the United States, and certainly most living overseas, had never even heard of Charlottesville. After that fateful weekend, many people would never forget it. At the airport in Copenhagen, a guard examining my travel documents as I checked in for my return flight asked me where I lived. "Charlottesville, Virginia," I said, trying to hide my panic-stricken face, as recognition lighted his. "Ohhh," he said. Just as Columbine and Sandy Hook have become indelible symbols of the intractability of US gun violence, Charlottesville immediately became shorthand for one of the most hateful displays of racism in modern US history.

Upon my return, as I fielded phone calls from concerned family and friends, most were confused about why this racist mob had chosen Charlottesville and UVA. I explained that the city had recently approved the removal of a General Robert E. Lee statue, after a petition was brought forward by Charlottesville High School student Zyahna Bryant. The city's determination to remove the statue immediately led to a lawsuit intended to block its removal. This brought national attention to Charlottesville and hate mail to Bryant and city officials, as protecting the statue quickly became the cause célèbre of myriad white supremacist groups, national and local. (Up until its ultimate removal in 2021, an armed faction guarded on rotation the park where the Lee statue stood.)[5]

Yet the conclusion that I have drawn after seven years of reflection on that tragic weekend is that none of this was really about the statue. It was the sad outcome of the United States' inability to reckon with its founding in white supremacy. UVA and Charlottesville in many ways remain merely the most arresting monuments of that inability and so the most fitting place, perhaps, for its unabashed eruption into public consciousness.

In August 2024, for example, the University of Virginia, founded by Thomas Jefferson in 1819, announced it would suspend guided services of the campus's famous grounds, following complaints by a conservative alumni group called the Jefferson Council. Among the Council's numerous objections were that the guides acknowledged the university to have been built by enslaved Africans on land originally stolen from the Monacan Indian tribe and that they often stated that Jefferson himself was an enslaver.[6] While the university's suspension led some prominent alumni families to decry UVA's "immense hypocrisy,"[7] suppressing, downplaying, or outright ignoring Jefferson's direct participation, maintenance, and protection of slavery—facts hardly in dispute today—is wholly in keeping with the university's ethos. As Maurie D. McInnis wrote in her coedited volume about slavery at the university, *Educated in Tyranny*, "The central paradox at the heart of UVA is also the central paradox of the nation, the unresolved paradox of American liberty." "How is it that the nation that defined the natural rights of humankind did so within a system that denied those same rights to others based on the color of their skin?" she asked. "And what does it mean to have a public university founded to preserve those democratic rights that is likewise founded and maintained on the stolen liberty of others?"[8]

But what if there is no paradox at all? What if the United States is not the nation that defined the natural rights of humankind? What if, with all due respect to Frederick Douglass, he was wrong when he rejected outright the idea of "the pro-slavery character of the Constitution," in his much-quoted and exalted speech, "What to the Slave Is the Fourth of July?" "In that instrument I hold there is neither warrant, license, nor sanction of the hateful thing," Douglass insisted with adamance, "but interpreted, as it ought to be interpreted, the Constitution is a GLORIOUS LIBERTY DOCUMENT."[9] Douglass could not have known at the time he spoke these words, however, that more than 150 years after the Civil War ended the "hateful thing" called slavery, Black people in the United States would continue to grapple with the same disenfranchisement, wealth gap, and ingrained racism that emancipation was supposed to destroy; and he certainly could not have foreseen the long and violent fight Black Americans had to wage to achieve the vote and end legalized segregation during the civil rights movement, or ongoing redlining, seemingly unstoppable police killings of unarmed Black men and women across the country, and most profoundly, the "New Jim Crow," or the carceral system that disproportionately, by a wide degree, condemns Black men to lives in prison, toiling essentially for free in conditions little better than chattel slavery.

I must confess, it now seems hard to imagine things having turned out otherwise. The Thirteenth Amendment to that "glorious liberty document," passed shortly after the end of the Civil War, does not even outlaw slavery. It reads instead: "Neither slavery nor involuntary servitude, *except as a punishment for crime whereof the party shall have been duly convicted*, shall exist within the United States, or any place subject to their jurisdiction."[10]

Perhaps instead of reflexively, and unflinchingly, celebrating the founding principles of the United States, we would do better to rethink the idea that the Constitution—with its original and infamous three-fifth clause to describe how enslaved Black people would be counted for the purpose of representation—is a sacred document, filled with timeless, inestimable, and inviolable principles. Maybe the US Constitution merely reflects back to us, and uncomfortably so, the fact that the United States, and the University of Virginia, remain exactly the places their founders originally designed them to be: institutions that offer freedom for white people at the expense of Black, Native, and other nonwhite citizens.

FROM 1817 to 1825, more than one hundred enslaved Black men were forced to help build the University of Virginia. Hundreds more were enslaved there after the school opened its doors until general emancipation belatedly reached the state in the spring of 1865. As McInnis reminds us, "The university's existence was made possible by a large enslaved population."[11] The university tried to grapple with this fact, often phrased as a revelation, during the entire time I was employed there—I even witnessed the start-to-finish erection of a monument to the enslaved laborers who built the university. Yet this reckoning often felt performative. It seemed designed to acknowledge, only to dismiss, the painful reality that the university was, and remains, virtually a plantation.

UVA's *Memorial to Enslaved Laborers* is a steel structure that appears from a distance like a half-moon rising and fading out of the grass. It sits prominently below the Rotunda building across from the area that UVA students call "the Corner." Completed in 2020, the monument was designed to provide visitors space for reflection and encourage dialogue around the university's, and the nation's, slave past. As visitors circle the memorial, they read the names of the known enslaved laborers who built the university and encounter a timeline chronicling UVA's violent founding in slavery. The first plaque explains its raison d'être:

> As it enters its third century, the University of Virginia remembers the enslaved people whose labor and talents made possible the construction and operation of the Academical Village. Forced labor, incalculable suffering, and the struggle to live with dignity were the daily experiences of the enslaved African Americans who shaped the institution's first half century. This memorial is erected as a permanent tribute to them.

The monument also unwittingly stands testament to the university's own complicated relationship to acknowledging its founder, Thomas Jefferson, as an enslaver, one who consistently upheld white supremacy and who did nothing to bring about the universal abolition of slavery during his time as president. A plaque on the monument's timeline for the year 1776 reads, "Jefferson writes the Declaration of Independence proclaiming 'All Men are Created Equal.'" Just below, on the same plaque, we find the painful contradiction laid bare, "In his lifetime he holds over

600 African Americans in human bondage." Jefferson continued to force Black people into *inhumane* bondage for his entire life. A plaque covering the years 1826–29 leaves no doubt: "Several professors purchase enslaved people from Jefferson's estate after his death in 1826." With this pithy acknowledgment, the monument exhibits the same inability as the rest of the university to truly contend with the magnitude of Jefferson's crimes against humanity.

For the entire six years I worked at UVA, I heard Jefferson quoted seemingly endlessly as a prophet of peace and freedom because of his work to create the Declaration of Independence and because of the architectural significance of the Rotunda and the Academical Village. The latter comprises a UNESCO World Heritage Site, and at the same time, serves as the most visibly arresting symbol of slavery at the university; the buildings on the Lawn of the Academical Village were structured so that professors and students lived aboveground, with those they enslaved living below, out of sight, a tacit acknowledgment of the shamefulness of slavery. The year before I arrived on campus, students and professors had protested former UVA President Teresa Sullivan's particularly curious usage of Jefferson quotes—following Donald Trump's election to the presidency and the discovery of graffiti reading "terrorists" scrawled on a dorm room occupied by two Muslim students, for example. When national news outlets learned of the outcry against the Jefferson quotes, they deliberately distorted the logic behind the complaint, with the Jefferson Council responding that faculty who did not want to hear Jefferson quoted at the university he founded should simply quit. But using that logic, instead of siding with those who objected to hearing about slavery during the guided services tours, the Council might have asserted with equal vehemence that those who do not want to hear about slavery at UVA should probably not visit a university founded by an enslaver and built by enslaved hands.

As UVA Professor Lawrie Balfour told the campus newspaper, the *Cavalier Daily*, "The point is not that [Jefferson] is never appropriate. . . . The point is that the move that says, he owned slaves, but he was a great man, is deeply problematic, and I think it will continue to prevent us from being the kind of inclusive, respectful community that President Sullivan and the rest of us envision."[12] Balfour's comments unwittingly prophesied the problem with the university's attempt to use the monument to reckon with what cannot be reckoned: Jefferson's direct participation in the violent torture of other human beings for personal gain.

The memorial to enslaved laborers is not only contradictory but confusing. Imagine that an extraterrestrial is dropped onto the campus. They know nothing of the United States, Virginia, or Jefferson, but read these terrifying words on the monument under the years 1776–1865: "Virginia holds more enslaved people than any other state." Under the year 1850, they find out, "Three students attack a twelve-year-old enslaved girl in a field near UVA." Although the university expels these students, the visitor learns that in 1856, "An enslaved eleven-year-old girl is beaten unconscious by a UVA student. Claiming his right to discipline any slave, he suffers no consequences." After reading about at least a dozen more such atrocities, and that in 1861, "Virginia secedes from the Union invoking the federal government's oppression of the slaveholding states," our visitor might wander past the much more well-known Thomas Jefferson statue nearby. It depicts the former president reading the Declaration of Independence atop a liberty bell. Jefferson is surrounded by angels and the words "Vox Populi, Vox Dei" (the voice of the people is the voice of God). Scott Harrop, an adjunct lecturer in UVA's Woodrow Wilson Department of Politics and the Department of Middle Eastern and South Asian Languages and Cultures, has interpreted the statue as an homage to Jefferson's putative commitment to religious freedom and his desire to spread the principles of US-style democracy around the world. "For Jefferson, this was all about the survival of democracy—not just here in the U.S., but the whole world, having free education available to everyone," Harrop explained.[13] But could our extraterrestrial visitor, unfamiliar with Great Man theories and "Men of their time" excuses, come away from this experience believing the University of Virginia (and the United States, by extension) to be the birthplace of liberty, democracy, and education for all?

The memorial to the enslaved laborers makes clear that UVA's true founders were the enslaved Black people, who, in 1817, "begin to clear the land that will become UVA," and who, for decades afterward, denied the ability to enroll at the university, labored to maintain it, tragically, brutally, under conditions of great violence, such as that experienced in October 1825, when "rioting students beat a professor's enslaved servant," as another plaque reads.

Just as my colleagues who remonstrated against the Jefferson quotes faced derision, whenever I scoffed out loud at the patently absurd idea that Jefferson could ever be a symbol of freedom for a Black American like me—UVA did not admit its first Black student until 1950 and did not hire its first Black professor until 1967[14]—my protests were waved off as if I were an annoying fly. When I reminded the offended that Jefferson was an enslaver and a rapist, those promoting him as an icon of liberty usually asked me not to call him a rapist or condemn him for enslaving Black people since he merely did things sanctioned as legal by the (white) men of his time. But what does that mean? Does it mean we must excuse that Jefferson personally enslaved more than six hundred Black people during his lifetime, including Sally Hemings, the teenage girl with no legal ability to refuse to have sex with him, and who birthed at least six of his children (something the memorial fails to even acknowledge)?[15] Do we shrug off knowledge that enslaved children were whipped at Jefferson's infamous plantation, Monticello—a brutal terror tactic used by enslavers to exert domination and control?[16] And do we pretend that as head of state Jefferson was powerless to end slavery when other world leaders of the time managed to do so?

In day-to-day life, "man of his time" is a cliché often used to excuse past crimes, especially those of so-called great white men. For scholars, though, it's a meaningless phrase. Every person is of their time. What we're interested in is how people lived in their time. All of them. Not just a chosen few.

THE GREATEST war for liberty and humanity the world has ever seen happened in Jefferson's own time. It was neither the American nor the French Revolution. In August 1791, enslaved people in French Saint-Domingue (present-day Haiti) planned a huge rebellion. It was led by an enslaved man called Boukman Dutty, who encouraged the crowd to rebel against their "masters." Enslaved men and women subsequently drove out their enslavers by setting fire to the colony's northern plain. By 1793 the Black revolutionaries forced the French to formally end slavery on the island.

The enslaved liberators of Saint-Domingue lived in the same era as Jefferson. Yet while Jefferson bragged to George Washington that the birth of enslaved Black children at Monticello earned him 4 percent profit per year,[17] the Haitian revolutionaries endured genocidal violence as they risked their lives to permanently end slavery and achieve independence from France.[18]

Although it has become a standard rejoinder to argue that the actions of noteworthy figures from the past should not be judged by people living in the present,[19] it is perfectly possible to judge someone like Jefferson according to the opinions of people living in his time. In 1791, before joining the Haitian revolutionaries, a free man of color named Julien Raimond, a former plantation owner and enslaver, asked, "The father who creates another being only to enslave him, is he not a monster?"[20] And in 1807, three years after Haitian independence, the Haitian writer and statesman Juste Chanlatte, also from a family of former enslavers, made history when he declared slavery and the slave trade a "crime against humanity," a public condemnation of enslavers heard around the world for the first time.[21]

Jefferson also judged his own participation in the crime of slavery. He knew that slavery was monstrously wrong but feared that its end might bring about "the extermination of the one or the other race."[22] Jefferson's own words make it hard not to read as a double entendre what he later wrote about the Haitian Revolution to St. John Tucker in 1797. "If something is not done, and soon done," Jefferson warned, "we shall be the murderers of our own children."[23] Jefferson had good reason to be worried.

Haitian independence exposed an embarrassing truth about the American Revolution. The Haitian revolutionaries used the same practices of radical, and violent, rebellion as the American colonists to fully implement the American Declaration of Independence's putatively "self-evident" phrase, "all men are created equal." On January 1, 1804, under General Jean-Jacques Dessalines, Haiti declared its independence from France. As emperor of the new nation, Dessalines demonstrated that he was far more enlightened on questions of slavery and freedom than President Jefferson.[24] The 1805 Imperial Constitution of Haiti reads: "Slavery is forever abolished. . . . Equality in the eyes of the law is incontestably acknowledged."[25] This constitution circulated across the world, laying bare a damning contrast: It was infinitely possible to eliminate slavery during Jefferson's presidency, but Jefferson and his administration chose otherwise.[26]

While Jefferson and the other US founders, most of whom were also enslavers, were by turns too cowardly, depraved, or self-interested to end slavery, Haiti's founders saw "liberty" and "equality" as more than just pretty slogans. The result was that the US republic was founded on slavery, in great contrast to the empire of Haiti, founded on freedom.

In the nineteenth century, even as the country's successive rulers transformed it from an empire to a kingdom to a republic, Haiti was "the land of the free and home of the brave" to which other freedom fighters in the hemisphere, like Simón Bolívar, looked for inspiration.[27] As for President Jefferson, when he had the opportunity to support the people he once called "cannibals of the terrible republic," he did the opposite.[28] Jefferson so feared that Haiti's antislavery egalitarianism would spread to US shores that he tried to economically strangle the new nation with a trade embargo.[29] What the case of Haiti makes apparent is that we can only write off the crimes of enslavers as the deeds of "men of their time" if we leave out the story of their victims.

THE UNIVERSITY of Virginia teemed with slavery's victims: McInnis tells us that at UVA, "enslaved people were daily subject to the arbitrary actions of faculty, hotelkeepers, and students," whose "violent offenses" included "beating, kicking, whipping, and raping." These unfortunates, usually women and children, had no recourse against their assailants since the faculty did not consider enslaved testimony "admissible."[30] The fact that those in power at the time disregarded the protests and complaints of enslaved individuals is no reason for us to continue to do so today.[31] Enslaved men and women forced to silently suffer by those tyrants euphemistically called slaveholders and planters—including the enslaved who ran away or killed themselves—were also people of their time. So were the maroons who led slave rebellions across the Americas, including in the United States, as were the abolitionists who advocated for universal emancipation.

If there is one thing that teaching at "Thomas Jefferson's University" taught me, it is that those who defend the proslavery founders of the United States are not seeking moral clarity when they tell us not to judge Jefferson. It is absolution they want.[32] Yet this is something Jefferson could not give to himself, much less the nation he helped create. "I tremble for my country when I reflect that God is just; that his justice cannot sleep forever," Jefferson lamented in his 1785 *Notes on the State of Virginia*.[33] He clearly didn't tremble too much. George Washington freed all the people he claimed as his slaves in his 1799 will.[34] Thomas Jefferson, who died in 1826, freed only five in his. Sally Hemings wasn't one of them.[35]

Passing by the Jefferson statue on UVA's grounds one day nearly two years after the Summer of Hate, just following my promotion to full professor, I could not help but feel a little bit like my fictional extraterrestrial. I wondered how I got dropped into this place, at a university whose founder could never have even conceived of my promotion to the highest ranks of university faculty, let alone have approved of it. I marveled at how it is that so many of us live in countries where the cruel and inhumane see their rise to power praised in stone, while those they irreparably harmed to get there are relegated to the status of collateral damage.

Continuing my walk across the grounds, I could only shake my head as I thought about the way UVA's Black students, faced with numerous kinds of racial conflict, often evoke the history of Robert Bland, the first Black graduate (though not the first Black student) of the university. "Bobby stayed, then I can stay," they console one another and themselves.[36] But stay, I did not.

Notes

1. Howard Spencer, *Summer of Hate* (University of Virginia Press, 2019).
2. Meg Wagner, "'Blood and Soil': Protesters Chant Nazi Slogan in Charlottesville," CNN, August 12, 2017, https://www.cnn.com/2017/08/12/us/charlottesville-unite-the-right-rally/index.html; "Deconstructing the Symbols and Slogans Spotted in Charlottesville," *Washington Post*, August 18, 2017.
3. Meghan Keneally, "What to Know About the Violent Charlottesville Protests and Anniversary Rallies," ABC News, August 12, 2017, https://abcnews.go.com/US/happen-charlottesville-protest-anniversary-weekend/story?id=57107500; Denise Lavoie, "Life Sentence for Killing at Charlottesville Protest," AP, June 28, 2019.
4. Morgan Winsor, "Families of Virginia State Troopers Killed in Charlottesville Grapple with Painful Anniversary," ABC News, August 12, 2018, https://abcnews.go.com/US/families-virginia-state-troopers-killed-charlottesville-grapple-painful/story?id=57142770
5. Theresa Vargas, "The Girl Who Brought Down a Statue," *Washington Post*, July 18, 2021.
6. Stephanie Saul, "University of Virginia Suspends Tours Criticized for Emphasizing Ties to Slavery," *New York Times*, August 29, 2024.
7. Jason Armesto, "Family of Late Professor, Civil Rights Activist Calls Out 'Immense Hypocrisy' at UVa," *Charlottesville Daily Progress*, September 4, 2024.
8. Maurie D. McInnis, introduction to *Educated in Tyranny: Slavery at Thomas Jefferson's University*, eds. Maurie D. McInnis and Louis P. Nelson (University of Virginia Press, 2019), 4.
9. Frederick Douglass, "What to the Slave Is the Fourth of July?" Oration Delivered in Corinthian Hall, Rochester, by Frederick Douglass, Rochester, NY, 1852; Noelle Trent, "Frederick Douglass and the United States Constitution," *Black Perspectives*, November 28. 2018, https://www.aaihs.org/frederick-douglass-and-the-united-states-constitution/#:~:text=Under%20his%20new%20thought%2C%20Douglass,line%20with%20its%20founding%20intent.
10. Michelle Alexander, *The New Jim Crow: Mass Incarceration in the Age of Colorblindness* (New Press, 2010); The House Joint Resolution Proposing

the 13th Amendment to the Constitution, January 31, 1865; Enrolled Acts and Resolutions of Congress, 1789–1999; General Records of the United States Government; Record Group 11; National Archives, https://www.archives.gov/milestone-documents/13th-amendment#:~:text=The%2013th%20Amendment%20to%20the%20United%20States%20Constitution%20provides%20that,place%20subject%20to%20their%20jurisdiction.%22 (emphasis added).

11. McInnis, introduction to *Educated in Tyranny*, 16, 5.
12. Travis M. Andrews, "Group of U-Va. Students, Faculty 'Deeply Offended' by Thomas Jefferson Being Quoted at School He Founded," *Washington Post*, November 15, 2016; Richard Gard, "Unquoting Jefferson," *UVA Magazine*, Spring 2017; Bre Payton, "UVA Professors to UVA President: You Can't Quote Thomas Jefferson," *The Federalist*, November 15, 2016.
13. Lauren Jones, "Let Freedom Ring: U.Va. Professor Rediscovers Sacred Story Behind Jefferson Statue," *UVA Today*, July 2, 2014.
14. "Desegregating UVA," *Virginia Magazine*, October 12, 2009; Patrice Preston Grimes, "UVA and the History of Race: Allies of Integration," *UVA Today*, March 25, 2021.
15. "How Many People Did Thomas Jefferson Own?," "Slavery FAQs—Property," Monticello website, https://www.monticello.org/slavery/slavery-faqs/property/#:~:text=How%20many%20people%20did%20Thomas,bondage%20on%20Jefferson's%20other%20properties; "Thomas Jefferson and Sally Hemings: A Brief Account," Monticello website, https://www.monticello.org/thomas-jefferson/jefferson-slavery/thomas-jefferson-and-sally-hemings-a-brief-account/.
16. Martha Jefferson Randolph and Thomas Mann Randolph to Thomas Jefferson, January 31, 1801, Founders Online.
17. Henry Wiencek, "The Dark Side of Thomas Jefferson: A New Portrait of the Founding Father Challenges the Long-Held Perception of Thomas Jefferson as a Benevolent Slaveholder," *Smithsonian Magazine*, October 2012.
18. Marlene L. Daut, "Napoleon Isn't a Hero to Celebrate," *New York Times*, March 18, 2021.
19. For a summary of such positions, see Ta-Nehisi Coates, "The Myth of Jefferson as 'a Man of His Times,'" *The Atlantic*, December 2, 2012.
20. Julien Raimond, *Réponse aux considérations de M. Moreau, dit Saint-Méry, député à l'Assemblée nationale, sur les colonies: par M. Raymond, Citoyen de couleur de Saint-Domingue* (Paris, 1791), 56.
21. Juste Chanlatte, *"Avis," Gazette royale d'Hayti*, May 7, 1807.
22. Thomas Jefferson, *Notes on the State of Virginia*, ed. William Peden (Omohundro Institute of Early American History and Culture and University of North Carolina Press, 2011), 138.

23. Jefferson to St. John Tucker, August 28, 1797, Founders Online.
24. Julia Gaffield, "Meet Haiti's Founding Father, Whose Black Revolution Was Too Radical for Thomas Jefferson," *The Conversation*, August 30, 2018.
25. "Constitution de 20 mai 1805," Digithèque, MJP, https://mjp.univ-perp.fr/constit/ht1805.htm.
26. Deborah Jenson, "Dessalines's American Proclamations of the Haitian Independence," *Journal of Haitian Studies* 15, no. 1/2 (2009): 72–102.
27. Marlene L. Daut, "The King of Haiti's Dream," *Aeon*, July 14, 2020, https://aeon.co/essays/the-king-of-haiti-and-the-dilemmas-of-freedom-in-a-colonised-world; [Cinna] Marion, *Expédition de Bolívar, par le Senateur Marion aîné* (Port-au-Prince, Haiti, 1849).
28. Jefferson to Aaron Burr, February 11, 1799, Founders Online.
29. Jefferson to Rufus King, July 13, 1802, in "Jefferson Quotes and Family Letters," Monticello website, https://tjrs.monticello.org/letter/1741; for the trade embargo, see Julia Gaffield, *Haitian Connections in the Atlantic World: Recognition After Revolution* (University of North Carolina Press, 2015).
30. McInnis, "Violence," in *Educated in Tyranny*, 99, 103.
31. Sean Wilentz, "The Revolution Within the American Revolution," *New York Review of Books*, October 23, 2023.
32. James A. Bacon, "Jefferson Defended," Jefferson Council, October 29, 2021, https://thejeffersoncouncil.com/jefferson-defended/.
33. Jefferson, *Notes*, 163.
34. "A Decision to Free His Slaves," Mount Vernon website, https://www.mountvernon.org/george-washington/slavery/washingtons-1799-will/.
35. "Enslaved People Who Gained Freedom," Monticello website, https://www.monticello.org/research-education/thomas-jefferson-encyclopedia/slaves-who-gained-freedom/.
36. Anne E. Bromley, "Q & A with Sylvia Terry," *UVA Today*, July 7, 2009.

Hidden in Plain Sight

The George Rogers Clark Statue at the University of Virginia, 1921–2021

ALLISON BIGELOW AND TERESA R. POLLAK

It was uncomfortably hot, that sticky Saturday of July 10, 2021, as the sun bore down relentlessly. But we were in the backyard anyway, sweating buckets and swatting mosquitoes, because the COVID-19 pandemic was in full force, and sitting outside was the only way to be together. The adults were vaccinated, but pediatric vaccines would not be available for another year. So, in a time when nothing was normal, it was a typical weekend: lunch on a friend's deck, with chairs spaced generously apart, parents eating in shifts as we chased toddlers who were fighting naps. And then, suddenly, it became a day like no other. At 12:51 p.m., reporter Katherine Knott announced on Twitter (now X) that the George Rogers Clark statue would be removed from the University of Virginia at 8:00 a.m. the next day. This was news to us, the faculty, students, community members, and administrators who had spent six months developing a plan for the statue. Our phones blew up, and we spent the next twenty-four hours drinking from a firehose, trying to make sure that Tribal citizens could witness the event safely.

Earlier that morning, joyful crowds observed the removal of two monuments of Confederate Generals Robert E. Lee (1807–1870) and Thomas "Stonewall" Jackson (1824–1863), and one commemorating the Lewis and Clark expedition (1804–6), which depicted Shoshone knowledge holder Sacajawea (1788–1820) in a disrespectful, subordinate position, crouching on the ground. The twenty-four-foot-tall bronze of General George

Rogers Clark (1752–1818), shown charging against three Indigenous adults and one infant, nestled in a woman's cradleboard, was the last to fall. The timing was fitting, in some ways, since Clark and his statue were the least famous of the lot, and many people often confused him with his younger brother, William (1770–1838), of the aforesaid Expedition. In contrast to William's formative role in early American history, the second-oldest Clark brother, George Rogers, was almost immediately forgotten after the Revolution. Before we served on the statue committee, we only had a hazy idea of who Clark was, and we imagine that you're in a similar boat. During his lifetime, Clark was most famous for a civilian massacre of Ottawa and Lenape men in 1779 at the British fort of Sackville, in present-day Vincennes, Indiana, which helped to weaken Native Nations' alliances with the Crown. Afterward, he drifted out of public memory until the Jim Crow era, when monuments of men like the Clark brothers and Confederate generals were erected throughout the United States, and especially in the South. Charlottesville's four statues were installed between 1919 and 1924 with a gift of $145,900 (more than $2.5 million today) from local businessman Paul Goodloe McIntire (1860–1952), who made substantial donations to the university around the same time.[1]

Two of the monuments celebrated settler colonialism in the US West by emphasizing the heroic triumphs of white men and erasing Native Americans, and two reinforced the Lost Cause, a romanticized interpretation of Southern history that ignores its role in a nationwide system of racial capitalism, rape, and land theft. These imagined histories of vanished Indians and happily enslaved Black families went hand in hand. At UVA, the Clark statue was built at a busy intersection where the campus became city, kitty-corner from a Confederate-era hospital that desegregated in the 1960s, after a long period of research and clinical practice in eugenic medicine. Speaking at the statue's dedication on November 3, 1921, mathematics professor Archibald Henderson (1877–1963), who traveled from University of North Carolina–Chapel Hill for the occasion, called Clark "the Stonewall Jackson of the Revolution" for his westward charges against "copper-hued foes."[2] Henderson presumably referred to Clark's military campaigns of the 1770s and 1780s, but it could not have been lost on the crowd that the four Native figures on the statue before them, male, female, and infant, all staring down the barrels of Clark's guns, were cast in bronze.

Although they were supposed to represent distinct moments of revolutionary, pioneer, and Civil War history, the four statues converged into a narrative that celebrated the past, present, and future of white supremacy. Public monuments have a way of doing that. They tell us less about the periods they depict and more about the time they were built. The Clark statue has very little to do with 1776, or 1779, and everything to do with 1921, a period that was characterized by voting restrictions, segregation, and laws like Virginia's Racial Integrity Act (1924). This act made it illegal to be recognized as a Native, Latinx, or Asian American citizen—and, thus, it became extremely difficult for Native Nations to claim rights as sovereign peoples, since no official records of their traditions of governance, economics, social service programs, or even their very lives as people existed for much of the twentieth century.

Spanning multiple chronologies and forms of memory, public monuments offer unique opportunities to reflect on the contradictory legacies of the Revolution in our own time. In the Jim Crow era, the statues were hallmarks of the City Beautiful movement, which introduced art and greenways into urban life to improve conditions in working-class neighborhoods—and often forced people from their homes and land kin to do so.[3] By 2019, when a presidential commission on slavery examined the "misalignment" between UVA's historic landscape and its "current mission and values," and the city voted to remove the Lewis and Clark statue after consulting with descendants of Sacajawea, few citizens saw anything beautiful in these statues.[4]

In 2012, faculty like Grace Hale, a professor of history, and students like Bethany Gordon, a freshman in engineering, suggested the statues should remain in place, perhaps with recontextualization, as evidence of the nation's discriminatory past.[5] Gordon—now Dr. Gordon, an assistant professor of civil engineering at the University of Washington focusing on climate resilient, community-driven infrastructure and Black women engineers—has thought a lot about her statement over the years, as she told us by email. The reporter came to her dorm and needed an immediate response. After one month on campus, Gordon "had no context for what was happening in Charlottesville," but she wanted to help a fellow student meet a deadline. Her words remind us that there is always more to a story than what is printed on a page, and that beliefs about statues change, even as the monuments seem frozen in time.

In Gordon's senior year, during a nationwide reckoning with Confederate monuments after a white supremacist massacre in the Mother Emmanuel Church of Charleston, South Carolina, UVA students once more debated the campus statue. Brandon Brink, a junior, drew from his experiences as a Black student to argue that it should be removed, as "a disgrace upon our community." Alexander Mink, also in his third year, responded that Clark was "an American hero" whose "greatest successes were bloodless victories where he convinced Native Americans and settlers to stay neutral in the war between the British and Americans."[6]

Historians view Clark differently, as a general who used what his biographer calls "psychological warfare" against Native people.[7] Clark's reputation has shifted over time, but he remains most famous for a using a civilian massacre to compel allegiance to the American side—or, at least, to dissolve British alliances.[8] On February 24, 1779, in Vincennes, Indiana, just outside of British-controlled Fort Sackville, Clark released two Frenchmen from a captured search party. He marched the remaining four men, Lenapes and Ottawas, into the town center, where he tomahawked, scalped, and threw them into the Wabash River. By all accounts, including Clark's own, everything about his anti-Native violence was intentional. The English name "Wabash" is derived from a French approximation of the Myaamia term *waapaahšiiki*, "it shines white," referring to the limestone beds found elsewhere in the river that connected diverse peoples.[9] Clark sought the greatest visibility for his execution and disposal of Native men so that word would spread.

Scholars disagree on the extent to which Clark's campaigns worked in the "prosperous Indian world" of the Ohio River Valley, where multiple Native Nations—including historic rivals—"banded together" to combat American settler colonialism and imperial encroachment from France, Spain, and England.[10] By 1776, Native Americans had a century-long history of participating in armed conflict with and against American settlers and European empires. Whereas Native soldiers joined colonial militias as early as King Philip's War (1675–76), the brutal Anglo victory against the Wampanoag Confederation caused Indigenous people in New England to rethink such alliances, and word spread with strategies to resist, regroup, and survive.[11] When the Revolution came to the greater Ohio Valley, most Native Nations stayed neutral. The largest, including the Miami, Wyandot, and Ojibwe, saw Americans and British as equally untrustworthy. Others, such as the Shawnee, Mingo, and Delaware, reluctantly aligned with the British "because they felt the immediate pressure of American land hunger."[12]

Whereas the statue declares Clark to be the "CONQUEROR OF THE NORTHWEST," historians agree that "no conquering occurred." Indigenous people regrouped and found new ways to thrive in the early years of the new republic. They are still here. As for the Revolution, the victories for which Clark was most famous "were won against weakly fortified enemies" with "little bearing on the war's outcome."[13] By 1793, Clark offered to "expatriate" himself from an "ungrateful" country and become a French mercenary, capable of delivering "all of Spanish Louisiana and perhaps New Mexico."[14] In other words, the statue of Clark that was commissioned for UVA in 1919 and finished in 1921 celebrated a conquest that did not happen, and it memorialized a revolutionary patriot who, fourteen years after his most famous victory, offered to abandon his country for a small stipend and license to form his own army.

Individual activists had long advocated for the statue's removal, but student organizations began to weigh in after August 11–12, 2017, when white supremacists marched on campus and in the city to defend the statues. Antiracist protestors were assaulted, harassed, pepper-sprayed, and hit by a car; one, Heather Heyer (1985–2017), died from the impact, as did Trooper Pilot Berke Bates (1977–2017) and Lieutenant Pilot Jay Cullen (1969–2017) when their surveillance helicopter crashed. Two weeks after the deadly rally, the Native American Student Union (NASU) held a cleansing sage ceremony and collaborated with student groups, community members, and elders on marches, petitions, and teach-ins to highlight challenges facing Indigenous people around the world, from South America to the shadow of the statue.[15] Research shows, though, that public attitudes don't often matter in the creation or removal of such statues—one more sign of their undemocratic histories. For more than two hundred years, "scholars, activists, artists, and ordinary citizens have continually criticized American monuments for showing non-white Americans as inferior," but many are removed "only when those who hold political power find them personally insulting," often using legal processes "of a system that they also control."[16]

In many ways, our committee fits this pattern: We were a presidential committee with senior leadership from Kevin McDonald, vice president for diversity, equity, and inclusion; Lewis Nelson, vice provost for academic outreach; and Alice Raucher, university architect. The committee was charged with executing a vote by the Board of Visitors in September 2020, in response to an executive task force. And yet, because of the decision-making model that we adapted from trauma theory, called "ring theory" or "circles of impact," the people most affected by the statue—those historically furthest from power—had the greatest say in the outcome.[17] Virginia Busby, a community representative, UVA PhD, and expert on Tribal consultation, recommended the approach, which we used to identify three "circles" to balance the competing imperatives of inclusion and impact. In the first circle were Native students, represented by NASU copresidents Zac Russell (Cherokee) and Samantha Solomon (Monacan). In the second circle were citizens of Virginia Tribes, represented by chiefs or their delegates. The third circle included Tribal Nations outside of Virginia whose ancestors had been harmed by Clark. Students in the first circle served on the committee; representatives in the second and third circles consulted with us in a formal, four-month process of dialogue and debate.

For UVA employees, including landscape architects Mary Hughes and Rachel Lloyd, and faculty cochairs Barbara Brown Wilson and Allison Bigelow, these committees are more or less part of the job. For Professor Jalane Schmidt, the committee was an extension of her public scholarship and community activism. Another, Walt Heinecke, was named as a faculty alternate, but Dr. Schmidt never missed a meeting. The final committee member, Teresa Pollak (Monacan), served in memory of her best friend, Monacan citizen Karenne Wood (1960–2019), who led a twenty-year fight for curriculum building, Tribal recognition, and statue removal. One UVA alumnus, Anthony Guy Lopez (Crow Creek Sioux), joined with Dr. Wood on a removal campaign during his graduate coursework in 2009. When the statue was removed in 2021, he called it "an exorcism of state violence."[18] Mr. Lopez wondered, though, how UVA would repair the harm it caused, one of the central questions of a working group he formed ahead of the presidential committee, which included many of the same people.

Monuments are symbols, but they matter in ways that extend beyond the physical: They divert resources from other programs, shape interactions with built and ecological landscapes, and influence policy and curriculum. Many of us have become so accustomed to seeing these monuments that we no longer stop to think about them. But this was not always the case. Before 1865, there were few historical markers or memorials anywhere in the United States.[19] Today, our landscape looks quite different—especially in the South, where more than 90 percent of the roughly 2,089 Confederate memorials are located.[20] Their violent iconography bleeds into national conventions. According to a recent study of five hundred thousand historic properties maintained by federal, state, local, and Tribal governments in the United States and its territories, the national landscape is "dominated by monuments to figures who would be considered white, male, and wealthy in our common understanding today," and violence is the "most dominant subject of commemoration." The findings of the Mellon Foundation's Monument Lab, part of an ambitious $250 million initiative, which doubled to $500 million in 2023 to support landscape reform and collective storytelling, are both shocking and consistent with what we see all around us.[21]

Mellon's research and investments illustrate the paradoxes of public statues: Private philanthropy, compounded through generations of family wealth, business savvy, and political ties, is now undoing the work of earlier waves of wealthy donors. Are we any more democratic now than we were in 1921? The committee may have been more inclusive, but the imperative for change still came from the top. None of this is simple or straightforward. And maybe that is how the statues help us think about the promises of democracy and its unsound history in the United States.

The day that the statue came down, everything flew by, with peaks and valleys of feelings too complex to name. We were thrilled the monument was gone, and frustrated that UVA did not invite Native leaders to commemorate the moment—especially the family of Dr. Karenne Wood. We were happy to watch the Black-owned construction crew, based two hours away in Newport News, work with a specialized crane brought down from Connecticut, and we were on edge about what might happen if white supremacists arrived, as they had in August, 2017. We were excited to tell our stories, and worried that our recommendations on scholarships, hiring, and the land back movement would be cut by journalists who were stretched thin and needed to amass clicks from the immediacy of the statue, told as a straightforward victorious narrative of removal rather than the slow work of repair, in which UVA was complicit in a ninety-nine-year, nine-month history of permitting the impermissible.

After the last flatbed drove off at 10:11 a.m., cheered out of town by victory cries, none of us knew what to do. The flurry and frenzy of texts, calls, and media was gone, as abruptly as it had started. We walked a few doors up, ordered obscenely large plates of pancakes and eggs, with a couple of drinks, and tried to take it all in. Phase one of the committee's work was done. Phase two, Tribal consultation, would lead us into new, open-ended opportunities to create a park and academic programs. As far as anyone could remember, this was the first time UVA had handed control of a project and its vision to Indigenous people.

Because the statue does not contain markers of Tribal identity, we aimed to be as inclusive as possible in identifying affected Nations.

We used digital archives, databases, and interviews with twenty-five historians and Tribal resource officers, held mostly by email and a few by phone or Zoom during kids' naptimes, to document sixty-seven Nations whose ancestors were harmed by Clark. Each time we spoke, we asked for recommendations of other affected Nations so that the list would reflect interviewees' input and expertise. The university president then wrote letters to the chiefs of each sovereign nation. Leaders in Virginia were invited to engage on anything that mattered to their people, whereas invitations to the third circle were scoped to the project. Most did not have the bandwidth to allot staff time during the pandemic, but thirteen Nations did: Monacan, Pamunkey, Nansemond, Mattaponi, Chickahominy, Eastern Chickahominy, Cheroenhaka-Nottoway, Upper Mattaponi, Nottoway, Rappahannock, Occaneechi-Saponi, Lenape, and Cherokee. The Cherokee citizen, Zac Russell, now a second-year law student at the University of Oklahoma focusing on Tribal law, was appointed by Native students, not his Nation, but his chief friended him on Facebook one month into the process, which he said was pretty cool.

In our first meeting, we developed a decision-making framework and survey to guide conversations at the second meeting, where we identified priorities and points of consensus. At the third meeting we workshopped proposals for landscape reform, a speaker series, and outreach initiatives, and at the fourth meeting we decided who would have final review before submission. We spent serious time discussing the double bind of state and federal recognition. On the one hand, working with recognized Tribes allowed UVA to affirm their sovereignty by engaging in leader-to-leader frameworks that are the hallmarks of Indigenous diplomacy and governance. On the other, this approach tied us to settler colonial protocols to determine who "counted" as Native.[22] Were Tribes who hadn't yet been recognized somehow "less Indigenous" than those with formal status? Should we include unaffiliated citizens, like local individuals with Native heritage, or city residents whose Nations did not interact with Clark? These questions have no easy answers. After a lot of listening, Tribal consultants voted that state- and federally recognized Tribes with the institutional capacities and the express decision-making authority of their people should have final say. They defined sovereignty as does Anishinaabe scholar Leanne Simpson: a collective fabric that "comes from an abundance of healthy, responsible, respectful relationships with all of our relations."[23] They understood it as a flawed system, one that had been worked out by previous leaders as a necessary compromise to get things done and, hopefully, open doors for future opportunities to create something better. Our healthy disagreement on an imperfect solution felt like a test of true democracy.

With a similarly practical approach, they voted 66 percent to 33 percent to hire a non-Native landscape architectural firm whose budget included a Tribal Advisory Council. When presented with the option for an extensive bidding process, which could have resulted in a proposal from a Native-owned firm located somewhere in the United States, or an expedited process for a local company with an established term contract, they voted for the latter. The first option, consultants noted, did not guarantee that a Native-owned firm would secure the bid, and given the unstable, highly polarized political environment that we navigate today, they opted for practical certainty rather than a possible ideal. At the time of this writing, the four-member advisory council, which includes Pollak, Monacan educator Victoria Ferguson, Nottoway chief Lynnette Allston, and Nottoway council member and seed keeper Beth Roach, have worked with the Wolf Josey Landscape Architecture firm for two years, leading site visits, consultation with elders and knowledge holders, and trading design ideas.

Tribal politics are complicated, with the generational trauma of settler colonialism, boarding schools, family separation, erasure, and dehumanization layered on top of the competing perspectives that govern all human debates. The committee was uneasy about every step, and uncomfortable with the role that we played as a predominantly white institution, and a historically bad neighbor, that was trying to work with sovereign nations to build respectful relationships. How could UVA take responsibility and empower Native citizens without putting the burden back on them? It felt like there was no road map, which is part of the reason why we wanted to write this essay. Our guiding principle, the thing we kept coming back to, was the use of trauma theory to repair harm. We kept the most affected people at the center of shared decision-making. By agreeing to that principle from the start, we created an environment to hash things out, dissent, and feel seen in disagreement. Some Tribal consultants wondered why we were spending so much time and energy on a hunk of brass when there were more pressing issues facing their people, like food insecurity, job training, healthcare, affordable housing, and scholarships. We understand this view, and we said the same thing before serving on the committee. But in researching the layers of power that made the statue, and seeing how it became a catalyst for a whitewashing of American history from public schools to Hollywood studios, we were convinced that monuments matter.

By 1912, George Rogers Clark had fallen into what President Theodore Roosevelt (1858–1919) called "deserved obscurity," but when renowned sculptor Robert Ingersoll Aitken (1878–1949) was commissioned to make the statue seven years later, Clark was vigorously reinserted into public life.[24] Between 1920 and 1921, he appeared in volumes 12, 14, and 19 of the fifty-volume series *Chronicles of America*, a monumental effort to narrate US history from 1492 to 1918, which soon became the source for undergraduate surveys at Yale University and films that were screened nationwide, with free teaching aids to facilitate use in public schools.[25] Five years after the release of *Vincennes* (1923), the federal government earmarked $2 million (north of $35.6 million today) for a memorial to Clark in Illinois, marking the height of a decades-long period of monument building in his name. Today, there are twenty-five commemorations of him, ranging from statues and plaques to bells, signs, and gates, making Clark one of the fifty most memorialized individuals in the country.[26] The first went up in 1884, on a plaque for Simon Kenton, an Ohio-born soldier who fought with Clark, but the most concentrated period of activity was 1921–32, when eight memorials were installed in Illinois (1), Indiana (1), Kentucky (2), Ohio (2), and Virginia (2), idealizing Clark as a revolutionary and pioneer hero.[27] By the 1940s, against the backdrop of World War II, historians revised these celebratory depictions, but by the 1950s Clark was once again heroized in academic scholarship.[28]

History is not just a record of what happened—it's the way we tell about what happened. More than facts we're forced to memorize, history is a dynamic network of relationships and interpretations that we exist within and help to shape. It is, in this way, much like landscape, what Kasey Jernigan (Choctaw), UVA's first tenure-track assistant professor of Native and Indigenous studies, calls "a *spirit-scape*," or "place filled with the resonance of our actions from generations past." Today's landscape exists because of history; what we and it do now will shape everything to come. In a careful dynamic of respect and reciprocity, we exist in relationship with the land and all kin who share it. Monuments like the one to Clark rupture those relationships. Standing before the statue, Jernigan wondered, "Do people not understand what this sculpture represents?"[29] Our research indicated that, yes, people understood exactly what it meant.

The statue is unmistakably violent in its twenty-four-foot depiction of Clark, and there's a reason we waited this long to describe it. Clark is at the center of the statue but not the center of this story. When viewed from the perspective of a pedestrian on West Main Street, taking in the statue from left to right, as you might words on a page, the first thing you see is men loading gunpowder into rifles. They pass one to Clark, who reaches back to meet their outstretched arms. He is mounted on horseback in the middle of the scene, an eighteen-foot-wide series of figures that extend twelve feet into the air. The statue is massive, and it hurts your neck to look at it if you get too close. This embodied discomfort was by design. The original plans called for a smaller work, nine feet by fourteen feet, but the committee overseeing the monument called for something more "impressive."[30] The guns are aimed at the four Indigenous people who stand, sit, and kneel in front of Clark. Three figures are adults: two men, and one woman, on her knees, holding a cradleboard with an infant nestled inside. At the statue's dedication, reporters noted favorably that the Native woman's cries were "inviting the mercy of the invaders and begging for the protection of her young baby" while Clark explained "the futility of a resistance."[31]

The first recorded removal of a public monument in the United States occurred on July 9, 1776, when, at the behest of elite white men and women, enslaved and free African American men pulled down a statue of King George III (1738–1820) at the intersection of Broadway and Bowling Green in New York City.[32] Since the earliest days of the US republic, we have debated statues as indexes of public memory, historical narratives, and democratic participation, and we have lived with their contradictions.

Today, if you walk in the park once occupied by the George Rogers Clark statue, you will find a few benches, a semi-circular paved path, and, growing in the grass where the granite base tried to flatten the earth, resilient native plants that are reclaiming the space. They are the seeds of what is to come, a transformed landscape built around Monacan land ethics of relationality: To the west, referencing Monacans' spatial relationship with Virginia Tribes, a botanical garden will be curated by rotating groups of Tribal citizens for mutual exchanges of knowledge, with plants named in English, Latin, Algonquian, Iroquoian, and Tutelo-Saponi. To the east, parkgoers will find two forking ways to enter the site: a woodland path that winds through groves and clearings, the future home of workshops and teach-ins with room for 160 people, or a sidewalk that runs along the northernmost edge, punctuated by plazas dedicated to the borders of the Monacan world, the Blue Ridge Mountains and Fall Line. In the southernmost section of the park, pointing in the direction of the Monacan homeland on Bear Mountain, pine trees will gather stories from which future generations of students will learn. Throughout the park, walking paths will promote contemplation through movement, and benches will offer spaces for quiet reflection. Multilingual historical markers will tell about the past, and installations by contemporary Indigenous artists in Virginia will inspire shared visions of resilient futures. We are currently fundraising to support those installations, so at the time of this writing, the work of rebuilding, re-creating, and repairing remains ongoing. The Supreme Court's decision in 2023 to prohibit the use of racial data in admissions decisions—even though Native Nations are defined by citizenship and sovereignty, not US paradigms of race—has slowed the process of awarding waivers to Indigenous students who have paid tuition several times over through stolen land. The more recent elimination of federal funding to support public art presents an additional challenge, one that we did not anticipate in 2021 or 2024, but must now confront head-on in our collective efforts to realize the full potential of an inclusive, democratic society. The statue may be gone, but there is much more to do.

Notes

1. James Collier Marshall, "The Gifts of Paul Goodloe McIntire, 1867–1958," MSS 9137, Harrison Small Special Collections Library, University of Virginia.
2. Archibald Henderson, *The George Rogers Clark Statue* (University of Virginia Press, 1921), 5, 10, Albert and Shirley Small Special Collections Library, University of Virginia.
3. Betsy Gohdes-Baten, "National Register of Historic Places Registration Form: George Rogers Clark Sculpture," US Department of the Interior—National Park Service 104–0252 (1996), 7, https://www.dhr.virginia.gov/historic-registers/104-0252/; Michael A. Tomlan, *Historic Preservation: Caring for Our Expanding Legacy* (Springer, 2014), 1.
4. University of Virginia President's Commission on the University in the Age of Segregation, "Memorialization and Mission," September 25, 2019, https://segregation.virginia.edu/memorialization-and-mission/.
5. Christina Leas, "Local Monuments Pepper Charlottesville Cityscape," *Cavalier Daily*, October 24, 2012.
6. Brandon Brooks, "Remove Culturally Inappropriate Statues," *Cavalier Daily*, March 16, 2016; Alex Mink, "George Rogers Clark Was an American Hero," *Cavalier Daily*, March 23, 2016.

7. Lowell H. Harrison, *George Rogers Clark and the War in the West* (University Press of Kentucky, 2001), 59.
8. Bernard W. Sheehan, "'The Famous Hair Buyer General': Henry Hamilton, George Rogers Clark, and the American Indian," *Indiana Magazine of History* 79, no. 1 (1983): 20.
9. William Bright, *Native American Placenames of the United States* (University of Oklahoma Press, 2004), 537.
10. Susan Sleeper-Smith, *Indigenous Prosperity and American Conquest: Indian Women of the Ohio River Valley, 1690–1792* (University of North Carolina Press, 2018), 10.
11. Brian D. Carroll, "'Savages' in the Service of Empire: Native American Soldiers in Gorham's Rangers, 1744–1762," *New England Quarterly* 85, no. 3 (2012): 384–85.
12. James Fisher, "A Forgotten Hero Remembered, Revered, and Revised: The Legacy and Ordeal of George Rogers Clark," *Indiana Magazine of History* 92, no. 2 (1996): 126.
13. Sleeper-Smith, *Indigenous Prosperity*; Christian McMillen, "The George Rogers Clark Statue and Native Americans," in *After Emancipation: Racism and Resistance at the University of Virginia*, ed. Kirt von Daacke and Andrea Douglas (University of Virginia Press, 2024), 111, 110.
14. Fisher, "A Forgotten Hero," 128.
15. Charlie Teague, "Five Student Organizations Held a March to the George Rogers Clark Statue in Honor of Indigenous Peoples' Day," *Cavalier Daily*, October 16, 2019; Maryann Xue, "PLUMAS Holds Discussion on Climate Politics in Brazil and Bolivia," *Cavalier Daily*, November 20, 2019.
16. Erin L. Thompson, *Smashing Statues: The Rise and Fall of America's Public Monuments* (Norton, 2022), 33, 24.
17. Susan Silk and Barry Goldman, "How Not to Say the Wrong Thing," *Los Angeles Times*, April 7, 2013.
18. Teo Armus and Hannah Natanson, "Charlottesville Takes Down Two More Statues, Deemed Offensive to Native Americans, in Weekend of Removals," *Washington Post*, July 11, 2021.
19. Kirk Savage, *Standing Soldiers, Kneeling Slaves: Race, War, and Monument in Nineteenth-Century America* (Princeton University Press, 2018), 4.
20. Southern Poverty Law Center, "Whose Heritage? Public Symbols of the Confederacy (Third Edition)," February 1, 2022.
21. Monument Lab, "National Monument Audit," September 29, 2021, Mellon Foundation Presidential Initiatives, 5, 17, 21, https://www.mellon.org/report/interrogating-our-monument-landscape.
22. Angela L. Riley, "Native Nations and the Constitution: An Inquiry into 'Extra-Constitutionality,'" *Harvard Law Review* 130, no. 6 (2017): 173–99.

23. Leanne Betasamosake Simpson, "The Place Where We All Live and Work Together: A Gendered Analysis of 'Sovereignty,'" in *Native Studies Keywords,* ed. Stephanie Nohelani Teves, Andrea Smith, and Michelle H. Raheja (University of Arizona Press, 2015), 22–23.
24. Fisher, "A Forgotten Hero," 115.
25. The Chronicles of America Photoplay: Yorktown, Aids and Lesson Materials Used in the Troup Junior High School 1927, Eighth Grade (1927), Special Collections, UVA.
26. Monument Lab, "National Monument Audit," 12.
27. Monument Lab, "National Monument Audit: Interactive Map Data," https://monumentlab.com/audit.
28. Fisher, "A Forgotten Hero," 114, 117–18.
29. Kasey Jernigan, "Nanta ish ikhvna ha? Kucha hoh ilhkoli (What have you learned? Go outside)," in *After Emancipation,* ed. von Daacke and Douglas, 118–19.
30. Robert Ingersoll Aitken, "Letter from New York to E. A. Alderman about the George Rogers Clark Monument, by the Sculptor," MSS 3359, November 19, 1919, Special Collections, UVA.
31. General Alumni Association of the University of Virginia, "The George Rogers Clark Group," *University of Virginia Alumni News* 10, no. 3 (September 1921): 326.
32. Monument Lab, "National Monument Audit," 15, https://www.mellon.org/report/interrogating-our-monument-landscape.

PART THREE

Political Foundations

Original Intentions, Unintended Consequences

PETER S. ONUF

British-American colonists did not know they were fighting a war for independence until they finally declared themselves independent on July 4, 1776, and sought recognition from the "powers of the earth." Patriots who spearheaded resistance to British efforts to reform imperial administration, curb the autonomy of provincial legislatures, and impose new taxes on colonists decried the "unconstitutional" policy initiatives of "wicked" and ill-informed ministries, rejecting the novel pretensions of a supposedly sovereign insular Parliament to deprive them of the rights they claimed as overseas Britons. When resistance turned to rebellion in April 1775, members of the Continental Congress insisted on their undying loyalty to King George III. Historians describe the preceding decade as the "imperial crisis," an escalating and converging sequence of controversies about the constitution of the British Empire. The belated decision to break with Britain marked the failure of British-American patriots to vindicate their claims within the empire. Original intentions had led to unintended consequences. Revolutionary Americans then invoked the "common sense" of a self-declared people as they fulfilled the providential design of their "new order of the ages."

American colonists always thought of themselves as Britons. In the wake of Britain's decisive triumph over France in the Seven Years' War (1757–63), British-American patriots embraced an exalted conception of a greater British, imperial identity. Provincial contributions to the victorious war effort fostered patriotic attachments, situating colonists in the vanguard of what they saw as the empire's glorious and irresistible "westward course." Subsequent controversies only reinforced that identity, even as misguided British policies threatened to strip them of their rights and reduce them to "slavery." In characteristic creole mode, patriots drew heavily on metropolitan norms and practices in defense of their distinctive provincial interests. Defending the jurisdiction and parliamentary privileges of their assemblies led to claims for the autonomy and sanctity of colonial and state constitutions, bulwarks of their rights as Englishmen, and to a broader and more inclusive claim for an imperial constitution. The transprovincial, imperial community Anglo-American patriots imagined was thus constitutional.

Political mobilization in the Anglo-American provinces was precipitated by metropolitan reformers' tentative and incoherent efforts to rationalize imperial administration. If supposedly "paranoid" provincials exaggerated the malign intentions of wicked ministers, patriots had good reasons to discern dire consequences for their liberties in the halting progress of imperial state formation. Resistance to imperial reform democratized provincial politics, enhancing the legitimacy of local representative institutions while fostering popular participation in an expanding, extraconstitutional regime of committees, conventions, and crowd action. Successfully immobilizing royal government across the continent, patriots sought to fill the vacuum of legitimate authority. Political and military mobilization was an ad hoc, improvisational, bottom-up response to imperial state formation. The means patriots adopted to resist unconstitutional encroachments on their rights modeled the new republican governments they would constitute when the empire collapsed. Vindicating independence meant securing those governments against future threats, thus transforming the *means* of resistance into the Revolution's ultimate, justifying goal, or *end*.

Anglo-American patriots' constitutional commitments grounded their creole identity as displaced Britons in an imagined greater British imperial community. Creole constitutionalism in turn facilitated the transprovincial mobilization that prepared revolutionary patriots to embrace a new national identity and construct a federal-republican state that would fulfill their neoimperial ambitions.[1] The Declaration of Independence announced the birth of a new nation, founded on "self-evident," *universally* applicable principles. Yet it also acknowledged the failure of its patriotic authors to fulfill their original, *imperial* intentions.[2]

Sovereignty

The premise of Parliament's reform efforts in North America was that it had the capacity to command compliance of distant provincial subjects to new regimes of taxation and administration. Policymakers thus overlooked and imaginatively dissolved colony "constitutions," preemptively incorporating creole subjects within the ambit of its sovereign authority, presuming on the legitimacy it had achieved in its insular ascendancy. The concept of "virtual representation" expressed the triumphant ascendancy of a putatively "sovereign" Parliament, but it also betrayed Parliament's increasingly conspicuous *unrepresentative* character and its distance from the "people" of metropolitan Britain as well as from Britons in the American provinces. In the wake of their Glorious Revolution, establishment Whigs in the home islands might believe that the king-in-Parliament embodied or represented the British people: After all, good Whigs everywhere agreed that Parliament was the "palladium" of their liberties. But how were Anglo-Americans "present" in a supposedly imperial Parliament or the Crown's administrative apparatus or the Court itself? Exponents of parliamentary supremacy presupposed the existence of an imperial state that their controversial policy initiatives sought to create. Virtual representation was thus countersuggestive, conjuring up its "actual" antithesis and enhancing the legitimacy of the provincial assemblies.

The king-in-Parliament was self-evidently incapable of representing, and therefore exercising authority over, the American provinces. In response, creole patriots sought to extricate the king *from* Parliament—abstracting him from the insular constitution—and domesticate prerogative by inserting him in their own constitutions. Americans thus appealed to George III to exercise his prerogative *on behalf* of the colonies and their constitutions rather than serve as the executive, administrative arm of an all-powerful Parliament. Calling on the king to protect them, they invoked traditional, customary conceptions of the British (and imperial) constitution that still commanded wide support in the metropolis. Betraying the protection covenant, George III instead chose to make war on his loyal American subjects.[3]

Advocates of parliamentary supremacy celebrated the coercive, war-making capacity that secured Britain's dominant position in the European state system. But the synthesis of the branches and the emergence of a powerful fiscal-military state eliminated the negotiable middle ground of the customary constitution. The apparently impeccable logic of parliamentary sovereignty thus generated resistance, revolution, and replication in the American provinces. Notwithstanding patriots' original intentions—and the conventional scholarly wisdom—the American Revolution entailed the modernizing transformation of sovereignty, not its negation.

The juxtaposition of American *liberty* and limited government against British *power* and the "modern" idea of sovereignty is misleading. For revolutionaries, popular legitimacy preceded and enabled expanding state capacity. Convincing a broad political public of the unconstitutionality and illegitimacy of British policy, patriots developed the extraconstitutional infrastructure of popular political and military mobilization. The practical progress of state building in an emerging "state of nature"—that is, of war with their former sovereign—set the stage for American statesmen and constitution-writers to declare independence and assume the status of a "power of the earth."[4]

Popular sovereignty was the most significant unintended consequence of the Revolution. When they resisted parliamentary sovereignty claims, Anglo-American patriots appealed to the customary constitution of distinct orders, divided government, and a plurality of polities in imperial union, thus enabling them to mobilize support in the metropolis as well as across the continent. Yet the resistance movement should not be construed simply as a reactionary turn to an outdated seventeenth-century conception of the constitution, rendered irrelevant by the Glorious Revolution. To the contrary, adherents of the newly orthodox view of Parliament's illimitable authority failed to understand and accommodate the dynamic political and constitutional realities of an expanding empire. At a distance, on the imperial periphery, creole patriots could see more clearly the implications of constitutional development in the metropolis. Britain's growing capacity to make war was not matched by the incorporation of its far-flung provinces into the imperial state. The empire collapsed because of that discrepancy in a protracted crisis of legitimacy that led Americans to declare themselves an independent people, the unintended, nation-making consequence of Parliament's claims to sovereignty.

Constituting the People

Revolutionary claims to independent nationhood derived from provincial patriots' identification with, rather than divergence from, the mother country. Resistance to ministerial taxation and administrative reform initiatives was animated by an emerging conception of an inclusive British imperial community. Mobilizing on behalf of American claims to English rights, patriots imaginatively collapsed the distance between provincial periphery and metropolitan center. Their claim to equality *within* the empire justified resistance to policies they feared would strip them of their rights and reduce them to a condition of servile subordination. Antithetical visions of incorporation framed the imperial crisis: Metropolitan reformers sought to expand the authority of the imperial state to tax, govern, and protect Britain's overseas provinces; their provincial counterparts sought recognition of their equal standing as members of a transatlantic national community by securing the autonomy of provincial governments and negotiating a constitutional settlement or "more perfect union" for the empire as a whole.[5]

Patriot mobilization was *not* based on the idea that "Americans" were—or inevitably would become—a "people." To the contrary, American nationhood was the unintended consequence of a protracted struggle over how (or if) provincial Americans would be incorporated in the British Empire. The surprising emergence of a new people—an autonomous corporate entity, or body politic—reflected the alien and autonomous character of a punitive Parliament that no longer pretended to represent rebellious Americans, even virtually, and a king who spurned their allegiance. The arguments that brought patriots to the threshold of independence were predicated on their professed British identity. In the midst of a war against a king who no longer recognized them as subjects, these stateless outlaws were no people at all. They had no choice but to declare themselves a new people.

Abjuring allegiance to the Crown, Americans were bound to protect themselves against an alien, despotic power. Declaring themselves a people was a conscious, commonsensical, consensual response to pervasive existential threat. Dedication to their common cause confirmed the equal rights claims of provincial Anglo-Americans in the imperial crisis, shifting the imagined community from the nominally vertical and hierarchical order of the old regime to a horizontal, republican plane. Making republican citizens required a reductive and homogenizing process, stripping provincial Anglo-Americans of prior statuses, allegiances, and identities: making them equal. The imperial crisis thus challenged the ongoing concentration of wealth and consolidation of authority in the provinces, as Anglicizing elites distanced themselves from their humble neighbors. Spurned by the metropolis, genteel patriots enlisted support from the people "out of doors," fashioning a progressively more inclusive, "democratic" conception of political community.

Mobilizing resistance to British reform efforts depended on leveling distinctions and promoting the active engagement of fellow patriots. Consent was the threshold of commitment. Where persuasion failed, the people's power was unleashed on its timid and recalcitrant enemies. Popular sovereignty may have been "fiction," but it proved powerful enough to topple the provincial-imperial old regime and authorize the constitution of new republican governments. Political and military mobilization expanded state capacity and connected Americans to the exercise of authority in substantive ways. The "constitutional origins" of the American Revolution culminated in an empire-wide crisis of legitimacy that set the stage for nation-making, constitutional consequences in Britain's North American provinces.[6]

A new conception of what a constitution was emerged from the imperial crisis. The unintended consequence of revolutionary regime change was to expose the radical insufficiency of the customary constitution and the holistic, descriptive account of the body politic (provincial or imperial) it entailed. Hoping and failing to negotiate and make explicit the terms of imperial union, American patriots began to think of constitutions as texts—beginning with their protoconstitutional charters and culminating in the alliances they forged within and among their new states. Fixed in a specific text, a constitution came to be understood as a higher or fundamental law that authorized a structure of responsible governance and distribution of power over and in the name of the "people." If (in most cases) the peoples of the new states wrote their own constitutions, bringing them to life and giving them legitimacy, their constitutions (or charters that continued to function as constitutions) made or constituted them *as* peoples.[7]

The famous circularity of the Declaration of Independence (in which Americans, acting as if they were *already* a people, declared themselves to be one) also characterized the new state constitutions. What is significant about these transactions is not their circularity: What else could they have done? It was instead the resulting distinction between the "people" in their constituent power and the "people" who would thereafter submit to their own constitutional authority or, more simply put, between governors and government. Thomas Paine made this distinction in *Common Sense* when he juxtaposed "society" (which is natural) to "government" (a man-made contrivance). This was *not* to say that government was unnecessary but rather that to be legitimate it had to be responsive and responsible to the people—that is, constitutional. The state was conceptually autonomous: distinct from, and therefore potentially alien or foreign to the people. This was the fate of Britain's failed efforts to construct an imperial state apparatus in North America. For Americans to win and secure their independence, they would have to construct states and a postimperial union of states that rose to the high bar of legitimacy that Americans incorporated in their constitutions. The governments a free, self-governing people constituted were subject to their own ultimate authority.[8]

Thomas Jefferson captured this fundamental distinction when he conjured up the homely image of a constitution as an article of clothing, fitted to a people at a particular moment in its history. "We might as well require a man to wear still the coat which fitted him well when a boy," he wrote fellow Virginian Samuel Kercheval in 1816, "as civilized society to remain under the regimen of their barbarous ancestors." If republican revolutionaries *became* a people by writing a constitution, it was incumbent on latter-day patriots to write new constitutions, better calibrated to their own distinctive circumstances, in order to *sustain* their collective, national identity across generations. Mobilization was the touchstone for Jefferson. War-making and constitution-writing were inextricably linked in the revolutionary process of nation-making. A people's existence could never be taken for granted but was the historically contingent product of the "course of human events." By reconstituting themselves as a people on a predictable, generational schedule, self-governing republicans would make their own history.[9]

Jefferson's conception of generational sovereignty is easily dismissed as theoretical foolishness; his strong commitment to citizen engagement and participatory democracy gets much better marks. But both themes express Jefferson's emerging understanding of the rebellious resistance and revolutionary war that destroyed the empire and turned his familiar provincial world upside down. If popular military and political mobilization were wartime imperatives, the people or peoples who emerged in their wake could not be imagined away when peace finally came: The provincial old regime could not be restored. Patriots had to create new governments with sufficient capacity and legitimacy to sustain the war effort (if not to win the war) on multiple fronts, internal as well as external, and to manage the formidable challenges of postwar reconstruction.

The premise of Jefferson's democratic constitutionalism was that the new American republics would *always* face existential threats, in peace as well as war. In future crises, the virtues citizen-soldiers had displayed in the Revolution would be the republic's ultimate resource and recourse. This would be the modern republican return to first principles. A properly constituted people would mobilize in self-defense under the aegis of "the strongest Government on earth."

Consequences

Jefferson's democratic constitutionalism and his celebration of the irresistible power of the sovereign people have made him seem like a prophet to later generations of Americans. But Jefferson's genius was to grasp the unfolding logic of their war for independence, not to articulate its leading ideas or chart its course. The belated break with Britain marked the frustration and ultimate failure of the provincial patriot's original intentions to reform the empire. As the imperial crisis unfolded, anglicizing provincial patriots affirmed their transimperial, inclusionary, greater British imperial identities, envisioning their vanguard role in an expanding "empire of liberty"—even as resistance to imperial reform enabled interprovincial collaboration and ideological convergence. Jefferson *became* a "democrat" when he pivoted toward the people, embracing the dynamic progress of popular political and military mobilization. Means became ends: Vindicating American independence suddenly became the "self-evident" point of more than a decade of resistance to unconstitutional assaults on the rights of overseas Britons and their provincial governments.

The Declaration of Independence mobilized the ideas that animated resistance into regime principles, presuming the preexistence of a self-declared people (or peoples). Provincial patriots' identification with Britain set the stage for identification with each other, enabling them to transcend conflicting interests, disputed boundaries, and provincial prejudices. Their original intentions thus survived in mutated form in affirmations of neoimperial union. As Jefferson later wrote, the Declaration also constituted the original union of Britain's former North American provinces—another unintended consequence of patriot mobilization. Mobilization also had significant democratizing effects, expanding the ambit of political participation in discomfiting ways for elite patriot leaders. Citizens claimed respect, demanding recognition as equals in their patriot commitments; the "better sort" descended from their high horses and met them on the common ground of battlefields and public assemblies. The "people" was an existential imperative, not an abstraction. The "common cause" dissolved distinctions, putting a high premium on collective action while bringing the consenting citizen into sharp focus. The Declaration's bold assertion that "all men are created equal" was a call to action.[10]

Patriot mobilization promoted transprovincial and cross-class solidarity; American independence required an inclusive and expansive postimperial national identity. As the imperial crisis came to a head, revolutionary leaders synthesized grievances and invoked universal, natural rights principles. Jefferson's language in the Declaration expressed what he called the "American mind" at a specific, culminating moment in a protracted crisis. These "Americans" were an embattled, self-declared "people" who spoke with one voice only because the voices of so many of their provincial countrymen were suppressed. The inclusionary promise of mobilization—the invitation to join the people's struggle for independence and share the fruits of victory—was also an exclusionary threat. When independence was finally secured, that invitation and the exalted terms on which it was offered to the oppressed and benighted peoples of the world came to define the new national narrative and the intentions of its founders for subsequent generations of Americans. But the new nation, belatedly declaring itself into existence in the midst of war, was also defined in enduring ways by its wartime enemies. The Declaration of Independence was also a declaration of war against Britain's counterrevolutionary allies, "merciless savages," rebellious slaves—a captive nation within the new nation—and of all other un-American enemies of the people.[11]

Looking outward, seeking recognition and support from the "powers of the earth," Americans claimed the rights that sovereign nations exercised under the law of nations. However exceptional they might imagine themselves to be, Americans could only secure their independence and make their own history by becoming a sovereign "power"—and thus take on the form of the powers that recognized them. Making wars, the United States created a new and improved, neoimperial federal state and developed the capacity to colonize the continent and dominate their world. The provincial-imperial patriots who set the stage for a nation-making war had no such original intentions. Defenders of traditional liberties and customary constitutions who mobilized against monarchical despotism and parliamentary sovereignty, they unintentionally modeled the legitimating link between nation and state that has—for better and for worse—transformed the modern world.[12]

Notes

1. Benedict Anderson, *Imagined Communities: Reflections on the Origin and Spread of Nationalism*, rev. ed. (Verso, 2006).
2. David Armitage, *The Ideological Origins of the British Empire* (Cambridge University Press, 2000); Eliga H. Gould, "A Virtual Nation: Greater Britain and the Imperial Legacy of the American Revolution," *American Historical Review* 104 (1999): 476–89.
3. Jack P. Greene, "The Case Against Parliamentary Sovereignty, 1765–1776," paper delivered at "The Declaration of Independence at 250" conference, Durham, NH, November 2023.
4. Jack P. Greene, *Peripheries and Center: Constitutional Development in the Extended Polities of the British Empire and the United States, 1607–1788* (University of Georgia Press, 1986).
5. Alexander Boulton, "The Declaration of Independence and the Language of Slavery," *Journal of the Early American Republic* 44 (2024): 1–26.
6. Edmund S. Morgan, *Inventing the People: The Rise of Popular Sovereignty in England and America* (Norton, 1988); Jack P. Greene, *The Constitutional Origins of the American Revolution* (Cambridge University Press, 2012).
7. Jonathan Gienapp, *The Second Creation: Fixing the American Constitution in the Founding Era* (Harvard University Press, 2018); James F. Hrdlicka, "War and Constitution-Making in Revolutionary Massachusetts, 1754–1788" (PhD diss., University of Virginia, 2016).
8. Jacques Derrida, "Declarations of Independence," in *Negotiations: Interventions and Interviews, 1971–2001* (Stanford University Press, 2002), 46–54; Thomas Paine, *Common Sense: Addressed to the Inhabitants of America*, 3rd ed. (Philadelphia, 1776), https://www.gutenberg.org/cache/epub/147/pg147-images.html.
9. TJ to Kercheval, July 12, 1816, in *Thomas Jefferson: Writings*, ed. Merrill D. Peterson (Library of America, 1984), 140; First Inaugural Address, March 4, 1801, ibid., 493.
10. Robert Parkinson, *The Common Cause: Creating Race and Nation in the American Revolution* (University of North Carolina Press for the Omohundro Institute of Early American History and Culture, 2016).
11. TJ to Henry Lee, May 8, 1825, in *Thomas Jefferson: Writings*, ed. Peterson, 1501; Peter S. Onuf, *Jefferson's Empire: The Language of American Nationhood* (University of Virginia Press, 2000), 147–88; Parkinson, *The Common Cause*.

12. Eliga H. Gould, *Among the Powers of the Earth: The American Revolution and the Making of a New World Empire* (Harvard University Press, 2012); Max M. Edling, *A Revolution in Favor of Government: Origins of the U.S. Constitution and the Making of the American State* (Oxford University Press, 2003); Max M. Edling, *Perfecting the Union: National and State Authority in the US Constitution* (Oxford University Press, 2021).

Appeal for a New Revolutionary Narrative

The Curious Tale of *The Crisis*

T. H. BREEN

THE EVIDENCE is clear. The American Revolution began in the New Palace Yard, Westminster, Great Britain, around one o'clock in the afternoon on March 6, 1775. That was the day that Crown authorities executed an infamous publication known as *The Crisis*. This striking claim about timing may seem far-fetched. After all, how could a political transformation as sweeping as the American Revolution plausibly be linked to a single incident, much less one that occurred on the other side of the Atlantic Ocean? The answer exposes how little we know after more than two centuries about the wellspring of popular mobilization on the eve of independence.

A renewed awareness of the significance of *The Crisis* to our own history may liberate us from two increasingly stale narratives of revolution that dominate the literature and reflect largely the ideological concerns of the current generation rather than those of the people who actually created a new republic. On the one hand, we continue to focus inordinate attention on a small group of so-called founding fathers who put forth impressive historical and constitutional arguments for rights and liberty. We should applaud these efforts. After all, scholars such as J. G. A. Pocock, Bernard Bailyn, and Jack P. Greene have traced in impressive detail the evolution of republican ideas from the Renaissance to the American Revolution.[1]

Nevertheless, an explanation for revolution based largely on intellectual genealogy does not help us to understand why thousands of ordinary Americans risked their lives for independence. Other modern commentators, of course, are content to concentrate on a bundle of noble principles they insist should define our modern political culture. To be sure, even while the most patriotic writers recognize our failure to live up to these abstract values, they insist that a set of fundamental core ideas remains—or should remain—the foundation of American exceptionalism. In other words, from this perspective, our revolution was unlike any other major revolution in world history, and that was a good thing.

On the other hand, a counternarrative has recently gained traction. In this story the founding fathers deserve no special respect. They championed their own economic interests, which in many cases meant owning enslaved people and ignoring how their celebrated rhetoric about equality might have been extended to Native Americans and women, as well as to African Americans. This work has long been overdue. It has forcefully reminded modern Americans that an understanding of the Revolution must include people traditionally excluded from the story of independence.[2] One can understand the disappointment in discovering how so many revolutionary Americans accepted practices that we would condemn today. Sadly, such a standard of judgment would reveal that every other revolution—the French and Russian, for example—betrayed original goals in the name of crass pragmatism.

Both interpretations of the American Revolution reflect contemporary concerns. The way forward is certainly not to try to find some elusive middle ground. After all, whether we recount how the United States rose from colonial status to a great nation based on the founding principles of freedom and liberty or how the country has repeatedly ignored the universal call for rights and freedom, the historical narrative is still teleological—a tale of progress or fall over time—and neither story provides much insight about why young men would have flocked to Bunker Hill. We need to explore how the Revolution actually worked. If we insist on awarding good or bad grades to the revolutionary generation, we will not be able to address pressing and comparative questions about popular mobilization, about the emotional energy driving political resistance, or about how a sense of marginalization, betrayal, and revenge was required to transform everyday political grumbling into large-scale armed resistance to authority.

The challenge of weaving a new understanding of popular political mentality into the story of their own revolution alerts us to the enduring relevance of a shrill, often crude, completely forgotten London publication entitled *The Crisis.*[3] Of course, it is quite a leap from broad questions about the motive for effective revolutionary mobilization to a series of essays described at the time simply as a "periodic paper." Although *The Crisis* has been erased from modern historical scholarship, it became briefly, and powerfully, intertwined with the development of widespread armed resistance in the colonies, and more than any other title available at the time, it helped to explain not only why a comfortable imperial world suddenly came unraveled but also why people who probably had never encountered a learned pamphlet on constitutional law or read early modern political theory accepted violence in defense of a common cause.[4]

The Crisis had an extraordinary history. The first number of this periodic paper reached the streets of London on January 20, 1775, bearing the provocative heading "The Altar of Despotism is Erected in America, and We Shall be the Next Victims of its Lawless Power." *The Crisis* adopted an unusual format, possessing some characteristics of a pamphlet, some of a newspaper. It appeared weekly in small folio, four to eight pages, and although each issue contained a discrete essay on some political topic, the continuing numbers were paginated consecutively like a book. Its low price indicated that the printer, T. W. Shaw of Fleet Street—an obscure figure—aimed to reach a large readership. About the author or authors of *The Crisis* we know almost nothing.[5]

The initial number set the tone for the entire run of ninety-one segments. Shrill, intemperate, adversarial, *The Crisis* sounded an alarm. The survival of the British Empire hung in the balance. Time was running out; the end of political freedom was at hand. "It is in your defense," proclaimed *The Crisis,* "I now stand forth to oppose, the most sanguinary, and despotic court that ever disgraced a free country."[6] *The Crisis* could not claim literary merit. Its descriptions of contemporary political figures were vulgar and heavy-handed. Indeed, the publication made its mark through the force of rhetoric. It did not worry about evidence, or, in fact, about the logic of argumentation. Like the publications that even today titillate the members of fringe political groups, *The Crisis* cried out against a vast and evil conspiracy.

After only a few weeks, the paper had a marvelous piece of luck. Parliamentary spokesmen declared the third number, entitled "To the King" and dated February 4, 1775, so insulting to George III that they proposed, in both the House of Commons and the House of Lords, prosecuting *The Crisis* for treason, a capital offense. The episode probably saved the publication. If the authorities had considered the situation with greater care, they would probably have ignored *The Crisis*. But, like so many other government figures who over the centuries have mistaken toughness for insight, British officials—including the government's solicitor general, Alexander Wedderburn, who earlier had humiliated Benjamin Franklin—apparently reasoned that they might silence harsh and unwelcome dissent through intimidation. After a short debate, the members of the House of Commons concluded that "the said Paper is a false, scandalous, and seditious libel, highly and unjustly reflecting on His Majesty's sacred person, and tending to alienate the affections, and inflame the minds of his Majesty's subjects against his person and Government."[7]

The Crisis flagrantly pressed the limits of acceptable political dissent. The troublesome third number recounted fourteen years of the king's "shameful and inglorious reign." The monarch had encouraged corruption; he had appointed petty despots to positions of power. And during the long night of misrule, the people had suffered patiently, waiting for relief and liberation. The moment of reckoning had now arrived. In words that seemed to condone regicide, *The Crisis* announced that the king might not be able to preserve himself from the "vengeance, of a brave and mighty people, with law, justice, heaven, and all its sacred truths on their side." The political slate must be cleaned. And so, in the last days, George should know that "the people" will "treat you, Sir, with as little ceremony, as little respect, and as little mercy, as you and your minions have treated them; for, Sir, whenever the state is convoluted by civil commotions, and the constitution totters to its center, the throne of England must shake with it; a crown will then be no security, and at ONE STROKE *all the gaudy trappings of royalty may laid in the dust.*"[8]

Crushing *The Crisis* proved extremely difficult. Agents reported to Wedderburn that they "hath not been able to make any further Discovery as to the Author or Printers of the Crisis but all the Numbers of the Crisis are still publickly sold by a young girl at a little Stall in Fleet Street." Frustrated authorities instructed the common hangman to burn the third issue of *The Crisis* at the New Palace Yard, Westminster, on March 6, 1775. The next day the procedure was to be repeated before the Royal Exchange. Whatever the official plans may have been, the entire event quickly turned into a fiasco. When the hangman and two high sheriffs arrived at the place where the publication was to be executed, they encountered people handing out broadsheets entitled "The Last Dying Speech of the Crisis."[9]

As the crowd swelled, the hangman went about his business as best he could, laying down dry wood and arranging *The Crisis* for destruction. But as he prepared to light the fire, the people dramatically intervened to save the paper. According to the *Gentleman's Magazine*, "There was a prodigious concourse of people, some of whom were at first very riotous; they seized and threw about the first brush and faggots which were brought, and treated the city marshal and the hangman very ill; but more faggots being sent, which were dipped in turpentine, they immediately took fire." The flames failed to discourage the people. The *Kentish Gazette* reported, "As soon as the fire was lighted . . . it was immediately put out, and dead dogs and cats thrown at the officers."[10] And so, it must be said, like so many doomed figures throughout history who have ridiculed authority, *The Crisis* achieved martyrdom in death.

No one possibly could have anticipated the next chapter in the adventitious history of *The Crisis*. Winds transported it across the Atlantic Ocean, where it soon found a market far larger and more receptive than anything it had enjoyed in England. The first indications of a spectacular reception in the colonies were not evident until the last days of April, about two and a half months after Parliament had originally announced its intention to have a common hangman publicly execute *The Crisis*.

Colonial printers distributed the London paper in two forms. In eight cities—New York, Philadelphia, Hartford, Newbern, Williamsburg, Norwich, Newport, and New London—*The Crisis* appeared exactly as it had in England, in other words, as a periodic paper or series of independent essays released on a weekly schedule. These American publications carry no date, making it impossible to establish precisely when the periodic papers first went on sale. Demand must have been substantial, however, for in at least two cities—New York and Norwich—colonial printers produced multiple editions of certain early numbers of *The Crisis*.[11] In the colonies this level of commercial print activity was without precedent. For the sake of comparison, we might note that the formal political pamphlets that have received so much scholarly attention usually had only a single printing, a total press run of perhaps no more than a thousand copies.[12] The figures for *The Crisis*, however, during some weeks between April and July 1775 must have reached as many as eight to ten thousand.

That is only part of the story. At least fourteen American printers ran selected numbers of *The Crisis* as newspaper articles. The essays appeared as far south as Charleston, South Carolina, and as far north as Portsmouth, New Hampshire. Most New England journals carried at least eight numbers. They seem also to have enjoyed wide popularity in New York, Philadelphia, and Baltimore. *The Crisis* was politically sensitive, a hot item that needed to be put before the public as swiftly as possible. The editor of the *New-London Gazette* explained the situation to his own readers. "We have obtained eight Numbers of this valuable Paper," observed Thomas Green, "and published Seven of them in a Pamphlet, (which may be had for 14d. or 2d. each Number); several of our Customers choose to have them continued in this Method; but as we conceive they would be more generally read if published in a News-Paper, and better to serve the cause of LIBERTY, we propose to publish the succeeding Numbers (as they may come to Hand) in the Gazette."[13]

With this additional information we can more accurately estimate how many copies of newspapers containing *The Crisis* reached American readers during the late spring and early summer of 1775. An advertisement that appeared in the *Virginia Gazette* provides a clue. In that announcement the editor for a new Baltimore journal claimed that he could not successfully launch his enterprise—the *Maryland Gazette and Baltimore Advertiser*—unless he had a guaranteed list of one thousand subscribers.[14] If we take this figure as a rough guide, we can account for another seven to eight thousand copies of *The Crisis*. These are conservative estimates. And, of course, if we multiply the new results to obtain a general sense of American readership, then we begin to realize that by any measure *The Crisis* was a genuine bestseller, a publication that in terms of circulation alone must place it with Thomas Paine's *Common Sense* as a major determinant in the shaping of political opinion before independence.

The timing of its arrival goes a long way toward explaining the extraordinary popularity of *The Crisis* throughout the colonies. The Americans had been angry before this moment, of course—in a few port cities so angry that they had rioted, torn down the houses of imperial officials, and thrown a small fortune in East Indian tea into the Boston Harbor. But the killing of ordinary people by an army of occupation raised the emotional stakes. Like 9/11 or Pearl Harbor in modern times, Lexington and Concord forced the members of communities throughout America to think more seriously about the burden of resistance than they had ever done before. Within a few weeks, the deaths of Americans turned protest into insurgency. Nothing in the traditional accounts of revolution can adequately explain this remarkable transformation.

Within this volatile political environment, *The Crisis* spoke the language of the people. Newspaper editors throughout America recognized immediately that these essays—more than any other publication then available—explained to colonial readers unschooled in the history of political thought not only who was to blame in England for the oppressive imperial policies but also what they must now do to save America.

The Crisis itself thus sparked a sudden surge of popular political energy. The editor of the *Connecticut or New-London Gazette* introduced the first number of *The Crisis* by noting, "The Tyranny of the King and Parliament of Great-Britain, hath been lately exposed in a periodical Paper called 'the CRISIS' in very bold and explicit Terms; which has given such great Offense as to produce an Order of the House of Lords for burning the same by the Hands of the common Hangman." The *Pennsylvania Evening Post* was even more explicit, announcing, "This DAY is PUBLISHED, and SOLD, by the Printer hereof, THE CRISIS EXTRAORDINARY, Proving unanswerably, that there is a faction against the laws and constitution, and that the AMERICANS are not REBELS." Samuel Hall, publisher of the *Essex Gazette*, a newspaper printed in Salem, Massachusetts, declared in the June 3 issue, "We have received six numbers of a periodical paper, published in London, entitled the CRISIS:—Because they contain too great truths—truths that the ministry would conceal from the people, the Printer, in England, was prosecuted and the production burnt by the common hangman by order of the House of Lords."[15]

For at least one editor, *The Crisis* dramatically brought home just how swiftly the character of political resistance had changed in America. On May 23, 1775, the publisher of the *South Carolina Gazette and Country Journal* decided to run what was in fact the fourth number of *The Crisis*. The piece opened with a declaration that "the steady and uniform perseverance in a regular plan of despotism, since the commencement of this reign, makes it evident to the meanest capacity, that a design was formed . . . for subverting the religion, laws, and constitution of this kingdom, and to establish upon the ruins of public liberty, an arbitrary system of government."

Such extreme rhetoric shocked Charles Crouch, who managed this Charleston journal. "There was a Time," he reflected only a month after Lexington and Concord, "and that not very far back, when the Editor would have thought the following Paper gross and licentious, too violent to lay before the Public." But terror of an army of occupation in America had altered political sensibilities. Writing in the third person, Crouch explained that "the Adoption of the late iniquitous ministerial Measures has convinced him, that this is not a Season to lisp, and whisper, to cog, and frown, and flatter; when plain truths are to be argued, plain direct Language is absolutely necessary; therefore without further Introduction or Apology he inserts the ensuing Extract." Two issues later, a letter submitted to the *South Carolina Gazette* described *The Crisis* as a "fiery piece . . . wr[itten] professedly in favor of Liberty and America, and which, from its freedom, has suffered martyrdom at Westminster . . . by order of a prostituted Parliament."[16]

The words of *The Crisis* resonated just as persuasively in New England. In late October, for example, the editor of the *New-Hampshire Gazette*, a newspaper published in Portsmouth, decided to print *The Crisis* number twenty-two, entitled "BLOOD calls for BLOOD." The essay offered a grim and gory description of American suffering at the hands of a British administration that had lost control over imperial policy, and in its floundering incompetence had come to rely on state-sponsored violence against its own subjects. "Consider the gloomy, the dreadful Prospect before you," urged *The Crisis*. "The Plains of America are running with the BLOOD of her Inhabitants, the Essence of the English Constitution destroyed, and nothing but the Form, the mere Shadow of it remains." The New Hampshire editor could not resist adding for local readers, "'Tis worthy of Observation that this CRISIS was printed in London, the Day of the Battle of Bunker Hill." It was as if *The Crisis* knew in advance what was going to happen in America.[17]

Considering the incendiary character of *The Crisis*—in other words, a widely circulating print statement capable of injecting inchoate ideas and feelings about the abuse of power with the passion necessary to sustain armed revolution—it is strange how little scholarly attention it has received. The publication was always hiding in plain sight. Probably the major reason why *The Crisis* has gone missing from modern accounts of the Revolution is that it reflected a raw, angry aspect of public opinion that may make uneasy those who fancy that the American Revolution was exceptional—unlike so many other revolutions that have shaken the world—and was on the whole a reasoned, genteel affair. No matter how popular *The Crisis* may have been throughout revolutionary America, the rain of cats and dogs does not fit comfortably in the story we like to tell ourselves about the country's origins. Its rediscovery injects a welcome new element of complexity into our founding narrative.

The larger argument advanced here is not simply that revolutionary Americans were receptive to vulgar conspiratorial rhetoric. Of course, they were. They were not unlike the sansculottes who stormed the Bastille or the Russian workers who attacked the Winter Palace. Had they not been so, resistance to Great Britain would have failed. A more challenging question is why a raw appeal to violence—blood for blood—did not lead to a subsequent breakdown of civil society. During many revolutions in modern times, the release of popular passions has yielded chronic instability, even anarchy. And so, a new appreciation of *The Crisis* compels us to pose a very different question. How, we might ask, did so many angry Americans manage to establish a reasonably stable republican government based on the will of the people? It is an achievement we take for granted today at our peril.[18]

Notes

1. J. G. A. Pocock, *The Machiavellian Moment: Florentine Political Thought and the Atlantic Republican Tradition* (Princeton University Press, 1975); Bernard Bailyn, *The Ideological Origins of the American Revolution* (Harvard University Press, 1967); Jack P. Greene, *The Constitutional Origins of the American Revolution* (Cambridge University Press, 2012).
2. For example, Woody Holton, *Liberty Is Sweet: The Hidden History of the American Revolution* (Simon & Schuster, 2021); and Robert G. Parkinson, *The Common Cause: Creating Race and Nation in the American Revolution* (University of North Carolina Press, 2016).
3. Much of the description of *The Crisis* appeared originally in T. H. Breen, *American Insurgents, American Patriots: The Revolution of the People* (Hill and Wang, 2010), 262–74.
4. For almost two centuries the only serious recognition of *The Crisis* in revolutionary America was Paul Leicester Ford, "The Crisis," *Bibliographer* 1 (1902): 139–52. Anyone doubting the popularity of this work should look at the full listing of the publication of *The Crisis* in the colonies as a separate "periodic paper" in Charles Evans, ed., *American Bibliography*, 14 vols. (Blakely Press, 1903–14), 5 (1774–78): 112–25. More recently, Neil L. York has revived interest in *The Crisis*. See "George III, Tyrant: *The Crisis* as Crisis of Empire, 1775–1776," *History* 94 (2009): 434–60. Also relevant is York's impressive edition of the entire run of the

publication, *The Crisis: A British Defense of American Rights, 1775–1776* (Liberty Fund, 2016).

5. See C. W. Sutton, "Thicknesse, Philip 1719–1792," in *Dictionary of National Biography*, ed. Sidney Lee, 22 vols. (Macmillan, 1909), 19:612–13. See also Public Record Office, London, SP. 37/12. I want to thank Nick Rogers for bringing these manuscript documents to my attention.
6. *The Crisis*, no. 1.
7. Cited in Ford, "The Crisis," 144. See also *Journals of the House of Commons from November 29th, 1774 [. . .] to October the 15th*, 56 vols. (London, 1803), 3:158–59; and *Parliamentary Register; Or History of the Proceedings and Debates of the House of Commons*, 17 vols. (London, 1775–80), 1:235. The extraordinarily shrill character of the popular press in London during this period is described in John Brewer, *Party Ideology and Popular Politics at the Accession of George III* (Cambridge University of Press, 1976), 154–66, 252–54.
8. *The Crisis*, no. 3.
9. Ford, "The Crisis," 144–46, 148.
10. Ford, "The Crisis," 146–48.
11. See, Evans, *American Bibliography*, 5:112–25.
12. Thomas R. Adams, *American Independence: The Growth of an Idea. A Bibliographical Study* (Jenkins and Reese, 1980), introduction.
13. *New London Gazette*, June 9, 1775. In addition, some numbers of *The Crisis* appeared in the following American newspapers: *Connecticut Courant* (Hartford), *Connecticut Journal* (New Haven), *Norwich Packet*, *Boston Gazette*, *Boston Evening-Post*, *Massachusetts Spy* (Worcester), *Essex Journal* (Salem), *Essex Journal* (Newburyport), *New-Hampshire Gazette* (Portsmouth), *Providence Gazette*, *Pennsylvania Evening Post* (Philadelphia), *Constitutional Gazette* (New York), *North Carolina Gazette* (New Bern), *Maryland Journal and Baltimore Advertiser* (Baltimore), and *South Carolina Gazette and Country Journal* (Charleston). This geographic distribution indicates that *The Crisis* had a much wider readership than did the often-cited prerevolutionary constitutional pamphlets.
14. *Virginia Gazette* (Hunter and Dixon), April 1, 1775.
15. *Connecticut or New-London Gazette*, June 9, 1775. See also *Norwich Packet*, October 9–16, 1775; *New-England Chronicle, or Essex Gazette*, May 18, 1775; and *Pennsylvania Evening Post*, April 22, 1775, and October 14, 1775.
16. *South Carolina Gazette and Country Journal*, May 2, May 9, and June 6, 1775.
17. *New-Hampshire Gazette*, October 10, 1775.
18. See. T. H. Breen, *The Will of the People: The Revolutionary Birth of America* (Belknap Press of Harvard University Press, 2019), 195–222.

The Declaration of Independence, Institution Building, and the Orderly Transfer of Power in Revolutionary America

ROSEMARIE ZAGARRI

I REALLY BEGAN to worry when all ten living former secretaries of defense published an opinion piece in the *Washington Post* on January 3, 2021, warning that the US military should play no role in impeding the peaceful transition of power from one president to his duly elected successor.[1] Why, I wondered, was such an extraordinary warning necessary? Ever since November, President Donald Trump had blustered about "rigged elections" and claimed that he, not Joe Biden, had actually won the contest. During the intervening months, however, dozens of courts rejected Trump's claims of fraud and found no basis to doubt the election's outcome. Surely now, I thought, even Trump would admit that the game was over.

And yet on January 6, 2021, Trump, speaking at a rally, urged his supporters to march to the Capitol and—in his ominous words, "fight like hell." Something was up. I turned on the television and watched in horror as Trump's supporters assaulted Capitol police officers, invaded the building, and rushed toward the chambers where members of Congress were in the process of certifying the presidential election. Far more than a simple protest that got out of hand, Trump had incited an insurrection in hopes of preventing lawmakers from performing their official governmental duties. After decades as a historian of the founding era, I was aghast. Although partisan bitterness, animosity, and division had surfaced in many previous presidential elections, I could not believe what was happening right before my eyes.

The Trump insurrection of January 6, 2021, violated one of the most basic, long-standing, and fundamental principles of American democracy: a respect for the peaceful and orderly transition of power. George Washington first established this precedent when he relinquished command of the Continental Army at the end of the American Revolution, and then again in 1797, when he retired to Mount Vernon after serving two terms as president. Despite any formal constitutional requirement, all subsequent presidents, until Franklin Delano Roosevelt, abided by this norm. Even in hotly contested elections, presidents honored the official electoral results without resorting to violence. Although it took thirty-six ballots in the House of Representatives to decide the outcome of the election of 1800, neither Federalists nor Democratic-Republicans took to the streets to contest the result.[2] More recently, despite the gap between the Electoral College and the popular vote in the presidential elections of 2000 and 2016, Democrats did not turn to mob violence to overturn the results.

This tradition of an orderly transfer of power can even be seen in a most unlikely place, during the years immediately preceding America's separation from Great Britain. Even as Americans were shedding their allegiance to the mother country, they attempted to adhere to norms regarding a respect for the rule of law and the orderly transition of power. To do this, colonists engaged in a process of institution building that would ensure the continuation of government by the people, even amid the violence of war and the instability of rebellion. Ironic though it may seem, Americans attempted to stage a rebellion in the most orderly manner possible.[3]

At the end of the French and Indian War in 1763, few American colonists—and even fewer British officials—contemplated the prospect of American independence. Americans considered the British monarch to be their protector and guardian, the most important link uniting the colonies with the British Empire. Parliament exercised little direct authority over the colonies, passing legislation primarily related to the regulation of international trade and the waging of war against common enemies. Each of the thirteen North American British colonies had its own representative assembly, with a popularly elected lower house and (in most colonies) an appointed upper house and royal governor. Only the colonists' individual legislatures could authorize taxes—and then only for the inhabitants of their own particular colony. Americans were proud to be British subjects, believing that they lived under the freest, most beneficent form of government in the world.[4]

Yet after 1763, a number of factors converged to change the status quo. The British East India Company had recently conquered vast new territories in India. To oversee its newly expanded empire, British officials decided to streamline imperial administration throughout its extensive holdings, to make its dependencies more productive and self-sustaining. At the same time, ever since the Glorious Revolution in 1688, Parliament's power had grown while the monarch's power had declined. Parliament, not the monarch, had become supreme. Unchecked by the king, Parliament began to claim that authority to represent not only the inhabitants of Great Britain but those in its North American British colonies as well. Most important of all, in the wake of the French and Indian War, the British government was deeply in debt and desperately in need of additional funds. Though Parliament had never before directly taxed the American colonies, the body now began to do so. In a series of laws passed between 1764 and 1776, Parliament not only attempted to extract revenue from the colonies but also imposed increasingly onerous restrictions on the lives and freedoms of Britain's North American subjects.

Both political elites and ordinary colonists reacted with outrage to what they perceived as Parliament's unwarranted intrusion into colonial affairs. Political leaders in the colonies sent protests to the king, the House of Lords, and the House of Commons. Newspapers and pamphlets raged against the injustices. Crowds gathered in towns and cities to hear orations denouncing Britain's latest travesties. Groups, such as the Sons of Liberty and Daughters of Liberty, formed to provide a means of collective resistance. Mob violence erupted, resulting in riots, threats to individuals, and attacks on private property.

From the beginning, American political leaders realized that they would have to walk a fine line in resisting Great Britain. Although they knew they needed the power of the people behind them, they also knew that the crowd might be hard to control. Crowds could easily become mobs, unleashing bloodshed, chaos, and the threat of anarchy. In addition, American society at this time was a seething cauldron of race, class, and ethnic tensions.[5] The existence of a significant enslaved population and restive Indians on the frontier complicated matters further. Britain would systematically try to exploit these divisions in an effort to undermine American unity. As John Adams remarked, the British "Ministry [sought to stir] up Tories, Landjobbers, Trimmers, Bigots, Canadians, Indians, Negroes, Hanoverians, Hessians, Russians, Irish Roman Catholicks, [and] Scotch Renegadoes." These groups, along with women, he feared, were now "demand[ing] new Privileges and threaten[ing] to rebell."[6] Such divisions might well undermine their cause from within, leading colonists to destroy one another.[7]

Throughout the decade prior to independence, American political leaders knew they must incorporate new constituencies into the resistance against Great Britain; at the same time, they also must control and contain popular outrage. As historian Kenneth Owen puts it, revolutionary leaders struggled with "the difficulty of fixing a relationship between politically motivated violence and a government based on popular sovereignty."[8] American colonists found a new way out of the dilemma: by grassroots institution building. Within each colony and among the thirteen colonies, Americans began to create new, ad hoc, extralegal institutions, including local committees of safety, intercolonial committees of correspondence, provincial assemblies, and the Continental Congresses. Though unofficial, these institutions would maintain order, handle the affairs of governance, and provide guidance to the citizenry as the formal monarchical structures withered away. These new organizations reflected a common belief, based on the colonial experience of representative government, that the people were the basis of government and that government was based on the consent of the governed.

Parliament's passage of the Stamp Act in 1765 inaugurated a new era in the colonies' relationship with Great Britain. As colonists began to devise a response to the statute, inhabitants initially turned to the lower houses of their colonial legislatures for assistance. As the popular branch of government (that is, elected by "the people," meaning propertied white males), these bodies were considered the most sympathetic to, and reflective of, the voice of the people. The legislatures became the first vehicles of resistance. Many of the assemblies passed resolutions declaring their principled objections to the Stamp Act tax and demanding its repeal. "[N]o Taxes ever have been, or can be imposed on them," insisted the New Jersey Assembly, "but by their own Legislature."[9] To do so, maintained the Virginia House of Burgesses, "is illegal, unconstitutional and unjust, and have a manifest Tendency to destroy British as well as American Liberty."[10] In addition to passing such decrees, many legislatures also sent petitions to Britain—to the king, the House of Commons, and the House of Lords—to demand a redress of their grievances.

At the same time that colonial leaders were devising a political response to the Stamp Act, popular protests erupted in many towns and cities throughout the colonies. The Sons of Liberty denounced British infringements of their rights and liberties. Angry crowds gathered at local "Liberty Trees" or "Liberty Poles" to demonstrate their opposition to the tax. Not infrequently, peaceful protests turned violent. Stamp Act commissioners were hanged in effigy or threatened with tarring and feathering. In a fit of rage, mobs in the summer of 1765 attacked the house of Massachusetts Lieutenant-Governor Thomas Hutchinson, demolishing his possessions and stealing the valuables they didn't destroy. Hutchinson and his family barely escaped with their lives.[11]

Colonial leaders knew that violent protest would be counterproductive. Yet when the legislatures resisted, the governors often tried to quash dissent. They refused to call the assemblies into session, or dissolved their gatherings, sending the legislators back home to prevent the discussion of controversial topics.[12] In February 1768, for example, Governor Francis Bernard ordered the Massachusetts Assembly to retract its "circular letter," sent to the other colonies to oppose the Townshend Acts. When representatives rejected the governor's request, the governor promptly prorogued the assembly and prohibited the assembly from meeting. In Virginia in 1774, when the House of Burgesses began to discuss methods of resisting the hated Coercive Acts, Virginia's governor, Lord Dunmore, refused to allow the debate and closed down the official gathering. Such incidents, repeated in colony after colony, undermined the people's trust in the royal authority and, more generally, eroded their faith in royally sanctioned institutions.[13]

As early as 1765, however, American political leaders realized that unity would bring strength. Their protests would be more powerful if they joined with the other North American British colonies to express their grievances to Britain. As a result, in September 1765, nine of the thirteen colonies sent representatives to New York to consider a collective response. Speaking on behalf of all the colonies, the Stamp Act Congress produced a set of resolutions that outlined the colonists' legal and constitutional objections to the Stamp Act. The body also sent a set of petitions to the king, the House of Lords, and the House of Commons, requesting the law's repeal. Finally, and perhaps most importantly, the Congress called for economic sanctions against Britain, formulating a plan to institute a unified boycott on the importation of British goods. Since the colonies purchased almost half of all British exports, such a boycott would, it was believed, put immense economic pressure on Parliament to repeal the act.[14]

Operating outside the bounds of officially sanctioned royal institutions, the Stamp Act Congress possessed no official standing or legal authority. It had only the authority that ordinary people gave it. Yet the Congress's recommendations achieved widespread popular support. Throughout the colonies, merchants and ordinary folk alike applauded the body's actions and rallied to support the boycotts. Less violent forms of protest against the Stamp Act became more common. When November 1, 1765, came, the date the Stamp Act was to go into effect, not a single stamp was sold. In March 1766, Parliament agreed to repeal the hated statute.[15] Collectively, the Stamp Act Congress had succeeded, at least temporarily, in unifying the colonies. Just as importantly, the gathering had achieved another goal: harnessing popular outrage and redirecting it through institutional channels.

In the following years, Parliament's passage of additional laws—including the Townshend Acts of 1767, the Tea Act of 1773, and the Coercive Acts of 1774—fanned the flames of popular hostility against Great Britain. Instead of being a temporary misunderstanding, or a simple error of judgment, Britain's actions appeared to be part of an ongoing and deliberate attempt to undermine the colonists' rights and liberties—to reduce them, in the language of the time, into the condition of slaves. The British also increasingly turned to the use of force to intimidate the colonists into submission. In 1768, two British regiments arrived in Boston, intensifying tensions with the civilian population. On March 5, 1770, an angry mob gathered around the royal Customs House in Boston. Armed British soldiers stood outside the building, muskets at the ready. Snowballs were thrown, scuffles ensued, and gunfire erupted. Five colonists lay dead in the so-called "Boston Massacre"—victims, as the colonists saw it, of British oppression.[16]

As tensions with Britain increased, colonial political leaders realized that they must control and contain popular resistance toward Great Britain and find an institutional expression for their collective grievances. By the early 1770s, more and more colonial leaders wished put into place a semipermanent means of communication between and among the colonies. In 1773, Massachusetts led the way by establishing the Committee of

Correspondence. By identifying like-minded thinkers in other colonies, political leaders could more easily exchange news and coordinate their responses to developing events. This system soon proved its efficacy. In December 1773, Bostonians responded to Parliament's passage of yet another outrageous law, the Tea Act, by dumping imported tea worth ten thousand pounds sterling into Boston Harbor. In response, Parliament passed the Coercive, or Intolerable Acts, to punish the colony. Extremely harsh in nature, the laws altered the Massachusetts charter, ended certain elements of representative government, closed the port of Boston, and required citizens to pay for the destroyed tea. Though directed only against Massachusetts, the other colonies rallied behind their sister colony. They protested against the colony's loss of political rights. They sent food, supplies, and money to prevent Bostonians from starving. They made common cause with the New Englanders. If Parliament could deprive Massachusetts of its most fundamental rights and liberties, then Britain might well do the same to the others.[17]

Once again, political leaders decided that a collective response was called for. In September 1775, representatives from twelve of the thirteen colonies (only Georgia did not attend) gathered in Philadelphia in what came to be known as the First Continental Congress. As in previous gatherings, American leaders issued resolutions objecting to the Coercive Acts, sent petitions to the king, House of Lords, and House of Commons, called for repeal of the acts, and promoted economic pressure against Britain in the form of nonimportation and nonexportation agreements. No longer content with simply issuing directives, the Congress also called for the creation of a "Continental Association" that would enforce compliance with the boycott in local communities. Yet, as was the case with the Stamp Act Congress, the Continental Congress possessed no official legal standing. Existing outside of official channels of government, the Continental Congress assumed the powers of governance unto itself in the midst of a crisis. Many Americans, elites as well as ordinary people, embraced the new Congress and recognized its authority. They echoed their support for its resolutions and abided by its directives, including the boycott. In place of royal institutions, they were creating new institutions of governance of their own making.[18]

Significantly, before returning home, delegates to the First Continental Congress did something that previous intercolonial gatherings had not done: They agreed to reconvene the following spring to assess the impact of their actions. The intervening months proved to be decisive. British troops continued their siege on Boston, starving and harassing its population. In April 1775, shots were fired at Lexington and Concord. Colonial militia streamed into Boston, ready to fight the British. The question was, Would American leaders be able to control and contain the colonists' anger toward Britain, or would the colonies simply explode into random, unchecked violence? In May 1775, delegates to the Second Continental Congress gathered in Philadelphia, knowing that the imperial crisis was coming to a head.[19]

Like the First Congress, the Second Continental Congress had no official legal standing. Yet its very existence reflected the colonists' loss of faith in the king and Parliament. Though not yet prepared to declare independence from Britain, the Congress decided to put the colonies on a war footing, to prepare to defend their rights with force, if necessary. One of its first actions, in June 1775, was to appoint George Washington at the head of what was called the "Continental Army." Soon the Congress assumed other functions of government including seeking aid from France, requesting loans from the Dutch, sending diplomats to Canada, and mustering the resources for armed conflict with Britain. Unlike the first Congress, members did not simply pass a few resolutions and then disperse. From that time on, they essentially assumed the responsibility for overseeing the interests of the united colonies.[20]

By 1775, many of the individual colonies also devised new institutions of governance that were separate and distinct from Crown institutions. Building on colonial traditions of representation, they took the business of government into their own hands. At the local level, they created ad hoc, extralegal institutions such as committees of correspondence or committees of safety. These organizations enforced the boycott against Great Britain, met to discuss issues of pressing concern, and maintained order within their communities. At the colony-wide level, inhabitants began to bypass their official colonial legislatures and hold separate elections for representative bodies of their own choosing. When North Carolina's governor, for example, failed to call its assembly regular into session in 1774, Representative Joseph Hawley declared that "the people will convene themselves. . . . The people will have some government or other."[21] Variously referred to as "provincial congresses," "provincial conventions," or "provincial assemblies," these institutions helped provide a kind of shadow government, operating outside the bounds of official authority. Without the restrictive oversight of the royal governors, these assemblies continued to manage the colonies' internal affairs, including the collection of taxes, while also being free to debate their changing relationship with England.[22]

Such developments alarmed royal officials. Massachusetts Governor Thomas Hutchinson warned London officials that "a general dissolution of the established government in all the colonies" had occurred, producing new, extralegal bodies that had come into being "by the meer act of the People."[23] Thomas Jefferson staunchly defended the creation of such organizations: "When [legislatures] are dissolved by lopping off one of their branches [that is, the lower house], the power reverts to the people."[24] Although their existence was assumed to be temporary, until more regular forms of government could be established, such bodies provided a critical source of order, continuity, and stability within the colonies. By early 1776, groups in some communities had decided to debate the question of announcing their independence from Britain for themselves. In fact, ninety or more local declarations of independence were issued, many of which appeared before Congress's own declaration in July 1776.[25]

Yet the individual colonies did not go it entirely alone. As royal authority continued to deteriorate, colonists increasingly turned to the Second Continental Congress for guidance and assistance. Popular impatience with Britain was turning into outright hostility. Violence was increasing, especially in the Western backcountry and on the frontier. Lord Dunmore's Proclamation in Virginia heightened the prospect of slave revolts.[26] With the threat of war looming, colonists needed a source of common leadership and unity. Turning away from discredited royal institutions, they looked instead to the Continental Congress.

The colonies also turned to Congress to authorize their own experiments in governance. As dissatisfaction with British government grew, colonists wished to alter the framework of government within their individual colonies. They wanted to replace a system based on the king and Parliament with one based directly on the consent of the governed. It would be, in other words, an experiment in republican government. In June 1775, for example, the inhabitants of Massachusetts asked the Continental Congress for permission to create a new government for their colony. In response, Congress recommended that the colony vacate its current charter and revert, at least temporarily, to its earlier, more liberal Charter of 1691.[27] Similarly, in late 1775, leaders in both South Carolina and New Hampshire asked Congress whether they might abandon their existing royal charters and create new civil governments for their respective colonies. Congress agreed to these requests, suggesting that the people should create systems that would, "in their judgment . . . best produce the happiness of the people, and most effectually secure peace and good order in the colony, during the continuance of the present dispute between Great Britain and the colonies." Around the same time, Congress urged Virginia to form a new government as well.[28] These were important steps. By recognizing Congress's authority over them, the colonies were, in effect, acknowledging that Congress had become, as Massachusetts put it, "the representative body of the continent."[29] To be sure, not everyone in all the colonies was eager to grant Congress such extensive authority. Nonetheless, with war on the horizon, it was clear that a more formal kind of superintending authority, to replace British imperial authority, would be necessary. The Second Continental Congress filled that void.

Once independence was imminent, Congress issued a directive ordering each colony to establish a new framework of government within its borders. As John Adams's May 15 resolution put it, each colony should establish a form of government "that shall, in the opinion of the representatives of the people, best conduce to the happiness and safety of their constituents in particular, and America in general."[30] Each colony was, in effect, to vacate its colonial charter, create a new government, and write a state constitution based on the consent of the governed.[31]

With this change, the "colonies" became "states." Just as importantly, this action confirmed Americans' commitment to both the rule of law and the orderly transfer of power. As Adams and other delegates well knew, the success of the revolutionary cause would depend, in no small part, on the ability of the newly united states to secure popular allegiance and maintain order among its citizens. Delegate Caesar Rodney contemplated the necessity of good government to the task. "No prudent man," he said, "would choose to Trust himself long without the Security of a Regular Established Government. The Civil and Municipal Laws, for want of a proper Authority to Execute them, will grow into disuse and Contempt. All the Evils of Anarchy may then prevail and the most wanton depredations be Committed." If the country collapsed into chaos, the goal of achieving self-government might well collapse with it. "Love of order and Obedience to those Laws," Rodney declared, "are Essential bands of Society."[32] Significantly, John Adams himself called the May 15 proposal for the creation of state governments—not the motion for independence from Great Britain—"the most important Resolution, that was ever taken in America."[33]

Under the new system, the state and federal governments would have different spheres of authority. While the Continental Congress would be responsible for overseeing the war effort, requesting money and soldiers from the states, and conducting foreign affairs, state governments would maintain control over their own internal affairs. They would hold elections for their individual assemblies, collect taxes, raise troops, police their inhabitants, and send delegates to represent them at the Continental Congress. Though united with the other states for defensive purposes, each state would retain an enormous degree of autonomy and self-determination.

The May 15 order also served another purpose: to legitimate the authority of the newly created institutions of government. If the colonies/states chose to recognize Congress's authority over them while at the same time Congress recognized the authority of colonies/states to govern themselves, each gained legitimacy from the other's recognition. As a result, a new federal system replaced the imperial system of government. The revolutionaries, however, also emphasized another crucial point: In this system, the people themselves were the ultimate source of authority and the basis of all government. Thus, when the Second Continental Congress finally issued the Declaration of Independence on July 4, 1776, they could justify their claim to speak on behalf of the American people, asserting that their pronouncement was made by "the Representatives of the united States of America, in General Congress, Assembled, [acting] in the Name, and by Authority of the good People of these Colonies."[34]

Paradoxical though it may seem, even as Americans attempted to overthrow what they called British "tyranny," they wished to do so in the most orderly manner possible. During the first years of resistance against Britain after 1765, they tried to control and contain mob violence. As time went on, both ordinary people and their leaders joined together to create extralegal institutions that redirected popular sentiment into new forms of governance. This is not to minimize the violence or destructiveness of the American Revolution. Particularly in the South, the Revolution was a vicious affair, entangling Indians, Blacks, and whites in bloody cycles of violence and retribution.[35] Nonetheless, even before declaring independence Americans had already created new frameworks for governing that provided a critical source of stability and continuity throughout the upheavals of war.

Historically, since the time of the American Revolution, the orderly transfer of power has become both a hallmark and a symbol of the American system of government. Unlike many other countries that have been caught up in a revolutionary whirlwind, the United States did not experience a complete collapse of their governmental institutions during the War for Independence. Except at specific times and places, the country did not devolve into the extremes of violence and chaos that characterized many other early modern revolutions, such as the French Revolution or the Haitian Revolution. Nor, unlike in many Latin American revolutions of the nineteenth century, did the United States revert to strong-man rule or military despotism. This deep commitment to the rule of law and an orderly transfer of power persisted for over two centuries. On January 6, 2021, however, Donald Trump incited an insurrection in an effort to overturn the peaceful and orderly transition of power—a betrayal on top of a betrayal of what the American Revolution stood for.

Notes

1. Ashton Carter, Dick Cheney, William Cohen, Mark Esper, Robert Gages, Chuck Hagel, James Mattis, Leon Panetta, William Perry, and Donald Rumsfeld, "All 10 Living Former Defense Secretaries: Involving the Military in Election Disputes Would Cross into Dangerous Territory," *Washington Post*, January 3, 2021.
2. Joseph Ellis, *His Excellency: George Washington* (Knopf, 2004), 144–46, 230–40; Richard Hofstadter, *The Idea of a Party System: The Rise of Legitimate Opposition in the United States, 1780–1840* (University of California Press, 1969), 128–55.
3. This argument is made most explicitly Pauline Maier's classic work *From Resistance to Revolution: Colonial Radicals and the Development of American Opposition to Britain, 1765–1776* (Vintage, 1972).
4. Brendan McConville, *The King's Three Faces: The Rise & Fall of Royal America, 1688–1776* (University of North Carolina Press, 2006).
5. Woody Holton, *Liberty Is Sweet: The Hidden History of the American Revolution* (Simon & Schuster, 2021); Marjoleine Kars, *Breaking Loose Together: The Regulator Rebellion in Pre-Revolutionary North Carolina* (University of North Carolina Press, 2002); Brendan McConville, *Those Daring Disturbers of the Peace: The Struggle for Property and Power in Early New Jersey* (Cornell University Press, 1999).
6. John Adams to Abigail Adams, April 14, 1776, in *Adams Papers Digital Edition*, 1:382–83, Massachusetts Historical Society online, http://masshist.org.
7. At the same time, as historian Robert Parkinson has shown, colonial leaders themselves systematically tried to convince white people that nonwhite "others," especially Indians and enslaved people, were threatening to rise up against them. By emphasizing this common threat, American leaders

helped to solidify bonds of unity between and among the disparate colonists (see Parkinson, *Thirteen Clocks: How Race United the Colonies and Made the Declaration of Independence* [University of North Carolina Press, 2021]).

8. Kenneth Owen, "Violence and the Limits of the Political Community in Revolutionary Pennsylvania," in *Between Sovereignty and Anarchy: The Politics of Violence in the American Revolutionary Era*, ed. Patrick Griffin, Robert G. Ingram, Peter S. Onuf, and Brian Schoen (University of Virginia Press, 2015), 167.
9. New Jersey Resolves, November 30, 1765, in *The Declaration of Independence in Historical Context: American State Papers, Petitions, Proclamations & Letters of the Delegates to the First National Congresses*, ed. Barry Alan Shain (Yale University Press, 2014), 80–81.
10. Virginia Resolves as printed by the *Newport Mercury*, June 24, 1765, in *The Declaration of Independence in Historical Context*, 68–69.
11. Pauline Maier, *From Resistance to Revolution: Colonial Radicals and the Development of American Opposition to Britain, 1765–1776* (Vintage, 1972), 51–112; Bernard Bailyn, *The Ordeal of Thomas Hutchinson* (Harvard University Press, 1974); Alfred F. Young, Ray Raphael, and Gary B. Nash, eds., *Revolutionary Founders: Rebels, Radicals, and Reformers in the Making of the Nation* (Knopf, 2011); Alfred F. Young, *The Liberty Tree: Ordinary People in the American Revolution* (New York University Press, 2006).
12. Robert Middlekauff, *The Glorious Cause: The American Revolution, 1763–1789* (Oxford University Press, 1982), 108–76; John Phillip Reid, *Constitutional History of the American Revolution*, abridged ed. (University of Wisconsin Press, 1995), 49–72.
13. Jack P. Greene, *Peripheries and Center: Constitutional Development in the Extended Polities of the British Empire and the United States, 1607–1788* (University of Georgia Press, 1986), 128–50; Mary Beth Norton, *1774: The Long Year of Revolution* (Vintage, 2021), 124–70; Maier, *From Resistance to Revolution*, 169–70, 202, 224.
14. Edmund S. Morgan and Helen M. Morgan, *The Stamp Act Crisis: Prologue to Revolution* (University of North Carolina Press, 1963), 21–69; Maier, *From Resistance to Revolution*, 77–112.
15. Jane T. Merritt, *The Trouble with Tea: The Politics of Consumption in the Eighteenth-Century Global Economy* (Johns Hopkins University Press, 2017); Morgan and Morgan, *Stamp Act Crisis*.
16. Holger Hoock, *Scars of Independence: America's Violent Birth* (Crown, 2017); Timothy M. Barnes, Robert M. Calhoon, and George A. Rawlyk, eds., *Loyalists and Community in North America* (Greenwood, 1994).
17. Richard D. Brown, *Revolutionary Politics in Massachusetts: The Committees of Correspondence and the Towns, 1772–1774* (Harvard University Press,

1970), 210–12, 230–36; David Ammerman, *In the Common Cause: American Response to the Coercive Acts of 1774* (University Press of Virginia, 1974), 1–17, 103–24, 139–45; Norton, *1774*, 84–122, 149–58; Maier, *From Resistance to Revolution*, 228–70.

18. Jack Rakove, *The Beginnings of National Politics: An Interpretive History of the Continental Congress* (Johns Hopkins University Press, 1979), 42–62; Norton, *1774*, 192–208.
19. Merrill Jensen, *The Articles of Confederation: An Interpretation of the Social-Constitutional History of the American Revolution, 1774–1781* (University of Wisconsin Press, 1966), 54–103.
20. Jensen, *Articles of Confederation*, 80–103; Rakove, *Beginnings of National Politics*, 63–79.
21. Joseph Hawley, "Broken Hints to Be Communicated to the Committee of Congress for the Massachusetts" (1774), quoted in Gordon S. Wood, *The Creation of the American Republic, 1776–1787* (Norton, 1969),
22. Wood, *Creation of the American Republic*, 310–35.
23. Thomas Hutchinson, *Strictures upon the Declaration of the Congress at Philadelphia; in a Letter to a Noble Lord, & c.* (London, 1776), 15.
24. Thomas Jefferson, *A Summary View of the Rights of British America* (1774), http://avalon.law.yale.edu.
25. Pauline Maier, *American Scripture: Making the Declaration of Independence* (Vintage, 1997), 48–69; Norton, *1774*, 241–308.
26. Patrick Griffin, *American Leviathan: Empire, Nation and the Revolutionary Frontier* (Hill & Wang, 2007), 97–151; Norton, *1774*, 310–40.
27. "Response to Massachusetts Bay's Request for Instructions on Forming a New Government," June 2, 3, 9, 1775, in *Declaration of Independence in Historical Context*, 270–71.
28. "Congress, Response to New Hampshire's Request for Instructions on Forming a New Government, and Instructions for South Carolina and Virginia Concerning Forming New governments," November 3, 4, and December 4, 1775, in *Declaration of Independence in Historical Context*, 340–41.
29. "Response to Massachusetts Bay's Request for Instructions on Forming a New Government," June 2, 3, 9, 1775, in *Declaration of Independence in Historical Context*, 271.
30. "Congressional Recommendation to the United Colonies, Where Needed, to Adopt New Governments," May 10 and 15, 1776, in *Declaration of Independence in Historical Context*, 441.
31. Willi Paul Adams, *The First American Constitutions: Republican Ideology and the Making of the State Constitutions in the Revolutionary Era*, trans. Rita Kimber and Robert Kimber (University of North Carolina Press, 1980), 66–98.
32. Caesar Rodney to John Haslet, May 14, 1776, in *Letters of Delegates to Congress, 1774–1789*, ed. Paul H. Smith (Library of Congress, 1976–), 3:674.

33. John Adams to James Warren, May 15, 1776, in *Letters of Delegates to Congress*, 3:676.
34. Declaration of Independence, July 4, 1776, National Archives: America's Founding Documents, http://archives.gov.
35. Jim Piechuch, *Three Peoples, One King: Loyalists, Indians, and Slaves in the Revolutionary South, 1775–1782* (University of South Carolina Press, 2008).

What Does the American Revolution Mean to Me?

JOHN A. RAGOSTA

AMERICANS SEEM to have a general sense that religious freedom was an important outcome of the American Revolution and Constitution drafting that followed. But our lack of appreciation for the details of how American religious freedom developed can undermine our understanding of and support for that essential right. Lack of understanding has also contributed to modern efforts to use religious freedom as a bludgeon for political purposes.

It was through conflict and upheaval that religious freedom grew during the Revolution.

Personally, I came to appreciate the Revolution's impact on religious freedom in a rather circuitous way.

I WAS raised in a relatively conservative Catholic home with my ten brothers and sisters. I was an altar boy for eight years, often accompanying my father to daily mass during Lent. When a bit older, I regularly served as a lector at mass. There was an occasional offhand remark from a family member or friend that perhaps I would become a priest. Living in an area with a large Catholic population with southern and eastern European roots, religious freedom never seemed to be an issue.

With limited resources, I attended a very affordable, conservative Christian college. I was naïve, and it was a shock to realize that in some places in America even Catholicism was suspect. I came to realize that religion could be narrow, cramped, and cruel, applied as a weapon to exclude, a shield to hide from inconvenient truths, a means to disengage from productive discussions with others, and a tool for seeking political and economic power in this, rather than the next, world. Ironically, it was at that "Christian" institution that I came to value the need for religious freedom and separation of church and state.

My career took me in a different direction, but it was a lesson that I did not forget.

After practicing law for twenty years, I decided to earn my PhD in early American and legal history. Living in Culpeper, Virginia, I planned to study the Culpeper Minutemen: classic yeoman farmers and tradesmen who dropped their plows and tools, shouldered muskets, and walked 175 miles to Norfolk, Virginia, to win the December 1775, Battle of Great Bridge, the first battle of the Revolution in Virginia. While the question of "why did they fight?" was a bit out of vogue, I thought that the Culpeper contingent might have something interesting to say.

As I began my research, I came across Captain William McClanahan, an officer in the Minutemen, but also a Baptist minister who had been jailed in 1773 for preaching without a license. While I knew that the Church of England was technically the established church in colonial Virginia, I had read that it was a mild establishment, imposing little upon adherents or dissenters. But it was clear that Captain McClanahan might have felt differently. And why did he, a minister who was jailed by colonial leaders for preaching, march with his men to defend the new state led by some of the same people who imprisoned religious dissenters? My research topic changed.

What I learned speaks to what the Revolution means to me.

Conflicts over religious freedom had a long history in colonial British America. In the seventeenth century, Puritans came to New England seeking religious freedom, but it became obvious, certainly by the time of Quaker persecutions and the Salem witch trials, that Puritans meant freedom only to practice what they declared to be the "true" faith, freedom for themselves, but not for others.

Roger Williams, a Puritan outcast by 1635, had a much more capacious view of religious freedom, including a "wall of Separation between the Garden of the Church and the Wildernes of the world."[1] Unfortunately, much of his thought on religious freedom seemed to disappear by the end of the seventeenth century (being rediscovered near the end of the eighteenth century and into the nineteenth), and there is little evidence that he influenced the founders or the Revolutionary Era. (For example, no reference to Williams is found in the extensive correspondence of either Thomas Jefferson or James Madison, founders who played a central role in the development of religious freedom.) In any case, Williams was an anomaly.

As the Revolution approached in the wake of the First Great Awakening, each of the British colonies had an established church and/or imposed some form of religious discrimination. Taxes to support religion were common, as were religious requirements for holding office or for testifying in court. Given the centrality of religion in the culture and government, religion became a significant issue in the burgeoning dispute with Britain.

In New England, the "Bishop's Controversy"—the threat that Britain would ordain an Anglican bishop for America—fed concerns about Britain's waxing efforts to control the colonies and encouraged opposition to the Church of England. The Quebec Act—which, among other things, permitted Catholics in Canada to practice their religion—became another reason to break with Britain for intolerant New Englanders. As the war progressed, the need to ally with Catholic France encouraged tolerance, but tax-supported "Protestant" religious establishments continued, and they lingered well into the early national period in Connecticut, Massachusetts, and New Hampshire.

But while most of the focus by historians on the influence of religion on the Revolution has been on New England, the impact of the Revolution on religious freedom in the South proved to be far more consequential to the new nation.

Virginia, the largest, wealthiest, and most populous colony, had a long-standing establishment supporting the Church of England. Anglicans assured history of its "spirit of mildness," to use Edmund Randolph's phrase.[2] Historians have been too quick to accept that establishment view that Virginia's religious restrictions were weak and unintrusive. The reality for dissenters was quite different. Colonial Virginia imposed a substantial tax on all households, regardless of religious affiliation, to support the Church of England, the largest tax paid by most Virginians. Anglican vestries enforced laws requiring church attendance, regulating marriage, adoption, drunkenness, fornication, and profanity, and providing for poor relief. And those laws were applied in a discriminatory manner. "Little notice was taken" when an Anglican missed church, explained Baptist minister William Fristoe, but laws on church attendance—among the most actively enforced criminal laws in colonial Virginia—were more aggressively applied to religious dissenters.[3] Particularly galling was when church vestries sent dissenters' orphans to Anglican homes for upbringing.

When, in spite of such legal discrimination, dissent continued to grow, Virginia's establishment switched to open persecution in the 1760s. Dissenting ministers, mostly Presbyterians and Baptists, faced attacks on their meetinghouses, disruption of services, and physical assault. Baptist ministers were seized and dunked in ponds and rivers, almost to the point of drowning, in rude parody of immersion baptism. At open-air meetings, men on horseback whipped worshippers, especially African Americans. Stones were thrown. Foxhounds treed one beleaguered minister. A hornets' nest was thrown into a prayer meeting; another was interrupted with a snake.[4] Dissenting meetinghouses were desecrated, the "most slovenly things" done to one communion table.[5] When worshippers refused to disperse at the call of an Anglican magistrate that an unlicensed minister's prayer meeting was illegal, fines were imposed.

In 1768, with dissenting religion continuing to grow, the Anglican establishment—both a political and a religious entity—resorted to arrests. Baptists faced the brunt of arrests. By the time of the American Revolution, more than half of the Baptist ministers in Virginia had been jailed for preaching without a license or disturbing the peace. (Some ministers responded that they had a license from "King Jesus" and recognized no other authority over their calling.)

Seeing an opportunity to proselytize, many jailed ministers preached from their cells. Some were interrupted by burning pepper or sulfur, others by loud and drunken songs. One minister, in a partially below-ground cell in Culpeper, Virginia, had his face urinated on as he preached. Another, in Chesterfield, preaching from a barred window with his arms outstretched in prayer, had both arms cut with knives; he carried the scars to his grave. Worshippers gathered to hear jailed ministers could face men on horseback wielding whips to disperse a crowd.

James Madison, incensed with the harassment and jailing of ministers, famously referred to that "diabolical Hell conceived principle of persecution. . . . [T]o their eternal Infamy the [Anglican] Clergy can furnish their Quota of Imps for such business."[6]

Before the war, dissenters sought some relief from discriminatory laws and an end to the active persecution, but at that time, they grudgingly accepted the preferred status of the established church in the British Empire, even the church tax. All of this changed with the coming of the Revolution.

Facing the most formidable military of the eighteenth century, and with dissenters accounting for 20 to 33 percent or more of Virginia's white population, patriot leaders realized quickly that they needed dissenters' support in the war effort. (Government documents noted, for example, the need for support from those marksmen in the heavily Presbyterian Shenandoah Valley with the extraordinarily accurate long rifles who eventually made up the core of Daniel Morgan's riflemen at the Battle of Saratoga.) This recognition led to a remarkable negotiation—support of the war effort being offered by dissenters in return for religious freedom.

Dissenters' earlier pleas for some limited relief were replaced by demands for equal treatment: an end to the church tax; an end to Anglican control of marriage, orphans, and poor relief; exemption from military service for dissenting ministers. Religious freedom was tied to the sought-after support for the war. An early 1776 letter to the *Virginia Gazette* demanding religious freedom noted that unanimity was needed in the fight against Britain, concluding "a word to the wise is enough."[7] One Baptist petition calling for an end to the church tax and discrimination offered (and threatened) that "these being granted," dissenters would join the "common cause of Freedom."[8] The same veiled, but undeniable, connection was oft repeated: Presbyterians said that reforms would "blot out every vestige of British tyranny and bondage."[9] Militia from heavily Presbyterian Augusta County reminded Virginia's leaders that unanimity was needed to face Britain and "their unanimity will be ever preserved by giving equal liberty to them all." Listing needed reforms, Presbyterians concluded that, "this being done," it will inure to the "great honour and interest of the State." Requesting an end to the church tax, "*this granted,*" dissenters "shall ever wish well to the commonwealth, and shall always do every thing in their Power to defend it."[10] In November 1776, another letter to the *Virginia Gazette* (reportedly penned by Caleb Wallace, moderator of the Hanover Presbytery) asked rhetorically, "At a time when the salvation of our country confessedly depends on the aid and exertions of every party, does not policy loudly forbid any irritating refusal to the reasonable demands of thousands of valuable citizens?"[11] If there was any doubt about the quid pro quo, Anglicans dispelled it when they lectured that they would not adopt the tactics of dissenters and "withhold their concurrence in the common cause until their particular requests are granted, for by such conduct all may be lost."[12] The Anglicans were right, and political leaders knew it.

Negotiations and liberalization continued throughout the war. In 1776, the church tax on dissenters was ended (suspended for Anglicans, terminated in 1779). Marriage was somewhat liberalized. Poor relief and control of orphans, at least in areas with large dissenting populations, was made a governmental (rather than church) issue. Soldiers were permitted to choose dissenting chaplains. Dissenting ministers were exempted from conscription (while other exemptions were being eliminated).

After the war, some sought to whitewash the negotiations. Patriotic Americans had universally and willingly embraced the cause, or so the story went, a story endorsed after the war by many dissenters who did not want their patriotism to seem contingent. Anglicans insisted—never mind the historic record—that they had willingly abandoned their establishment, "cast[ing] the Establishment at the feet of its enemies," Edmund Randolph wrote.[13] More accurately, Thomas Jefferson recalled that these battles over religious freedom were "the severest contests in which I have ever been engaged."[14]

Still, with Britain defeated and the need for unanimity gone, there was an effort to claw back some of the reforms. One Anglican minister encouraged his colleagues, noting that while it would have been unwise to "interrupt that union" with dissenters during the war, now the time was ripe to seek government support for religion.[15]

But the new nation was religiously diverse. It was untenable to have the new government embrace one particular religious sect, but some hoped that government could support religion generally or at least all Christian sects, making the United States officially a "Christian nation." In the fall of 1784, a Virginia proposal for a multiple establishment of any Christian sect was initially endorsed by Patrick Henry, Richard Henry Lee, and other leading patriots. The Virginia General Assembly adopted a resolution that the people should "pay a moderate tax . . . for the support of the Christian religion, or of some Christian church."[16] Variations on such multiple establishments existed in several states.

But this proposal for a generic Christian establishment was met with a groundswell of pointed opposition led by eighteenth-century evangelicals. Opposing any effort to "unite the Church and the State" with a church tax, Chesterfield County dissenters admonished, "Let Jews, Mehometans, and Christians of every Denomination injoy religious liberty."[17] Montgomery County dissenters questioned, "Why then are Pagans & Mahomitans compelled to contribute to the Support of the *Christian* Religion?"[18] As Jefferson later explained, American religious freedom is for the "Jew and the Gentile, the Christian and Mahometan, the Hindoo and infidel of every denomination."

Our eighteenth-century forebearers realized that any limitation on who could receive a government benefit would set a dangerous precedent. The Hanover Presbytery wrote, "If the Assembly have a right to determine the preference between Christianity & the other Systems of Religion that prevail in the world, they may also, at a convenient time, give a preference to some favoured sect among Christians."[19] Madison made the same point: "Who does not see that the same authority which can establish Christianity, in exclusion of all other Religions, may establish with the same ease any particular sect of Christians, in exclusion of all other Sects?"[20]

Beyond the dangerous precedent, dissenters and their Enlightenment supporters insisted that government simply had no authority to interfere in religion, even providing support. This was a matter of both theology and politics. If the government had the power to act on religion, Accomack County dissenters warned, it could (and would) do more. A general assessment was the "first link which Draws after it a chain of horrid consequences, and that by Degrees it will terminate in who shall preach, when they shall preach, where they shall preach, and what they shall preach."[21] Rockbridge petitioners explained that religion was divine and not the subject of human legislation. The Hanover Presbytery warned that the General Assessment Bill was "a Departure from the proper line of Legislation."[22] Madison made the point emphatically: Religion simply cannot "be subject to . . . the Legislative Body"; this was part of "the great Barrier which defends the rights of the people. The Rulers who are guilty of such an encroachment, exceed the commission from which they derive their authority, and are Tyrants."[23] Baptists added, "For the men of the world to undertake to Legislate for his [God's] subjects in matters of Religion is Violating of his Kingly perogative."[24] Culpeper County petitioners explained that "any law fourcing people to pay for the Support of Religion is Contrary to the true principals of Republicanism, divinity, or our bill of Rights, and is Arbitrarily bigg with horrid Consequences."[25]

Government support for religion was also a theological trap for evangelicals. Presbyterians explained: "It is urged, indeed, by the Abettors of this [General Assessment] Bill, that it would be the means of cherishing Religion and Morality among the Citizens. But, it appears from fact, that these can be promoted only by the internal Conviction of the Mind, & its voluntary choice."[26] John Leland, the famous Baptist minister, was even more unequivocal: "Every man must give an account of himself to God, and therefore every man ought to be at liberty to serve God in a way that he can best reconcile to his conscience. If government can answer for individuals at the day of judgment, let men be controlled by it in religious matters; otherwise, let men be free."[27]

Facing a deluge of protests from evangelicals and others, the General Assessment was ignominiously abandoned. In its place, Madison introduced Jefferson's Statute for Religious Freedom—providing for broad religious freedom and a clear separation of church and state. The statute was adopted and became law on January 19, 1786.[28] Virginia, which started the war with a church establishment and active persecution of religious dissenters, ended the period with a strict separation of church and state.

These developments in Virginia took on an outsized role in the new nation. In the years to follow, Jefferson's Statute for Religious Freedom and Madison's Memorial and Remonstrance Against Religious Assessments were reprinted repeatedly around the country as state after state grappled with the meaning of religious freedom. Jefferson's vision was warmly embraced in other states, several modeling their own constitutional provisions on Jefferson's statute, and, under Madison's influence, the statute provided an important foundation for the First Amendment. In 1879, when faced with the first major case addressing the First Amendment's religion clauses—*Reynolds v. United States*, the Mormon polygamy case in which the court rejected the argument that religion provided a basis for an exemption from a neutral law—the Supreme Court unanimously declared that Jefferson's statute "defined" American religious freedom.

All of which brings us back to the questions posed: What does the Revolution have to say to us? How does it help us to understand religious freedom today? And what does the Revolution mean to me?

History makes clear that religious freedom was not simply a result of the Revolution; rather, it was fought for; it was contested. Without the war, and the need for dissenters' support, it is not clear if, when, or how real religious freedom would have developed.

Those who fought for religious freedom also had a very broad notion of what it meant. Led by evangelicals, Virginia rejected the idea of government involvement in, even support for, religion. There was a broad recognition that mixing government and religion would corrupt both; government had no business being in the religion business.

Today, that decision makes even more sense. If government is to support all religions, nondiscriminatory support for Rastafarians, Buddhists, Wiccans, and a host of other religions is needed. What about believers in "the Force" and Pastafarians? And who decides what is and what is not a legitimate religion for government support? (Are Swifties? Trump supporters?)

Some suggest that government support could be limited to Christians, but that is exactly what the Virginia evangelicals and founders rejected. In any case, that begs the question of who decides which "Christians" receive benefits—remember the dispute during the 2012 election campaign over whether Mormons were Christians?—and today, exclusion of Jews, Muslims, and others would be both ethically and politically untenable.

None of this has prevented several Supreme Court justices (Scalia, Rehnquist, Thomas) from simply inventing the idea that the government could provide benefits to monotheists, but this has no support in either our history or the language of the Constitution. Jefferson specifically included Jews, Muslims, Hindus, and "infidels" in religious freedom,[29] and evangelicals insisted on equal treatment of pagans and atheists.

This revolutionary history also speaks to the claim that the United States is a "Christian nation." As Presbyterian minister William Swan Plumer explained in the early nineteenth century when asked whether American was a "Christian Commonwealth," "If by these terms be meant that the great majority of our people, who profess any religion, profess the christian religion, then I do not object to the language. But if it be intended to create a belief that christians ought to be by our laws entitled to any civil, political, or religious privileges except in common with Jews, Deists and Atheists, if there by any amongst us, then I utterly reject it."[30] The founders and eighteenth-century evangelicals would agree.

Importantly, the evangelicals who rejected even nondiscriminatory government support of religion insisted upon a separation of church and state. Powhatan County Baptists opposed the General Assessment Bill so that "no law may pass, to connect the church & state in the future."[31] Botetourt dissenters added, "Civil Government and Religion are, and ought to be, Independent of Each other."[32] The danger was corruption, "entanglement" between the two. An early Baptist history quoted the minister Lewis Lunsford: "The unlawful cohabitation between Church and State, which has so often been looked upon as holy wedlock, must now suffer a separation and be put forever asunder."[33]

This history certainly puts the lie to the argument that separation of church and state owes its origin to a nineteenth century anti-Catholic movement, seeking to refuse funding to Catholic schools. Justice Thomas has embraced this ahistorical canard as an excuse for attacking the wall of separation. Yet, while anti-Catholicism undoubtedly fed support for separation in the nineteenth century, it was eighteenth-century evangelicals and Enlightenment thinkers who demanded separation, seeing it as essential for good government and good religion.[34]

Equally important, especially as we attempt to understand the Revolution more fully in this anniversary period, we should remember why Virginia gave up its establishment. While theological and philosophical arguments were important, it was a recognition that the state, facing a very difficult struggle, needed the support of all of its people that motivated the change. Jefferson and Madison made essentially the same point when they observed that "oceans of human blood" and "torrents of blood" have been spilt over dogmatic arguments because of government involvement in religious disputes and that these were inevitable as long as government involved itself with religion.[35] In a diverse nation, these founders realized that citizenship and legal rights could not depend upon religion. At a time when our nation faces enormous challenges, and when many people claim that the nation is hopelessly divided, increasing division by allowing government to take a side on religion would be very ill-advised. As former Supreme Court Justice Sandra Day O'Connor asked, "At a time when we see around the world the violent consequences of the assumption of religious authority by government, . . . [w]hy would we trade a system that has served us so well for one that has served others so poorly?"[36]

As a naïve young man, having grown up somewhat oblivious to such issues, I began to realize the importance of religious freedom. With my research, I was struck that when Americans were very familiar with church/state cooperation and the persecution that inevitably resulted from it, they rose and rejected it. In Virginia, evangelicals were particularly vocal in voicing the dangers of mixing church and state, how it corrupted both. They were joined in this by American statesmen. Having seen how religion could be used to divide Americans and attack the "other," the lived experience of Virginia's dissenters with the danger of mixing church and state is deeply important to me.

Today, the Supreme Court frequently seeks to justify its decisions on religious freedom based on history. The court has insisted that public funds (tax dollars) be given to religious institutions, often in violation of state constitutional prohibitions, in the name of religious freedom. The court's conservatives have attempted to justify religious exceptions to neutral laws, permitting exemptions from antidiscrimination laws for example, based on history. Religious displays in public buildings have been justified based upon a skewed view of history. These decisions fly in the face of the history of how American religious freedom developed. In the era of the Revolution, evangelicals, supported by Enlightenment statesmen, demanded a strict separation of church and state and supported neutral (Jefferson used the term "impartial") regulation without a religious exception. They concluded that tax dollars should not be used to support religion, even in a nondiscriminatory manner, and that mixing religion and government corrupted both. Speaking for both groups, Jefferson warned that when church and state mix, the church is "always in alliance with the Despot abetting his abuses in return for protection."[37]

As with so many of our founding principles, we still struggle to realize religious freedom fully. Those principles were aspirational, and so it is with religious freedom. There is much that still needs to be done. Informed by history, we must continue to fight for it.

I hope that, in some small way, my work has contributed to our understanding of the American Revolution and, more importantly, that our understanding will contribute to our commitment to religious freedom and separation of church and state as historically grounded and essential in a diverse nation such as ours.

Notes

1. Roger Williams, "Mr. Cotton's Letter Examined and Answered," in *The Complete Writings of Roger Williams*, ed. Perry Miller (Russell and Russell, 1963), 315, 392.
2. Edmund Randolph, *History of Virginia*, ed. Arthur H. Shaffer (University of Virginia Press, 1970), 158.
3. Rhys Isaac, "'The Rage of Malice of the Old Serpent Devil': The Dissenters and the Making and Remaking of the Virginia Statute for Religious Freedom," in *The Virginia Statute for Religious Freedom: Its Evolution and Consequences in American History*, ed. Merrill D. Peterson and Robert C. Vaughan (Cambridge University Press, 1988), 140–41.
4. The historic record tells us only that a snake was thrown into the meeting. I have speculated that throwing a black snake into a prayer meeting of eighteenth-century farmers would have been unlikely to elicit a report.

I believe the snake was likely a copperhead, a venomous occupant of Virginia's Piedmont.

5. Morgan Edwards, *Materials Towards a History of the Baptists in the Provinces of Maryland, Virginia, North Carolina, South Carolina, Georgia*, vol. III (1772), 70, microfilm, Special Collections, University of Virginia.
6. James Madison to William Bradford, January 24, 1774, https://founders.archives.gov/documents/Madison/01-01-02-0029.
7. *Virginia Gazette* (Purdie), April 26, 1776.
8. Garrett Ryland, *The Baptists of Virginia, 1699–1926* (Virginia Baptist Board of Missions and Education, 1955), 98, quoting Prince William County Petition (June 20, 1776). (Petitions, unless otherwise noted, are from the Library of Virginia Legislative Petitions database.)
9. Prince Edward County Petition (October 11, 1776).
10. *Virginia Gazette* (Purdie), October 18, 1776; Hanover Presbytery Petition, October 24, 1776; Albemarle, Amherst and Buckingham County Petition, October 22, 1776.
11. *Virginia Gazette* (Purdie), November 8, 1776.
12. Mecklenburg County Petition, May 29, 1777.
13. Randolph, *History of Virginia*, 263–64.
14. Thomas Jefferson, Autobiography (1821), https://founders.archives.gov/documents/Jefferson/03-17-02-0324-0002.
15. David Griffith to John Buchanan, Fall 1783, in Bishop William Meade, *Old Churches, Ministers and Families of Virginia*. 2 vols. (1857), reprint (Genealogical Publishing, 1978), 2:264–65.
16. Journal of the Virginia House of Delegates (November 11, 1784), 17.
17. Chesterfield County Petition (November 14, 1785).
18. Montgomery County Petition (November 15, 1785).
19. Miscellaneous Petition (Presbyterian ministers in convention) (November 2, 1785).
20. James Madison, Memorial and Remonstrance Against Religious Assessments (ca. June 20, 1785), https://founders.archives.gov/documents/Madison/01-08-02-0163.
21. Accomack County Petition (October 28, 1785).
22. Miscellaneous Petition (November 2, 1785).
23. Madison, Memorial and Remonstrance.
24. Chesterfield County Petition (November 14, 1785).
25. Culpeper County Petition (November 2, 1785).
26. James H. Smylie, "Jefferson's Statute for Religious Freedom: The Hanover Presbytery Memorials, 1776–1786," *American Presbyterians Journal* 63 (1986): 255, 371, quoting Augusta County Petition.
27. John Leland, The Rights of Conscience Inalienable (1791), reprinted in *The Writings of the Late Elder John Leland*, ed. L. F. Greene (New York, 1845), 181.

28. The statute received Senate approval on January 16, now celebrated as Religious Freedom Day, but it did not receive the Speaker's signature until January 19, 1786.
29. Jefferson's Autobiography, https://founders.archives.gov/documents/Jefferson/03-17-02-0324-0002.
30. William S. Plumer, *The Substance of an Argument Against the Indiscriminate Incorporation of Churches and Religious Societies* (Baltimore, 1847), 11–12.
31. Powhatan County Petition (November 6, 1783).
32. Botetourt County Petition (November 29, 1785).
33. C. C. Bitting, *Notes on the History of the Strawberry Baptist Association of Virginia, for One Hundred Years,—From 1776 to 1876* (Baltimore, 1879), 22.
34. Justice Thomas and his colleagues would be better served by asking why some American evangelicals abandoned their strong support for separation of church and state after *Brown v. Board of Education*. With lily-white, "Christian" academies springing up across the South, they hoped that government money might be used to support their racist schools if the wall of separation could be breached—a goal served by vouchers and "school choice" programs. Jerry Falwell Sr., for example, was one of the leaders of this about-face, emphatically demanding a strict constitutional separation until after *Brown*.
35. Jefferson to James Fishback (draft), September 27, 1809, https://founders.archives.gov/documents/Jefferson/03-01-02-0437-0002; Madison, Memorial and Remonstrance, https://founders.archives.gov/documents/Madison/01-08-02-0163.
36. McCreary County v. ACLU of Kentucky, 545 U.S. 844, 882 (2005) (O'Connor concurring).
37. Jefferson to Horatio G. Spafford (March 17, 1814), https://founders.archives.gov/documents/Jefferson/03-07-02-0167.

Embracing the Founders' Legacy

LINDSAY M. CHERVINSKY

I WRITE ABOUT old, dead, white guys. Not because I like them (though I sometimes do), but because they wielded enormous power. They drafted documents and crafted institutions that shape our world today. For better or worse, they are a central part of our nation's memory. They also offer a useful and accessible legacy for today.

The founding generation embraced a spirit of improvisation and improvement, from their creative collective protests against the British Empire to their overhaul of old governing charters and the creation of new constitutions. They hoped to create a system that would foster ingenuity and a persistent commitment to a more perfect union, despite the challenges and setbacks inevitable in the coming centuries. But they knew they could not possibly envision every challenge coming down the road, and they hoped that the spirit of improvisation and improvement would guide future generations. The 250th anniversary offers an opportunity to revisit the principles and the promise contained in the founding of the nation and live up to the founding generation's expectations.

When politicians, lawyers, and justices talk about the founding of the nation, they frequently reference the "founding fathers," by which they mean the elite white men who served in government institutions, the officer ranks of the Continental Army, and diplomatic posts around the world. "The framers" refers to the fifty-five white men who attended the Constitutional Convention. When discussing constitutional interpretation or intent, "framers" is a more accurate term. The founding generation includes the men, women, and children—enslaved, free, and indentured—who survived the tumultuous Revolution and the founding of the new nation. This essay largely focuses on the framers, as well as the elite white men who served in the federal government under both the Articles of Confederation and the new US Constitution, state legislatures, and ratification conventions. That framing inherently excludes most of the residents of North America. Accordingly, the ideas of the men discussed below should not be understood as universal.

Nonetheless, they should be taken seriously for two reasons: First, they used their expansive and concentrated political power to create founding documents and forge institutions that survive into the twenty-first century. Second, because of their innovations, they loom large in the debates over our national culture, judicial interpretation, and political discourse more broadly. Given their constant presence, they cannot be ignored. But neither should they be dismissed. Instead, we should actually understand their legacy of innovation and improvement, and embrace the positive and useful message it offers for today.

The founding legacy is one of change and reform. From the beginning, revolutionaries were trying to create something new with the Declaration of Independence. But they didn't stop there. They continue to tinker, rework, and revise governing charters and, critically, how they were interpreted. The framers of both the Articles of Confederation and the Constitution viewed their creations as imperfect and expected future generations to further innovate. Immediately upon taking office they set an example by experimenting with constitutional interpretation and amending the text.

Future generations of Americans picked up the mantle and worked to create a more perfect union. Amendments were a regular part of political life at the federal level until the mid-twentieth century. State constitutions underwent constant revision throughout the nineteenth century. The American people also reconsidered how they thought about the Constitution. Who counted as "we the people" was understood very differently in 1920 than it was in 1776. They understood that founding principles gave free rein to embrace change. We cannot go back to the founding era *and* stay the same—they are mutually exclusive.

The Declaration proclaimed "all men are created equal" but did little to make that principle a reality. The Declaration is not a governing document. It did not create institutions, nor did it have any binding legal authority. Instead, it had two purposes: First, it was a declaration of the principles upon which the new nation was created—or at the very least a promise to try to attain those principles. The second function was much more practical. It was an announcement of independence primarily intended for a foreign audience. It was crafted to explain to monarchies across Europe why the rebellion was justified and to assuage their fears that the Revolution might inspire the toppling of other hereditary governments.[1]

Recognizing the Declaration's limitations, Congress crafted the Articles of Confederation the following year to govern the new nation. Once it took effect in 1781, the governing charter was the first in a long line of innovations aimed at improving the legal relationships between the states, and the efficacy of the federal government, and the bond between citizens and the nation. The Articles largely concerned the powers of Congress and the relationship between the states. This focus made sense given that diplomatic, economic, and political coordination between the states had little precedent without the oversight of the British Empire. Personal liberty and equality received little attention except for one short line guaranteeing "all privileges and immunities of free citizens" to "the free inhabitants of each of these states, paupers, vagabonds and fugitives from Justice excepted."[2] In other words, citizens from Connecticut enjoyed the same privileges as citizens from Georgia even if they crossed state lines.

The Articles of Confederation provided just enough oversight to manage cooperation between the states during the war. As soon as the Treaty of Paris ended the conflict in 1783, however, the states no longer faced a common enemy. Over the next several years, the Confederation devolved into complete impotence. The Articles gave Congress no authority to compel taxation from the states. Without money, Congress could not repay its debts, engage in diplomacy, defend its borders, pay its employees, or suppress domestic insurrection. By 1787, many Americans had given up on the Articles and demanded reform.

In May 1787, delegates from twelve states gathered in Philadelphia (Rhode Island refused to participate). After establishing a quorum, they agreed to throw out the Articles just six years into its existence. The decision to create a new governance document from scratch was one born of necessity but also of a willingness to embrace change, even when tumultuous. Over the next three and a half months, the delegates locked themselves in Independence Hall and hammered out countless compromises. On September 17, the delegates signed the document and sent it to Congress.[3]

At the top, in large writing, was proclaimed, "We the People of the United States, in order to form a more perfect Union . . ." The opening line is a promise to try to live up to the principles put forth in the Declaration, and a recognition that the nation had failed to live up to those principles thus far. It also inherently recognizes the imperfection of the government it was forming, and any institution or government created and managed by imperfect humans. It does not say, "in order to form a perfect union," but rather calls for one slightly closer to perfect.

The promise to create a more perfect union reflected the cultural context at the time. Many of the framers at the Convention had served in Congress or had a hand in drafting the Articles of Confederation. They were humbled by the failure of the nation's first constitution and keenly aware that most nations don't get second chances. As students of history, they knew the risks of anarchy, military dictatorship, and authoritarianism.

The delegates also faced uphill battles within their ranks. They brought twelve states' worth of different cultural traditions, economic realities, religious factions, and political ideologies. The delegates quickly realized how much compromise would be required to merge these diverse backgrounds into one semi-legible document. They compromised on the structure of the legislature, the number of branches, the composition of the executive, which powers belonged to each branch, the methods of election, and the power granted to the federal government more broadly—just to name a few of the biggest issues.

The phrasing of "a more perfect Union" was not accidental, therefore, nor did it stem from undue humility. The delegates comprehended the document's flaws and acknowledged them. "The difficulty's which have ever arisen when attempts have been made to reconcile such variety of interests, and local prejudices as pervade the severeal States will render explanation unnecessary," Washington wrote to a friend as he left the Constitutional Convention. "I wish the Constitution which is offered had been made more perfect, but I sincerely believe it is the best that could be obtained at this time." Critically, Washington noted his expectation that it would change in the future: "As a constitutional door is op[e]ned for amendment hereafter—the adoption of it under present circumstances of the Union is in my opinion desirable."[4]

The other delegates shared Washington's disappointment. Everyone present had sacrificed an aim: The smaller states had agreed to population-based representation in the House of Representatives; the larger states had agreed to equal representation in the Senate; advocates of executive power had agreed to limitations on the presidency; and opponents of executive power had agreed to create a strong individual executive. Everyone present also understood that compromise was the only way they would get the document signed and ratified.

Edward Carrington, a member of Congress, acknowledged these challenges and the need for compromise upon receiving a copy of the draft Constitution. "I do not implicitly accede, in sentiment, to every article of the scheme proposed by the convention," he wrote to James Madison. "So long as I find it necessary to combine my strength and interests with others, I must be satisfied to make some sacrifices to the general accommodation."[5]

The delegates at the Constitutional Convention, therefore, understood the document to be a great jumble of compromises designed to ensure the maximum number of delegates would sign the document and the requisite states would ratify the document. We should also understand the document this way.

They also had very clear-eyed and realistic expectations for the Constitution's future. At most, they hoped the Constitution would last long enough to establish a firm foundation upon which the nation could build in the future. Their expectations for a short-lived document lasted longer than we might think. In April 1796, Vice President John Adams wrote glumly, "I see nothing better than a Crisis working up, which is to determine whether the Constitution is to be brought to its End this Year, or last a few longer."[6] They were not particularly humble men, but they had enough humility to acknowledge their own limitations. They knew they had left problems unsolved and that problems they could not possibly foresee would arise in the future.

Slavery was the most pressing problem, and the delegates knew they had punted it for future generations to confront. Few delegates had an appetite for abolition, but they collectively understood that it drove a wedge between Northern and Southern states. Gouverneur Morris, one of the most outspoken opponents of slavery, described the problem on July 11 as the Convention debated legal restrictions on the slave trade. The debated reduced him to "the dilemma of doing injustice to the Southern States or to human nature." Morris concluded that "he must therefore do it to the former. For he could never agree to give such encouragement to the slave trade as would be given by allowing them a representation for their negroes." At the same time, Morris "did not believe those States would ever confederate on terms that would deprive them of that trade."[7]

The Convention settled on a compromise that counted every five enslaved Americans as three citizens. This provision, known as the "three-fifths clause," inflated Southern representation in Congress and the Electoral College.

The delegates at the Constitutional Convention could not have predicted the exact twists and turns of the debate over slavery in the coming years, but they knew it would be a problem, and that they had probably exacerbated it. "Should a proportl. representation take place it was true, the N. side would still outnumber the other: but not in the same degree, at this time; and every day would tend towards an equilibrium," Madison had predicted in 1787.[8]

They desperately hoped future generations would craft a creative solution. Perhaps once the nation was more established, they reasoned, generations with more limitless imaginations could force a resolution. With that goal in mind, they included an amendment process in the text of the Constitution. Passing an amendment was a high bar, but not impossible, and provided a viable avenue to fix existing problems and ones they could not yet predict, as Washington had written to his friend Benjamin Harrison just a few days after the Convention had concluded.

In the years immediately following the Convention, many of the delegates demonstrated their commitment to ongoing improvement by participating in the amendment process. After the delegates submitted the proposed Constitution, many returned home to fight for ratification in their states. Many of the states, including New York, Virginia, and Pennsylvania, voted for ratification over the protests of vocal minorities.

Many Federalists (those in favor of the new federal Constitution) promised to consider amendments to secure support from their state legislatures or ratification conventions. James Madison's support for amendments helped secure the necessary votes in the Virginia convention. Although Madison had initially opposed amendments, he acceded to the wishes of his fellow Virginians.

In the spring of 1789, Madison took his seat in the new House of Representatives. Determined to keep his word, Madison spearheaded the drafting and passage of the first ten amendments to the Constitution.[9] The House approved seventeen amendments on August 24, 1789.[10] The Senate approved twelve of the amendments, and Congress signed a joint resolution on September 25, 1789.[11] On December 15, 1791, Virginia became the final state to ratify the ten amendments—now called the Bill of Rights.

Two years later, a court case revealed the need for another amendment. In *Chisolm v. Georgia,* the Supreme Court permitted a citizen of South Carolina to sue the State of Georgia. Congress quickly acted, passing the Eleventh Amendment, which proscribed federal judicial power to prohibit similar cases in the future.[12]

The first competitive election hinted that additional amendments were needed. In 1796, Federalist John Adams defeated Democratic-Republican Thomas Jefferson, seventy-one Electoral College votes to sixty-eight. Thomas Pinckney, the other Federalist candidate, came in third. As a result, Jefferson became vice president—the only time in American history the president and vice president represented competing parties. Observers immediately noted the closeness of the election; they had narrowly avoided a tie. They mused aloud and in letters about a constitutional amendment to clarify the process and ensure that future presidents and vice presidents would be selected from the same party. But then they failed to act.

The election of 1800 provided the necessary motivation to clarify the electoral process. On February 11, 1801, Congress opened the electoral returns from the states to reveal that the two Democratic-Republican candidates, Thomas Jefferson and Aaron Burr, had tied, with seventy-three votes each. John Adams came in third. After thirty-six ballots, the House of Representatives finally selected Jefferson as the next president of the United States. The peaceful transition from Adams to Jefferson was completed on March 4, 1801, but just barely. An extreme rump of the Federalist Party contemplated various legislative maneuvers to appoint a different president; Democratic-Republicans in Virginia and Pennsylvania readied militias on the border to intervene; and protestors gathered outside the Capitol Building, threatening to execute anyone who usurped Jefferson's place in the presidency.[13]

On December 9, 1803, Congress passed an amendment altering the method of election for the president and vice president by placing them on separate ballots. This amendment prevented a tie between the president and vice president of the same party. The states ratified the amendment on June 15, 1804.[14]

At this point, the Constitution had survived for sixteen years, and Congress had amended it twelve times. The nation was far from perfect. Women were mostly disenfranchised, Indigenous peoples were excluded from citizenship, slavery was on the march in the South, and many states still had property qualifications to vote. And yet, the founding generation had demonstrated an ongoing commitment to innovation. The amendment process they created and the amendments they passed indicate a belief that future generations would continue to improve on their initial foundation.

Since 1776, Americans have returned to the principles of the Declaration and the promise embedded in the Constitution for inspiration, especially in dark moments of turmoil. In those moments, they embraced the founders' legacy of innovation. In the depths of the Civil War, President Abraham Lincoln regularly referenced the principles in the Declaration. At a commemoration ceremony for the Battle of Gettysburg, Lincoln opened his remarks by saying, "Four score and seven years ago our fathers brought forth on this continent a new nation, conceived in liberty, and dedicated to the proposition that all men are created equal." He spoke to the living, reminding them of the "unfinished work" before them. He hoped that Americans would "take increased devotion to that cause" for which the fallen soldiers had given "the last full measure of devotion." Lincoln hoped the war would bring forth "a new birth of freedom" and would preserve the "government of the people, by the people, for the people."[15]

Lincoln's prosecution of the war effort went beyond his commitment to the principles contained in the Declaration of Independence, however. His war leadership was based on a fundamental loyalty to the Constitution and the promise to create a more perfect union. In 1861, he wrote, "I am exceedingly anxious that this Union, the Constitution, and the liberties of the people shall be perpetuated in accordance with the original idea for which that struggle was made."[16]

Preserving the Union was Lincoln's priority, and he pursued the Thirteenth Amendment as a means to that end. Lincoln abhorred slavery, but he did not enter the presidency pursuing emancipation. Instead, he gradually concluded that emancipation in the South was required as a war measure, by depriving the Confederate army of its enslaved workforce. Lincoln knew a constitutional amendment abolishing slavery would be required long-term to prevent the reenslavement of Black Americans and to force the Confederate states to rejoin the Union on his terms after the end of the war. The amendment's moral righteousness and its contribution to a more perfect union was a bonus.

The Fourteenth and Fifteenth Amendments continued these efforts after Lincoln's assassination by guaranteeing citizenship to anyone born in the United States and prohibited states from denying citizens from voting on the basis of "race, color, or previous condition of servitude." Although Republicans in Congress passed the amendments with political as well as moral motivations, they were a physical manifestation of the founders' legacy of innovation to pursue a more perfect union.

The war fought to end slavery, and the amendments to the Constitution changed the lives of millions of Americans, but it would not have been possible without a decades-long, bottom-up movement. The Fourteenth and Fifteenth Amendments expanded the legal definition of who counted as "we the people." Support for the constitutional amendments, however, first required that people change how they *thought* about who counted as "the people."

Abolitionists, both white and Black, free and enslaved, forced a reckoning of citizenship and belonging. Publications, including fiction like *Uncle Tom's Cabin,* and nonfiction slave narratives, forced white Americans to reckon with the horrors of slavery and the human suffering of those kept in bondage. These personal accounts made it impossible for Northerners to see slavery as an abstract institution; rather, it was comprised of millions of humans.

Orations like Frederick Douglass's July 4, 1852, speech challenge Americans to reconcile the promises of the Declaration of Independence with the lived reality. "Are the great principles of political freedom and of natural justice, embodied in that Declaration of Independence, extended to us?" he asked. "What, to the American slave, is your Fourth of July?" he challenged. He then answered, exposing the stark reality in front of them. The Fourth of July was "a day that reveals to him, more than all other days in the year, the gross injustice and cruelly to which he is the constant victim."[17]

Future generations built upon Douglass's vision for a more equitable America and demanded full participation. The Nineteenth Amendment and Civil Rights Act of 1964 enshrined civil rights into law for women and people of color, but like the amendments before them, they depended on campaigns of persuasion. Citizens had to first be convinced to interpret constitutional rights differently before they were willing to pass laws protecting those rights. These generations responded to crises, perhaps not the exact way the founding generation envisioned, but with the spirit intended—to try to make the nation just a tiny bit closer to perfect as the current generation understood it.

Today, the Constitution is revered as a quasi-religious relic handed down with infinite wisdom from high above. The idea of amendment or change is rejected or mocked as disrespectful to the founding intentions.

Celebrating the founders' contributions or remembering their legacy is not the same as immortalizing it. The founders have been celebrated since their deaths. The idea of a permanent, unfixable Constitution did not emerge until after World War II. As the world divided into two ideological camps in the Cold War, the United States wasn't just battling the Soviet Union for influence, power, and economic control. It was fighting a war to save democracy and defeat communism; to prove the American way of life was superior to the Soviet one. As a result, the founding of the United States took on a mythical status. The Constitution, which codified American democracy, became a semi-religious relic.

Out of this life-or-death battle emerged a dominant school of judicial philosophy called originalism, which is based on adhering to the law as it was intended when the Constitution was ratified. For example, in *New York State Rifle & Pistol Association, Inc. v. Bruen,* Justice Clarence Thomas wrote the majority opinion rejecting gun regulation in New York State on the grounds that it did not comply with the historical tradition. "The government must demonstrate that the regulation is consistent with this Nation's historical tradition of firearm regulation," Thomas wrote. "Only if a firearm regulation is consistent with this Nation's historical tradition may a court conclude that the individual's conduct falls outside the Second Amendment's 'unqualified command.'"[18]

The founders would be shocked and probably a little bit horrified. The idea that twenty-first-century America should be bound by eighteenth-century musket norms would have struck them as absurd. *They* did not consider themselves bound by eighteenth-century norms. They eagerly revised and adapted their own creations to better suit the needs of the contemporary moment.

That is their true legacy and one that better serves a twenty-first-century nation facing twenty-first-century challenges. By rejecting innovation and improvement—by rejecting the call to constantly seek a more perfect union—we are betraying the founding legacy.

Notes

1. Pauline Maier, *American Scripture* (Knopf, 1997).
2. Articles of Confederation, National Archives, https://www.archives.gov/milestone-documents/articles-of-confederation.
3. George Washington to the President of Congress, September 17, 1787, in *Papers of George Washington, Confederation Series* (University Press of Virginia, 1997), 5:330–33.
4. George Washington to Benjamin Harrison, September 24, 1787, in *Papers of George Washington, Confederation Series,* 5:339–40.

5. Edward Carrington to James Madison, September 23, 1787, in *Papers of James Madison,* (University of Chicago Press, 1977), 10:172–73.
6. John Adams to Abigail Adams, April 13, 1796, in *Adams Family Correspondence,* ed. Margaret A. Hogan (Harvard University Press, 2013), 11:250–51.
7. Gouverneur Morris, "Constitutional Convention Speeches," 1787, National Constitution Center, https://constitutioncenter.org/the-constitution/historic-document-library/detail/gouverneur-morris-constitutional-convention-speeches-july-5-and-11-and-august-8-1787.
8. "Rule of Representation in the Senate, [July 14,] 1787," in *Papers of James Madison,* 10:100–102.
9. "Amendments to the Constitution, [8 June] 1789," in *Papers of James Madison,* 12:196–210.
10. Annals of Congress, House of Representatives, 1st Cong., 1st Sess., 808.
11. Bill of Rights, National Archives, https://www.archives.gov/founding-docs/bill-of-rights-transcript#:~:text=The%20document%20on%20permanent%20display,10%2Damendments%20to%20the%20Constitution.
12. Amendment XI, United States Constitution, National Archives of the United States.
13. Lindsay M. Chervinsky, *Making the Presidency: John Adams and the Precedents That Forged the Republic* (Oxford University Press, 2024).
14. Amendments 11–27, National Archives, https://www.archives.gov/founding-docs/amendments-11-27.
15. US President Abraham Lincoln, "Gettysburg Address Delivered at Gettysburg[,] Pa.[,] Nov. 19th, 1863," https://www.loc.gov/item/rbpe.24404500/.
16. "Lincoln and the US Constitution," National Park Service, https://www.nps.gov/liho/learn/historyculture/constitution.htm.
17. Frederick Douglass, *Oration, Delivered in the Corinthian Hall, Rochester, July 5th 1852* (Rochester, NY, 1852).
18. New York State Rifle & Pistol Association, Inc. v. Bruen, 597 U.S. 1 (2022).

PART FOUR
Lived Experiences

The Presence and Absence of Religion in National Unity

KATHERINE CARTÉ

College students are a pretty good bellwether for changing times. Their blends of hyperawareness and youthful ignorance mark specific political moments with remarkable accuracy. In the past few years, certainly since 2020, my students are equally living with and wary of what the media calls "polarization"—the partisan divisions that have come to mark out nearly warring cultural camps in the United States' political life. Even though my students tend to be more career focused than politicized (or perhaps because of it), this political reality of their world makes them nervous and uncertain. They seem to worry that their fellow students, almost all fellow Americans, could be angered or hurt if any number of delicate topics are touched upon, and they are unsure if the political institutions that I was raised to see as rock-solid can possibly survive. Comfortable notions of political unity are foreign to their lived experience.

Unity. Historians usually tell the story of 1775 and 1776 as one of building national unity out of disparate colonies and disparate peoples. We recount the stirring scenes of Americans far away from Boston Harbor protesting the "Intolerable Acts." We celebrate the militias from across the countryside who marched toward Massachusetts after the Battles of Lexington and Concord. John Adams described the American Revolution as a time when "thirteen clocks were made to strike together" when he reflected on the era in 1818, with the obvious implication that it was no easy feat.

Americans, those older than the college students of 2026, frequently mourn the loss of that unity, though the passage of time means that they more often yearn for the culturally galvanizing moments of September 11, 2001, or, more distantly, of World War II, than for the days of the Revolution.[1] As a historian of religion, I am very conscious of how often those narratives of political unity are built out of religious building blocks. The slogan "united we stand" and its corollary, "divided we fall," conjure Mark 3:25: "And if a house be divided against itself, that house cannot stand." Thomas Paine referenced that Bible verse in his famous 1776 pamphlet *Common Sense*, and Abraham Lincoln memorably connected the phrase to the national crisis of slavery in the years before the Civil War. These were only two of the many times those stirring writers drew on Christian texts to inspire Americans to follow the "better angels of our nature," to use a quote that while *not* biblical, does feel like scripture to many Americans.[2]

It's an arguable question whether Americans today would be drawn closer together or pushed further apart by the kind of religious rhetoric that Paine and Lincoln used to conjure national unity. In 2024 the Pew Research Center found that 41 percent of Americans believe "it's best to just avoid discussing religion altogether." Furthermore, this is not just a matter of religious diversity, but one of politics. According to the influential work of sociologist Robert Wuthnow (first published in the 1980s), Americans are frequently more divided from coreligionists by politics—liberal Protestants from conservative Protestants, for example—than they are by the theological and cultural differences that mark the barriers between traditions such as Protestantism, Catholicism, Islam, and Judaism. The two political camps stretch across these various religions, according to Wuthnow, and the two sides have two "distinct civil religions . . . one favored by religious liberals, the other by religious conservatives."[3] Most visible on the political scene, some Americans are eager for national unity based in shared Christian faith; others find the very idea alienating and divisive.

The changing place of religion in American history weaves through the story of national unity and disunity. By attending to the timing and mechanisms of efforts to conjure religiously based national unity, it is possible to understand with greater clarity the role of religion in our challenged public moment. What follows, therefore, delves into the creation, failure, and re-creation of national unity based in religion during the founding era, with the goal of understanding how—or even if—it is possible that something that resembles religion might function to heal the national rifts of the twenty-first century.

Public religion—that is, government-endorsed Christian rituals—played a significant role in bringing colonists together in 1775 and 1776. That it happened was neither natural or accidental; it was orchestrated. Indeed, if historians were to seek out the *one* day when the most Americans were unified in their contemplation of the national project, it would likely be July 20, 1775. It's rarely remembered now, but the era's delays in communication made it nearly impossible for people across the country to share in events that weren't planned in advance. But people across the young nation experienced the July 20 national day of fasting declared by the Continental Congress, in effect our first national holiday, simultaneously. Held just under a year before the Declaration of Independence, the fast day was an explicit effort by political leaders to unify the nation through religion at a time of crisis and division. Congress passed the resolution calling for a fast day on June 12, 1775, just a few weeks into its sessions and while Boston was still under siege. The revolutionary governments of Connecticut, Rhode Island, Massachusetts, and New Hampshire then supported the precarious and extralegal Congress by declaring concurrent fasts. So too did British North America's largest Presbyterian body, the Synod of New York and Philadelphia.[4]

July 20, 1775, was widely commemorated, even if it was not universally *celebrated*. In other words, the act of public religion conjured ritualized performances, even when political opinion remained divided. As Adams wrote of Philadelphia: "The Fast was observed here with a Decorum and solemnity, never before seen ever on a Sabbath." In Newport, minister Ezra Stiles noted that the day saw "the most crouded Assembly that I ever preached to in my Meetinghouse. It has been a serious and solemn and I hope sincere Fast!" Another preacher, William Piercy, reported from New York that he "never remembered to have seen a Day that was observed with so much seriousness and solemnity as in this City. Every Thing and every Person wore the Appearance of Mourning and Lamentation." On the other hand, many Anglican clergy who had sworn allegiance to the king either avoided the day or marked it in protest. As historian Spencer McBride has described, Samuel Seabury closed the doors of his church in protest on the date. The event was widely shared, but its meaning was disputed.[5]

Why did so many people mark that day? With the benefit of hindsight, we can see that the moment of public religious unity achieved in 1775 was a relic of the colonial era, not a harbinger of events in the future United States. When Congress proclaimed the 1775 fast day, its members banked on the fact that religious leaders in the rebelling colonies would support them. It was a safe gamble, because in 1775, the Congress was still operating within the British Empire's structures of religious institutional establishment, if for no other reason than the population was used to them and colonial religious arrangements had not yet collapsed. In that system, political leaders determined the boundaries of legitimate religion by supporting certain denominations, tolerating others, and outlawing religious behavior that was disruptive or divisive. Colonial religious leaders—members of those privileged institutions—largely embraced the privileges they gained from Britain's Protestant establishment. Those institutional arrangements, still in place in 1775, were known and effective tools for times of political crisis, even though they were now put to revolutionary ends. Moreover, colonists were used to having political agendas—even war—cast in religious terms by preachers who had the imprimatur of government authorities. The scale of the shared experience produced by the July 20 fast day thus resulted from the structures of the ancien régime, rather than (principally) from enthusiasm for the revolutionary cause.[6]

Public religion was a readily available source of unity early in the war, but its power failed quickly when the structures that had built it waned. Tracing national days of fast and thanksgiving through the Revolutionary Era helps explain why the widespread commemoration of July 20, 1775, was not repeated. Although numerous such days were proclaimed by Congress between 1775 and 1784, the process of the Revolution wrenched Americans away from what the British called their "Constitution in Church and State." Amid the disruptions of war, political leaders chose not to attempt to re-create that establishment, but rather to separate church and state.

A major reason the United States' early leaders chose not to create a national church was the knowledge that religion could be just as divisive as it was unifying. Americans had been deeply divided along denominational lines, even when they shared commitments to Britain's Protestant empire. John Adams was one of the many politicians who recognized religion's potential for division. In 1818 he would write that the American clocks had struck together in the Revolution, but during the era itself, he used the same metaphor with a different message. Shortly before the Declaration of Independence he told a correspondent to "remember you cant make thirteen Clocks, Strike precisely alike, at the Same Second." With the next breath he advocated for "Toleration of all Denominations of Religionists" and said that he "hope[d] that Congress [would] never meddle with Religion, further than to Say their own Prayers, and to fast and give Thanks, once a Year. Let every Colony, have its own Religion, without Molestation." Adams knew that attempts at formal religious unity could and probably would backfire.[7]

Furthermore, political disunity based in religious difference became increasingly common after 1776—not just because of theological quarrels but because many people assumed religious labels could be used to predict political ones. As a result, the political conflicts of revolutionary partisanship were exacerbated by denominational difference. In New England, Baptists were accused of disloyalty to the American cause by their Congregationalist neighbors. Quakers in Pennsylvania were accused of Toryism for their pacifist sentiments; some were imprisoned or had their property seized. The followers of John Wesley were politically suspect in the colonies, as their English leader was an outspoken opponent of the fight for American independence. Anglicans often came in for suspicion, particularly in the North, where their numbers were smaller. In reality, members of all of these groups took a variety of political stances, and they changed those stances over time as they saw fit. That fact did not protect individuals from neighborly distrust and suspicion, however.[8]

Fears of political disunity caused by religion had consequences for the shape of the United States. Wise politicians sidestepped religion in moments when their goal was primarily to build and sustain political unity at the level of the newly forming nation. The most prominent such example is the Articles of Confederation, drafted by a committee that began its work shortly after the Declaration of Independence was signed. That first frame of government made virtually no reference to religion, or to forming national unity through public religion, despite the Continental Congress's considerable reliance on such tools in its early months. Initial sketches of the new national government omitted religion. Benjamin Franklin had proposed a plan in July 1775, but it said nothing about religion at all. A proposal from Silas Deane similarly made no mention of religion. Each of those plans included a reference to mutual defense—the essence of union in the context of war—but they asserted the colonies' willingness to protect one another's "liberties," without specification to type, thus neglecting the language of "civil and religious liberty" that was so common in British discourse. The absence of discussions of religion in any form in those early plans probably reflected a general sense that religion would not be an effective means to create national unity. The committee's draft of the Articles of Confederation, presented to Congress on July 12, 1776, added one reference to religion—that the colonies would defend one another from attacks "on Account of Religion." The statement vaguely conjured the days of Protestant-Catholic warfare and the idea that religion was worth fighting for, but it did nothing to unify Americans through religion.[9]

The 1787 federal Constitution followed the path laid out by the Articles when it came to religion, avoiding that which might divide the new nation. There is only one explicit reference to religion in the federal Constitution: the statement in Article VI that "no religious Test shall ever be required as a Qualification to any Office or public trust under the United States." The prohibition, included with several other measures as part of the article, passed without discussion.[10] The final act in this process, the First Amendment to the Constitution, adopted in 1791, furthered the trend set by the Constitution and the Articles before it. By banning any federal religious establishment and guaranteeing the free exercise of religion, it protected Americans' personal religious freedoms from the central government and eliminated the possibility of any formally unifying religious structure. Though the various states pursued many different paths, at each stage in the national process, the United States' leaders chose not to use religion as a means to unify their fragile nation. The 1796 Treaty of Tripoli used plain language to describe the situation, again in a context meant to avoid religious conflict: The United States "is not in any sense founded on the Christian Religion."[11]

A transition happened in the following decades, however, one that has suggested to many modern Americans who yearn for religious unity in their nation that the colonial-derived unity of 1775 was the real lesson of the Revolutionary Era, rather than the message from subsequent years that religion could be divisive. In the absence of any British-style religious structure capable of conjuring national unity, anxiety grew among those who believed religion—or at least a shared moral code—was essential to the survival of the republic. While he was president, the indomitable John Adams wrote: "Our Constitution was made only for a moral and religious People. It is wholly inadequate to the government of any other." Though he knew (or had known in 1776) that religion could divide the nation, he hoped—twenty years later—that it would somehow serve to restrain the worst and most destructive passions of the American people. Adams resurrected the use of days of fast and thanksgiving, but as formal church establishments had mostly collapsed, they were not widely celebrated. The creation of national unity based on religion thus passed out of the hands of government and into the hands of cultural leaders.[12]

In the next generation, some Americans—particularly Federalists and New Englanders—built powerful, unofficial Protestant establishments in an effort to bind the country together. They created a generic Protestantism that resonated with many people, perhaps even a majority, depending on who counted and who did the counting. Historians of American religion chart the gradual development of culturally powerful denominations and benevolent organizations, as well as the continued intermixing between church and state in the early decades of the nineteenth century. Blasphemy, for example, continued to be illegal in the United States in the antebellum era, despite federal protections for freedom of religion and freedom of speech. In 1844, the Supreme Court ruled that "Christianity" was part of common law [in Pennsylvania], so that "its divine origin and truth are admitted, and therefore it is not to be maliciously and openly reviled and blasphemed against, to the annoyance of believers or the injury of the public." Indeed, the court called the United States a "Christian country," a sharp veer away from the choices made by the nation's framers to avoid such language. When the Revolutionary Era finally gave way to the Jacksonian era, the idea that the United States was united by Protestant Christianity was cemented in the minds of many of its leaders and normative in much of its culture, though it took constant effort to maintain that fiction as Catholic immigrants arrived in great numbers, and even many Protestants found the nationalizing institutions of religious do-gooders irritating and intrusive. If the story of the nation's founding ends in 1791, no national unity based on religion could be pretended. If it ends in 1835, elites loudly protested the importance of Protestant Christianity to the nation, but they faced significant opposition.[13]

It is difficult for historians to skip over eras, impossible when doing so suggests false continuity. The early republic was a high-water mark of national religious unity on a cultural level, but if we're looking for lessons of the founding for the present, we must also recall that any such religious unity certainly disappeared by the Civil War. Notably, all the major national Protestant denominations divided over the issue of slavery, and those political fractures took the shape of deep theological divisions over questions of biblical interpretation and church polity. The ruptures were thus equally religious and political. In the years after the Civil War, Northern leaders called on religion to unify the country, but white Southerners invested in a separate, Lost Cause narrative that belied any facile national public religion in the decades that followed. Furthermore, the arrival of ever-larger numbers of non-Protestant and non-Christian migrants around the turn of the twentieth century, as well as sharp and increasing racial segregation in most religious organizations, ensured that religion was hotly contested territory. It defined and separated American communities from one another.[14]

The process of building national religious unity and then losing it recurred in the twentieth century. As religious diversity in the United States grew, a distinctive, Christian-inflected "civil religion," to use Robert Bellah's term, came to play an important role in public life. It resembled the hegemonic Protestantism of the early republic, at least insofar as it was a manifestation of an alliance between cultural elites and government institutions rather than a sign that Americans were *actually* coming to believe the same things or joining the same religious institutions. References to God and to the Bible increased in public rhetoric. Cold War fears of godless communists pushed many to embrace the notion that the "good guys" were both personally religious and accepting of other mainstream religious groups. The messages were not subtle. In 1945, a young Frank Sinatra crooned through a skit supporting religious toleration, and the short film won an Oscar. "Do you know what this wonderful country is made of?" Sinatra asks a bunch of rowdy boys in the process of bullying an outsider. "It's made up of a hundred different kind of people. And a hundred different ways of talking. And a hundred different ways of goin' to church. But they're all American ways."[15] To be American was to be religious and united in embracing mainstream religion. Like its predecessor in the early republic, however, the Cold War moment of religious unity was short-lived. The rhetoric of midcentury civil religion could not survive the political divisions of the 1960s and 1970s any more than the informal establishments of the early republic could hold together churches bitterly divided over slavery. By the 1980s and the rise of the Religious Right, religion had lost its power to promote national unity once again.[16]

Repeatedly, American leaders—a mix of those in office and those in pulpits—have attempted to use religion to create national, political unity. They did so in 1775, building on the tools of Britain's Protestant empire. That model gave hope to future generations. But the framers did not put those same institutions into the Constitution, so parallel performances have never again been possible. Powerful cultural brokers attempted to unify the nation through religion in the early republic and again during the Cold War. But neither of those moments survived engagement with the hard political issues that divided Americans.

Rituals of public religious unity were possible during the early days of the Revolution, but they offer no model for our present divisions, no matter how appealing they might be to people of faith. Religious affiliations and political perspectives both morph over time, with the former almost always following the latter. We should not assume Americans were united by faith at one halcyon point, only to lose it later. Nor should we assume that if somehow Americans could remember their shared values—something they could treat and describe as sacred—our political polarization would end.

From my perspective, as a historian of religion in the founding era concerned about polarization in the present, the message of 1776 for 2026 should be one of caution. Political union is fragile, and, as the founding generation knew, religion—with its normative proscriptions and its clarion teachings—can be deeply divisive. Avoid seeking a civil religious pablum that conjures common ground where there is none. Avoid empty protestations of shared belief when those beliefs do not resonate with audiences. Rather, do the hard and painful political work of identifying and solving political fissures.

Notes

1. Petula Dvorak, "Our Brief Moment of National Unity After the 9/11 Attacks Was Just That, Brief, Can We Ever Get It Back?" *Washington Post*, September 10, 2020.
2. Abraham Lincoln, First Inaugural Address, March 18161, https://www.loc.gov/resource/mal.0773800/?st=text.
3. "Religion's Role in Public Life," March 15, 2024, Pew Research Center, https://www.pewresearch.org/religion/2024/03/15/religions-role-in-public-life/; Robert Wuthnow, *The Restructuring of American Religion: Society and Faith Since World War II* (Princeton University Press, 1988), 13. Wuthnow has more recently argued that "religion is good for American democracy less because of the unifying values it might provide and more because of religion's capacity to bring diverse values, interests, and moral claims into juxtaposition with one another" (Wuthnow, *Why Religion Is Good for American Democracy* [Princeton University Press, 2021], 1–2).
4. Much of the material for this essay draws from Katherine Carté, *Religion and the American Revolution* (University of North Carolina Press, 2021), esp. chap. 4.

5. Spencer W. McBride, *Pulpit and Nation* (University of Virginia Press, 2016), 32–33.
6. Days of fast and thanksgiving had served to further both political unity and controversy long before the Revolution (see Brendan McConville, *The King's Three Faces: The Rise & Fall of Royal America, 1688–1776* [University of North Carolina Press, 2006]).
7. "From John Adams to Benjamin Kent, 22 June 1776," Founders Online (Original source: *The Adams Papers,* Papers of John Adams, vol. 4, *February–August 1776,* ed. Robert J. Taylor [Harvard University Press, 1979], 326.)
8. Carté, *Religion and the American Revolution,* 213–23. For Quakers' experiences in the war, see Sarah Crabtree, *Holy Nation: The Transatlantic Quaker Ministry in an Age of Revolution* (University of Chicago Press, 2015), 43–48.
9. See Carté, *Religion and the American Revolution,* 201–6. For discussions of religious liberty in British and colonial public life, see J. C. D. Clark, *The Language of Liberty, 1660–1832: Political Discourse and Social Dynamics in the Anglo-American World* (Cambridge University Press, 1993).
10. Frank Lambert, *The Founding Fathers and the Place of Religion in America* (Princeton University Press, 2003), 246–50. The federal Constitution also includes two references to religion that were not likely thought of as such by the framers, but which have received attention from Christian nationalists. These are the language of "in the year of our lord" in the date and the provision that Sundays would not be counted in the number of days the president has to approve (or veto) a law (see Michael I. Meyerson, *Endowed by Our Creator: The Birth of Religious Freedom in America* [Yale University Press, 2012], 144–46).
11. Treaty of Peace and Friendship Signed at Tripoli, November 4, 1796, https://avalon.law.yale.edu/18th_century/bar1796t.asp.
12. "From John Adams to Massachusetts Militia, 11 October 1798," Founders Online. The process of disestablishment was lengthy, varied, and unfolded mostly at the state level (see Carl H. Esbeck and Jonathan J. Den Hartog, eds., *Disestablishment and Religious Dissent* [University of Missouri Press, 2019]; and Charles Ellis Dickson, "Jeremiads in the New American Republic: The Case of National Fasts in the John Adams Administration," *New England Quarterly* 60, no. 2 [June 1987]: 187–207).
13. Vidal v. Girard's Executors, 43 U.S. 127 (1844); David Sehat, *The Myth of American Religious Freedom* (Oxford University Press, 2011), esp. 64–69.
14. Mark A. Noll, *Civil War as a Theological Crisis* (University of North Carolina Press, 2006); Charles Reagan Wilson, "The Religion of the Lost Cause," *Journal of Southern History* 46, no. 2 (1980): 219–38.
15. Robert A. Bellah, "Civil Religion in America," *Daedelus* (200): 134, 40–55 (originally published 1967), https://www.nypl.org/blog/2015/06/29

/house-i-live#; Frank Sinatra, *The House I Live In, American Rhetoric—Movie Speech* (1945), https://www.americanrhetoric.com/MovieSpeeches/moviespeechthehouseilivein.html.

16. There is a substantial literature on the rise of the Religious Right. See, for example, R. Marie Griffith, *Moral Combat: How Sex Divided American Christians and Fractured American Politics* (Basic, 2017); and Darren Dochuk, *From Bible Belt to Sunbelt: Plain-Folk Religion, Grassroots Politics, and the Rise of Evangelical Conservatism* (Norton, 2011).

Infectious Disease and the American Revolution

WOODY HOLTON

ABIGAIL ADAMS's letters to her absent husband John provide an intimate view of the dysentery epidemic that devastated Massachusetts during the summer and fall of 1775. With John away at Congress, Abigail was running the household alone. Dysentery carried off her servant girl and almost took little Tommy, who turned three in his sickbed. For Mrs. Adams, about the only bright spot was her mother Elizabeth's daily arrival to help feed the kids and scrub their soiled sheets. Barely a decade earlier, Elizabeth had sought command over her daughter, for instance trying to prevent her from marrying John. Astonishingly, given her acute understanding of how English common law treated married women, when Abigail married, she was "very thankful that I can do as I please now!!!"[1] But in September 1775 mother and daughter battled the affliction together, that is until Elizabeth contracted dysentery, undoubtedly from her grandchildren, and died on October 1.

The death of Elizabeth Quincy Smith revives an intriguing question. We know how the American Revolution affected women of color. It harmed most Indigenous women (and men), and it tended to drive African American women to one extreme (freedom) or the other (worse slavery than before or agonizing death from a disease such as smallpox). But was it a net positive or negative for nominally free white women?

That question will never be definitively answered, but it is at least possible to fill in both sides of the ledger. One debit that has attracted little attention from historians is that the Revolutionary War, like most wars, set thousands of people in motion, circulating pathogens that killed thousands of civilians as well as soldiers. In 1974, Howard H. Peckham offered what remains the reigning estimate of the number of American men (not counting loyalists) who died of their wounds during the seven-year war. The toll was seven thousand, which was fewer American deaths than in three days at Gettysburg. Edwin G. Burrows and others have shown that the body count rises to something like twenty-eight thousand when you add in the soldiers who succumbed to disease, primarily in British prisons.[2] No historian has tried to add up the number of women who succumbed to sickness in army camps, but it had to be in the hundreds, since exposure to contagious soldiers unsurprisingly killed more medical personnel than frontline troops.

It would be even more difficult to estimate how many civilians, male and female, died prematurely as a result of the war. I am not equal to that challenge, but I did get the chance to contribute my mite, thanks to a combination of narcissism among early American Puritans and the professionalization of the modern New England Historic Genealogical Society (NEHGS). Nearly every Congregational minister recorded all of his town's baptisms, marriages, and deaths, even among nonwhites. The NEHGS has not only made this data available to the public through its American Ancestors website but generously provided me a copy of the spreadsheet behind the site. Primarily because of an unusually lethal strain of dysentery, Massachusetts's annual death toll, which usually averaged around 2,300, increased by more than 50 percent to 3,900 in 1775.[3] Indeed, the number of Massachusetts women who died in the epidemic exceeded that year's battlefield deaths among men.[4]

No other colony or state recorded vital statistics as carefully as Massachusetts did, but a smattering of towns did. We are fortunate that one was Morristown, New Jersey, since Continental Army troops spent three winters there. No one in Morristown succumbed to smallpox between 1772 and 1776. But after the troops' first winter in town—1776–77—smallpox killed sixty-eight civilians. Even these surplus epidemic deaths were probably exceeded by those that came in twos and threes; think of the farmwife who entered an army camp to sell eggs, paused for a drink of water, and came home with typhoid fever. It seems likely, though it cannot be proven, that the war killed more civilians than soldiers—which certainly ought to be part of our discussion of whether the war was a net positive or negative for the era's free women.

Disease also intensified conflict between Continental Army officers and their men.[5] Northern troops were so worried about catching malaria or yellow fever that they often rebelled against Southern service. Indeed, this resistance preceded Congress's declaration of independence on July 2, 1776. The previous March, Virginia's Eighth Regiment, which hailed from the hilly and healthy northwestern corner of the colony, had been ordered to march to Charlestown (Charleston), South Carolina. The Virginians did not even make it fifteen miles into *North* Carolina before halting and refusing to take another step. As many as thirty deserted. Finally bullied on to Charlestown, the Eighth Regiment soon experienced the bittersweet taste of validation. A July 1776 return (census) of Continental troops in Charlestown showed a sick rate of 12 percent for South Carolinians and 33 percent for Virginians.[6]

The fit-for-duty soldiers of the Eighth were later sent to Georgia, where by October they as well as Continentals from North Carolina were "very uneasy to return home as they have so few men left and are all sick." With only seventy of the five hundred North Carolinians at one post able to bear arms, the Americans' Southern commander, General Lachlan McIntosh, himself a Georgian, determined that it would "be injuring the Service to detain them encreasing that dislike they have already but too much entertained to the Southern States if they should be ordered here again." McIntosh permitted the North Carolinians and other out-of-state Continentals to return to their homes, but it would be February 1777 before the remnants of the Eighth Regiment made it back to northwestern Virginia "in a shattered condition."[7]

Continental soldiers again resisted Southern service in each of the last four years of the war. In August 1781, George Washington marched half of his army from the Hudson River south to Yorktown in his own state only because his French allies essentially forced him to. One of Washington's primary objections to leading his mostly Northern soldiers to Virginia was their "objections to the climate" of the American South, especially during the summertime. Washington's French allies lent him enough money to mollify his troops with a month's pay in gold and silver coin—the first and only time they were paid in hard money.[8] Without French pressure and funding, the soldiers' anxiety about tropical disease might have prevented Washington from trapping Cornwallis at Yorktown.

Northern fear of Southern disease shaped the war in other ways as well. South Carolina and Georgia struggled throughout the conflict to fill their quotas of Continental troops. Most white men refused to leave their families vulnerable to reprisals from the African Americans they had enslaved and Native Americans whose land they had taken. Officials in both states tried to fill the labor gap with recruits from other states, but they could not overcome even North Carolinians' and Virginians' "prejudices respecting the climate" of the Lower South.[9] This was the context in which John Laurens, a Continental lieutenant colonel and briefly a member of the South Carolina Commons House, made a bold proposal. Believing, as did most whites, that African Americans did not share their susceptibility to tropical disease, Laurens argued that the Whigs should trade slaves freedom for military service. South Carolina enslavers rapidly rejected Laurens's scheme, but African Americans did end up playing a role in easing the South's recruitment crisis—not as soldiers but as bounties paid out to every white man who enlisted.[10]

One remarkable aspect of the soldiers' fear of Southern sickness was that they seemed to define the tropical disease zone differently depending upon where they lived. North Carolinians didn't want to march to Georgia, Pennsylvanians to North Carolina, and so on. The consensus definition of the tropics seemed to be, "everywhere south of me."

Latitude loomed largest in Americans' minds, but soldiers as well as officers also paid close attention to altitude. Beyond the windswept seashore, where mosquitoes had trouble alighting on human hosts, the Lowcountry, or Tidewater, was understood to be far less healthy than the Upcountry, especially in the summertime. Late in 1775, enslaved Virginians offered to fight for Lord Dunmore, their province's last royal governor, in return for their freedom. In July 1776, when soldiers of Dunmore's "Ethiopian Regiment" briefly landed in Maryland, Whig officials there figured the best militiamen to fight them would be those who lived in the state's westernmost county, Frederick. As experienced Indian fighters, the Frederick men were "compleatly armed, as well as good marksmen."[11] But just days after reaching the scene of action—St. Mary's County at the mouth of the Potomac River—the Frederick militia begged to be relieved, for several had already contracted Tidewater fevers.[12]

The contrast between east and west was at least as great in Georgia. There, late in the summer of 1777, General McIntosh took most of his men out of their Lowcountry bivouacs and sent them more than a hundred miles inland for the rest of the sickly season. These Continental soldiers thereby became climate refugees.[13]

Disease also rattled British commanders, but rarely as much as their counterparts on the American side, since most British soldiers had grown up in the more densely populated mother country, where they had obtained lifetime immunity to smallpox by surviving it in childhood.[14]

Many had also encountered other diseases at home and in their travels. Some had even been posted to the Caribbean, all but inevitably coming down with malaria and acquiring partial immunity. The one great health concern for British commanders was the thousands of Americans who fought on their side, especially the nearly ten thousand enslaved people who escaped their owners to fight for their king.

Huddled together on British warships and transports early in 1776, the men of Governor Dunmore's Ethiopian Regiment and their wives and children soon contracted smallpox. Some of the self-liberated soldiers were able to turn the epidemic to their advantage. One was recaptured by the Whigs but "not . . . so well guarded as he ought to have been, owing to the people's being afraid of the small-pox." Taking advantage of this lax supervision, he escaped back to Dunmore.[15] However, hundreds of Black soldiers died of disease. The governor was able to immunize his troops against smallpox, but no one could prevent the onset of "fevers," which mostly seem to have been typhus and dysentery. As lethal as these diseases were, Black Virginians and Marylanders, and even some enslaved people from other states, never stopped trying to reach the Ethiopian Regiment. But Dunmore and Admiral Andrew Snape Hamond, who commanded his naval squadron, abandoned the Chesapeake early in August 1776, their principal motivation being that fever had fatally weakened their mostly Black force.

Commanders on both sides never stopped worrying about illness disabling or even killing their American-born troops. During the second half of 1776, Continental officers also entertained an even greater worry: that potential recruits' fear of disease would dissuade them from signing up. The men already in service posed an even more alarming prospect. These valuable veterans' enlistments would expire at the end of the year, and the dread of contracting a fatal illness seemed likely to prevent many or most from re-upping. The problem was not just the diseases themselves but the wholly inadequate care provided in army hospitals, where a soldier was less likely to be cured of his illness than to be exposed to a new one. So hazardous were the army hospitals that when commanders tried to make up for the shortage of medical personnel by temporarily transferring troops to the medical corps, some deserted back to the front.[16] In a December 16, 1776, letter to John Hancock, the president of Congress, General Nathanael Greene pointed out that "the sufferings of the Sick" were bound to hurt the army as a whole: "Nothing will injure the recruiting services so much as the dissatisfaction ariseing upon that head."[17]

Early in 1776, Congress and Continental commanders overhauled the medical service. Most significantly, they acceded to nurses' and doctors' demands for higher wages. But they did not stop there. Elizabeth Fenn notes that in February, when Washington inoculated his army against smallpox, he saved it—not only by immunizing the existing force but even more by easing potential recruits' fear of contracting the virus.[18] Indeed, the numerous young men who had told recruiting officers that the dread of smallpox prevented them from enlisting probably deserve credit as coauthors of Washington's epochal mass inoculation decree.

Even after Washington immunized his troops against smallpox, potential recruits still had to worry about catching smallpox from militiamen or the women of the army, few of whom were inoculated until much later. "Enlisting goes on badly," Virginia Governor Patrick Henry observed nearly two months after Washington's mass inoculation began. "Terrors of the small pox, added to the Lies of Deserters &c, &c, deter but too many."[19] Would-be enlistees' fear of contracting a fatal disease in the army combined with other factors to prevent most of the states from meeting their enlistment quotas, and that in turn became the main reason that Congress and the states decided in 1777 to institute the draft.[20]

Disease even affected such major decisions as the stationing of troops. The United States directed its first offensive action of the war against Canada, but the Continentals' 1775–76 incursion into Quebec failed miserably after they came down with smallpox and other diseases. By early July 1776, the retreating Americans had reached the southern tip of Lake Champlain, where they had to decide whether to fortify Crown Point or Ticonderoga. It was an impossible choice, since each presented a distinctive threat. Smallpox had spread widely among the troops previously encamped at Crown Point, and the council of war called by Northern commander Philip Schuyler feared that a soldier might pick up the pox simply by grasping a door handle or tool—and then infect others. For that reason, the generals decided to make their stand at Ticonderoga. But the Northern army's field officers (colonels, lieutenant colonels, and majors) considered Ticonderoga even less healthy than Crown Point, primarily because of the numerous cases of malaria. Though Crown Point was only fifteen miles to the north, malaria was not as prevalent there, presumably because, as a peninsula protruding into Lake Champlain, Crown

Point enjoyed breezes as vigorous as those on the Atlantic coast. After the council of war issued its decree, the field officers took the extraordinary step of carrying their dissent to George Washington, who agreed with the field officers but sided with the generals. All along it had been clear that wherever the troops ended up, they would owe their new surroundings to their officers' conflicting concerns about disease.[21]

No one born after 2019 needs to be persuaded that pathogens and parasites can alter the trajectory of human history. And it comes as no surprise that in the American Revolution, as in other wars, infectious disease sometimes decided the fate of battles. But the more significant impact of illness was far subtler. Many studies of epidemics in the millennia before the germ theory deterministically depict *Homo sapiens* as little more than stalks for the Reaper's blade. But wars often add weight to human decisions—and not just those made by nominal leaders. Commanders often considered the dangers that came with lower latitudes and altitudes when designing their strategies. So did enlisted men and the women of the army, as they sought to minimize their exposure to the worst diseases. Many young men refused to sign up for military service—or to reenlist after a short stint—while others balked at orders to head south. Military-age men's imaginative strategies for avoiding fatal illness in turn provoked creativity from civilian and military leaders, all with the primary objective of keeping a respectable army in the field. One such reaction was to give up on the all-volunteer army and start drafting soldiers, a decision that produced its own massive round of plebian resistance.

We are starting to learn more about how infectious disease affected the Revolutionary War, but it will be a while before we understand the topic half as well as the Americans who faced its dangers.

Notes

1. Abigail Adams to Mary Smith Cranch, July 15, 1766, Founders Online.
2. Peckham, *The Toll of Independence: Engagements & Battle Casualties of the American Revolution*, Clements Library Bicentennial Studies (University of Chicago Press, 1974), 130–32; Burrows, *Forgotten Patriots: The Untold Story of American Prisoners During the Revolutionary War* (Basic, 2008), 197–204, 138.
3. Ministers attempted diagnoses of fewer than 10 percent of decedents, but in the cases where they did make estimates, deaths from respiratory illnesses continued to surpass those from dysentery, as did all of the various

fevers combined. But the largest source of the 50 percent mortality increase noted above was a surge in dysentery.

4. I wish to thank the New England Historic Genealogical Society for sharing with me the spreadsheets behind the Massachusetts death figures used in its remarkable American Ancestors website, https://www.americanancestors.org/. Those spreadsheets are the source of all Massachusetts death data cited here.
5. Carl L. Becker, *The History of Political Parties in the Province of New York, 1760–1776, Bulletin of the University of Wisconsin,* no. 286, History Series, vol. 2, no. 1 (University of Wisconsin, 1909), 22; Wood, "'Liberty Is Sweet': African-American Freedom Struggles in the Years Before White Independence," in *Beyond the American Revolution: Explorations in the History of American Radicalism,* ed. Alfred F. Young (Northern Illinois University Press, 1993), 149–84; Holton, *Liberty Is Sweet: The Hidden History of the American Revolution* (Simon & Schuster, 2021).
6. "Monthly Return of the Forces in South-Carolina, for July 1776," in *American Archives,* ed. Peter Force, 5th ser. (Washington, DC, 1848), 1:631–32.
7. McIntosh to Robert Howe, October 22, 29, 1776, *Papers of Lachlan McIntosh in the University of Georgia Libraries* (University of Georgia Press, 1968), 14, 18; Peter Muhlenberg to Washington, February 23, 1777, Founders Online; Charles Lee to John Armstrong, August 15, 1776, in *The Lee Papers [. . .] 1754–1811,* ed. Henry Edward Bunbury, Collections of the New-York Historical Society for the Year 1871–1874 Publication Fund Series, 4 vols. (New York, 1872), 2:230; Howe to Washington, May 14, 1777, in Washington Papers, Series 4, Library of Congress.
8. Washington, diary, May 22, 1781, Founders Online; Joseph Plumb Martin, *A Narrative of Some of the Adventures, Dangers and Sufferings of a Revolutionary Soldier; Interspersed with Anecdotes of Incidents That Occurred Within His Own Observation* (Hallowell, ME, 1830), 208.
9. Nathanael Greene to George Washington, January 24, 1782, Founders Online.
10. Virginia and Georgia also offered slaves as enlistment bounties. South Carolina congressional delegation and Daniel Huger (misidentified as Col. [Isaac] Huger), paraphrased in [Thomas Burke?], draft committee report, [before March 25, 1779], in *Letters of Delegates to Congress, 1774–1789,* ed. Paul Hubert Smith et al., 26 vols. (Library of Congress, 1976–98), 12:243; Greene to Washington, January 24, 1782, Founders Online; Edward Rutledge to Arthur Middleton, February 8, 1782, in "Correspondence of Hon. Arthur Middleton," *South Carolina Historical Magazine* 27, no. 1 (January 1926): 3, 4; William Johnson, *Sketches of the Life and Correspondence of Nathanael Greene: Major General of the Armies of the United States, in the War of the Revolution,* 2 vols. (Charleston [SC], 1822) 2:272–75; James Haw, *John & Edward Rutledge of South Carolina* (University of Georgia Press,

1997), 122; Justin S. Liles, "Thomas Sumter's Law: Slavery in the Southern Backcountry During the American Revolution" (PhD diss., University of South Carolina, 2011), 107–46, 234–35.

11. Maryland Council of Safety to Mary's County committee, August 9, 1776, "Journal and Correspondence of the Maryland Council of Safety: Aug. 29, 1775–Mar. 20, 1777," in *Archives of Maryland* (Baltimore, 1893), 12:190.
12. Captain Peter Mantz to Maryland Council of Safety, August 8, 1776, in *American Archives,* ed. Force, 5th ser., 1:831; Thomas Price to Maryland Council of Safety, July 29, 1776, NDAR, 5:1275.
13. Elbert to Robert Howe, July 18, 1777, Lachlan McIntosh, general orders, July 24, 1777, in "Order Book of Samuel Elbert, Colonel and Brigadier General in the Continental Army," ed. Wymberley Jones De Renne, *Georgia Historical Society Collections* 5 (1902): 46, 481–49.
14. Peter McCandless, *Slavery, Disease, and Suffering in the Southern Lowcountry,* Cambridge Studies on the American South (Cambridge University Press, 2011), 162.
15. Major Price to Maryland Council of Safety, July 23, 1776, in *American Archives,* ed. Force, 5th ser., 1:518.
16. John Morgan, *Vindication of His Public Character* (Boston, 1777), 47.
17. Greene to Hancock, December 16, 1776, in *The Papers of General Nathanael Greene,* ed. Richard Showman et al., vol. 1 (University of North Carolina Press for the Rhode Island Historical Society, 1976), 370; Heath to Washington, September 18, 1776, Founders Online.
18. Elizabeth A. Fenn, *Pox Americana: The Great Smallpox Epidemic of 1775–82* (Hill & Wang, 2001), 86–88, 92–93.
19. Henry to Stephen, March 31, 1777, in *Official Letters of the Governors of the State of Virginia,* ed. H. R. McIlwaine, 1:133, quoted in Fenn, *Pox Americana,* 87.
20. Michael A. McDonnell, *The Politics of War: Race, Class, and Conflict in Revolutionary Virginia* (University of North Carolina Press for the Omohundro Institute of Early American History and Culture, 2007).
21. Remonstrance of Colonel Stark and Other Field Officers to Major-General Schuyler, July 8, 1776, [John] Greaton to Gen. Heath, July 31, 1776, Col. Hurd to New-Hampshire Committee of Safety, August 3, 1776, Gates to Trumbull, August 11, 1776, Thomas Hartley to Horatio Gates, August 25, 1776, all in *American Archives,* ed. Force, 5th ser., 1:234, 697, 748, 899, 1154; Washington to Gates, July 19, 1776, Founders Online.

Legacies of the Revolution's Domestic Warfare

LAUREN DUVAL

In June 2020, as racial justice protests convulsed the nation, one image vividly captured the divisions that wracked the country: a barefoot, middle-aged white couple, the husband in a pink polo, clutching an assault rifle; his wife in a striped T-shirt wielding a tiny handgun, both pointing their firearms at the Black Lives Matter protestors walking past their sprawling St. Louis estate, located on a private street. As news of the incident spread, Mark and Patricia McCloskey were lauded by the Right for their armed defense of their property; they even garnered a speaking slot at the 2020 Republican National Convention. They were mocked by the Left as "bourgeois vigilantes," whose overreaction to the nonviolent, primarily Black protesters exemplified the very legacies of injustice that the protestors demonstrated against. The McCloskeys, however, were unrepentant. Defending their actions, they insisted that in protecting their property they had been championing "the values our country was founded on."[1]

The values our country was founded on. What, precisely, does this mean? Embedded in this justification, certainly, is an assertion of Second Amendment rights. But the incident in St. Louis is also deeply entwined with ideas about the rights of property owners, about the right to safety in one's home, and the right to defend one's house against attack. Collectively, these notions find legal expression in the modern castle doctrine—laws that, in states like Missouri, permit homeowners to employ force to protect their property. Castle doctrine, however, is not new. Derived from the seventeenth-century common law maxim, "an Englishman's house is his castle," castle doctrine retains residues of the patriarchal inequities that defined the early modern household, including property-owning (often white) men's legal authority over their wives, children, servants, and enslaved laborers. In practice, most households never fully conformed to this ideal; patriarchal power was always in flux, always contested.[2] Still, patriarchal property rights were a ubiquitous feature of revolutionary rhetoric. As John Dickinson asserted in his widely read 1767 *Letters from a Farmer in Pennsylvania*, "Let these truths be indelibly impressed on our minds—that we cannot be happy without being free—that we cannot be free without being secure in our property—that we cannot be secure in our property, if, without our consent, others may, as by right, take it away."[3]

As I watched the events in St. Louis unfold that summer, I was struck by the long shadow of the founding era. I was in the midst of writing my first book, an examination of the domestic experience of war during the American Revolution. Property, and its centrality to both the war and early national conceptualizations of independence, were themes very much on my mind. As I read about the incident in St. Louis, I couldn't help but draw parallels to my own research about how the wartime threat to white Americans' property in both land and people had contributed to the postwar veneration of the safe, protected patriarchal household as a symbol of American independence. The events in St. Louis underscored the urgency of my questions about the interplay between property, power, and the nation's founding and suggested that they remain deeply relevant in our contemporary moment. For if the concept of founding values—specifically, the rights of property owners—could be invoked to vilify activists demanding that the nation make real its promise that "all men are created equal" and entitled to "Life, Liberty, and the pursuit of Happiness," what then, I wondered, does this reveal about the significance of the Revolution in 2026?[4]

Interrogating the place of property in the American founding can, I believe, offer some instructive insights. The American War of Independence introduced real violence and terror to people's lives, resulting in a genuine desire to protect families and property. This wartime experience is, both explicitly and implicitly, embedded within our laws and national values. When the founders inscribed "domestic Tranquility" in the Constitution's preamble, they meant not only domestic politics, free from foreign interference, but also domestic life, free from the terror and chaos of the war years.[5] This duality continues to shape our understanding of the American founding. And so, if we are truly to wrestle with the Revolution's legacies in our own time, we must reckon more fully with the conflict as a chaotic, traumatic war that, among its other consequences, endangered private property and destabilized the privileges of race, gender, and status that property represented. Recognizing these dynamics allows us to better understand the Revolution's messy, contradictory legacy, and in so doing, to comprehend the deeply entrenched inequities concealed within some of our nation's so-called "founding values."

Since the war itself, it seems, property, and the more sentimental idea of the home, have been central to our collective commemoration of the Revolution. For centuries, Americans have flocked to Mount Vernon, where, after eight years of war, George Washington enjoyed the fruits of independence under his own vine and fig tree. Seeking to emulate the general's domestic repose in their own, newly independent households, in the early years of the nation, many white Americans looked to Washington to model the practice of independence. And many still do. Each year, one million people visit Mount Vernon; approximately half that number venture to Thomas Jefferson's Monticello, not to mention the estates of other founders scattered along the eastern seaboard.[6] Historic estates are where the public goes to touch history, to commune with the founders, to attempt to understand their lives, values, and intents. Given this, it is, perhaps, unsurprising that property holds such an outsized role in the public's conception of the founding of the United States.

Yet, my own research has shown just how removed the tranquil vision of the founding that visitors might glean from historic homes is from the actual experience of the Revolution. Reading family letters, personal diaries, military papers, and political correspondence, I came to understand that, for many people, the Revolution was characterized not by lofty principles, but by fear, hunger, chaos, and unpredictable violence. The American War of Independence was, first and foremost, an extended, brutal conflict fought among civilians. Soldiers and cannonballs regularly breached the walls of civilian houses, endangering individuals and threatening property in both land and people, with contradictory consequences for the varied residents of British North America. Whether by choice or force, inhabitants of all races and genders became embroiled in the military conflict, enduring battles, quartering, troop requisitioning, property destruction, and the threat of bodily harm. Laborers, both free and enslaved, fled Anglo-American households in droves, pursuing employment, and in the case of the latter, freedom, behind British lines. For many people, survival, the safety of their loved ones, and the preservation of their property outweighed abstract political ideals.

Yet, this messiness, this disruption, this widespread fear have largely been overlooked in popular understandings of the Revolution, which tend to focus on ideology rather than the realities of war. But the two are inextricable. The Revolution upended people's lives, sometimes for the better, but often for the worse. In the process, it destabilized their assumptions about how the world worked and their place within it. This wartime context is essential to understanding how Americans experienced the war, articulated its meanings, and conceptualized the promises of independence in the new nation.

For many colonists who resided in the thriving commercial ports and cultural centers that characterized Britain's North American seaboard, war was an alarming, anxiety-inducing experience. "No one knows where they are safest at this time," Christian Barnes worried from Marlborough, Massachusetts, as the colonies descended into civil war in the spring of 1775.[7] Unlike Western borderlands, where British patrols and conflict with Native nations were common, urban regions were largely sheltered from armed conflict in the decades preceding the war. All of this changed during the Revolution. For two centuries, Anglo-American colonists had been partners in Britain's colonial wars; now, for the first time, the full might of the British army was directed against them. During the war, British raiding parties ravaged American seaports—sometimes in search of supplies but also as a punitive measure to intimidate rebellious populations, invading homes, plundering resources, abusing inhabitants, and burning cities to the ground. The British army also occupied six of the largest cities in North America: Boston, New York, Newport, Philadelphia, Charleston, and Savannah. Often, the Continental Army was not far behind. As battles raged on the outskirts of cities, civilians and their property became casualties of civil war. As one Boston man lamented after the Battle of Bunker Hill, "It was a new and awful spectacle to us to have men carried through the streets groaning, bleeding, and dying."[8]

Urban warfare transformed American cities, damaging property and reshaping people's relationship to safety. The houses in Savannah, Elizabeth Johnston recalled, "were riddled with the rain of cannon balls."[9] In Philadelphia, Elizabeth Drinker described constant gunfire and explosions that shook the ground "like an Earth Quake."[10] For many people, it was a harrowing experience. During the siege of Newport in 1778, Mary Gould Almy ran through the streets with her six children as guns resounded above. "Men Women and chilldren all in as great a Consternation as myself," she recalled. "The ships fired continually. The women shrieking the chilldren falling down crying. . . . [I]t will Ever be in my rememberance."[11]

War eroded the sense of security that many civilians, particularly white inhabitants of the upper and middling classes, derived from their houses. "It is impossible for me to describe to you what I felt, while the British Army was on this side Ashley-Ferry," South Carolinian Mary Lucia Bull Guerard declared in 1779. "We never went in to our beds at night, had Candles constantly burning & were alarmed at every noise that we heard."[12] But even for people who had never felt safe in American households, war elevated the nature, duration, and frequency of violence. In search of safety, many people sheltered in cellars as cannonballs demolished the walls overhead. Even so, these domestic refuges—a privilege of the elite—were often illusory. During the 1779 siege of Savannah, one Continental officer was shocked by the gruesome civilian casualties, including many women and children. "They have all got into cellars; but even there, they do not escape the fury of our bombs," he grieved.[13]

But battles were not the only threat to property. Around urban garrisons, the British army demolished outlying houses and destroyed orchards to deprive their enemy of shelter and to make the landscape easier to surveil. Troops and camp followers of both armies plundered civilian residences in search of food, supplies, and valuables that could be sold or traded. Firewood was in particular demand. "Our very doors and window-shutters were taken from the house," Eliza Wilkinson lamented during the British occupation of Charleston.[14]

Civilians, particularly those residing near military camps, endured persistent looting. "We live—we sleep in constant fear," Andrew Eliot Jr. worried in 1781 from his Connecticut home, which lay within marching distance of both the British garrison at New York and a nearby Continental encampment.[15] In pursuit of both sundries and sport, soldiers (often drunkenly) raided civilian houses; it was not unusual for them to assault people of all ages, genders, and races—although the nature and consequences of these attacks varied considerably among these groups. Soldiers of both armies raped women; Black inhabitants, both free and enslaved, experienced comparatively more violence at the hands of troops, such as Mrs. Anderson, a New York woman who had a noose thrown about her neck by the British soldiers who ransacked her house in search of stolen goods.[16]

Politics could escalate these situations. Eager to assert dominance over rebellious colonists, many British soldiers felt, as Sergeant John Crusard proclaimed in 1777, "Dam them they are Rebels let us plunder them."[17] Continental troops likewise targeted loyalists. In South Carolina, Robert Gray recalled, "The unfortunate loyalist on the frontiers found the fury of the whole war let loose upon him. He was no longer safe to sleep in his own house."[18] Even the disaffected, who endeavored to remain neutral, were drawn into the conflict, such as twenty-two Philadelphia Quakers exiled by the Continental Congress in 1777 because, in accordance with their pacifist beliefs, they refused to choose sides by swearing allegiance to the United States.

Politics aside, male householders of all loyalties were often aligned in their resentment of military quartering practices, which they felt infringed upon their property rights and hindered their ability to care for their families—responsibilities that were integral to masculine independence in the patriarchal society of the American colonies. "Who is it that could urge to be received into my House," an exiled Henry Drinker thundered in 1778 after learning that a Scottish officer was quartered in his Philadelphia house alongside his wife and children. A pacifist Quaker, Drinker's faith intensified his opposition to the arrangement. Still, his primary concerns were for his family and his property: "How many of such intruders are there and what part of the House do they occupy, & do they demand Food, Firing &c. as well as House-Room[?]," he demanded to know.[19] Quartering made tangible what revolutionaries had long warned: British rule endangered the independence, property, and prosperity of American colonists.

Many revolutionaries deemed quartering, even by the Continental Army, incompatible with revolutionary values. "My House is forcibly entered & possessed by officers & Soldiers without my Consent," an anonymous revolutionary complained to George Washington in August 1776 after his residence was converted into a barrack and hospital for Continental soldiers. "The very chambers of my House which is ever considered a sanctuary to the owner, are not so to me, or my family," he protested. The man drew parallels between his own "intollerable" situation and Britain's "unjustifiable encroachment on [colonists] Liberty & Property." "I am doomed, by the strongest inconsistency with those Principles, to experience every Violence & Insult from those very *men*, who are the Strenuous Advocates of Liberty," he grieved.[20]

Nevertheless, the Revolution's domestic warfare held contradictory meanings for the varied residents of revolutionary households. For many domestic laborers, both free and enslaved, wartime disruption to daily routines and household power dynamics created an unprecedented moment to better their own lives and safeguard their loved ones.

In and around garrisoned cities, household servants, particularly young women whose domestic and sexual labors were in demand among the troops, pursued employment with soldiers. Laden with sexual overtones, a November 1777 advertisement in British-occupied Philadelphia illustrates the dual nature of nature of women's labor: "Wanted to live with two single gentlemen, a YOUNG WOMAN to act in the capacity of housekeeper, and who can occasionally put her hand to any thing. Extravagant wages will be given, and no character required."[21] For working women, military employment promised protection, access to rations, higher wages, and, perhaps, love or companionship. Many of these women later married soldiers and established households of their own. Yet life in military encampments was not without danger; nor were soldiers the most reliable employers. Violence, rape, and assault were commonplace; when armies moved on, many women were left abandoned and pregnant. Heightened wartime demand for women's labors nevertheless created a moment in which women who made their livelihoods as servants could alter the trajectory of their lives—for better or worse.

Among householders, however, servants' actions held far different meaning, exacerbating daily discomforts and heightening concerns about their diminished authority. In servants' absence, many employers were forced to fend for themselves. After living for only five weeks "without a servant," New Yorker Hannah Bancker was "worn to a skeleton with fatigue and sorrow." "See what a poor forsaken creature I am become," she moaned in May 1783. "I am at present so bewildered that I seem more dead than alive."[22]

As war disrupted household systems of oversight and threw daily routines into chaos, enslaved people similarly seized this moment to pursue their own interests and safeguard their loved ones. Lord Dunmore's 1775 Proclamation and the 1779 Philipsburg Proclamation, both of which promised freedom to enslaved people, made the British army a beacon of freedom. Still, flight was a gamble, and freedom was far from secure: Disease, crowding, and kidnapping lurked behind British lines. For many bondspeople it was, nevertheless, a chance worth taking. During the war, over twenty thousand people fled to British lines, often alongside their kin.

Proximity to British lines, combined with the army's emancipatory policies and the wartime erosion of slaveholders' power, made paths to freedom more accessible. These conditions facilitated family flight, a notable change from prewar patterns of escape. In 1777, for instance, Abraham and Moll fled the New York village of Pelham and carried their five-month-old daughter and three-year-old son to the British garrison on Long Island.[23] British emancipatory policies also led many women, such as twenty-year-old Dinah, who was "Big with child, and near the time of her lying in" when she escaped to British-occupied Philadelphia in 1778, to strategically give birth behind British lines.[24] Laws categorizing enslavement as a heritable condition passed from mother to child remained firmly in place in regions under revolutionaries' control; but no such laws applied to the self-emancipated refugees behind British lines. Reclaiming control of their bodies and their loved ones—the very things that enslavement endeavored to deprive them of—enslaved kin fled to British lines as an explicit rejection of enslavement, an act that had the potential to destabilize the very foundation of a system premised upon enslavers' co-opting of Black women's reproductive capabilities.[25]

The British army's promises of protection emboldened many enslaved people to forcefully reject enslavers' authority. Seventeen-year-old Quamina taunted his enslaver "to [his] face," before disappearing into the British army's Charleston garrison, that "he can go when he pleases, and [the enslaver] can do nothing to him."[26] Others, such as one self-emancipated South Carolina man, saw an opportunity for vengeance. In April 1782, he led a party of armed Black men to the plantation where he had been enslaved. His former enslaver, William Matthews, believed that the incident, which he described as "a most atrocious attempt on my Person & effects," was motivated by revenge. "I cannot think myself safe a single Night without this Offender punished," Matthews avowed.[27]

On multiple fronts, then, the warfare of the American Revolution subjected elite and middling colonists to a startling, perhaps unprecedented, lack of control over their property and the people they employed and enslaved. Quartering, looting, urban warfare, and material destruction endangered their property and their future prospects. The exodus of domestic laborers, both free and enslaved, unsettled their households and altered their daily lives in significant ways. Life became more uncomfortable; safety, more precarious. War exposed the fragility of property and the tenuousness of the financial, legal, and social relations that it underpinned—a distressing realization for many of those who benefited from these hierarchies.

Peace promised a return to normalcy. As Virginia Continental Congress delegate George Mason yearned in 1776, "May God grant us a Return of those halcyon Days; when every Man may sit down at his Ease under the Shade of his own Vine, & his own fig-tree, & enjoy the Sweets of domestic Life!"[28] Lauding private property and the safe, protected household as powerful emblems of American independence, such rhetoric promised that, after years of sacrifice and suffering, white citizens would never again suffer the invasions and assaults of the war years. Entwining idealized domesticity with white property rights, this veneration of domestic tranquility served important political purposes in the early republic. Acknowledging the very real trauma and loss of the war years, it also forcefully reasserted the patriarchal authority and property rights of white families, especially male householders, in the aftermath of a violent civil war in which many people had overtly rejected that authority. A desire to safeguard the assets of property-owning white citizens and bolster their diminished wartime power thus became a central feature of the laws and values of the new nation. Or, to put it differently, cloaked in the romanticized rhetoric of domesticity, a racialized, patriarchal understanding of property is concealed within our founding creeds.

The private home remains a potent political symbol in contemporary America. Yet simply equating private property with founding values overlooks a vital insight about the deeper significance of property in our founding moment. Property was not—is not—neutral; in the founding era, it was deeply entangled with the privileges of class, race, gender, and freedom. In many ways, the idealization of property was part of a broader a conservative backlash against the potential of the war years, when thousands of people pursued their own independence, their own happiness in ways that fundamentally challenged the financial, legal, racialized, gendered, and classed power that property and the patriarchal household represented.[29] The messiness unleashed during the war and the postwar efforts to contain it; to defuse it through law, custom, and the articulation of national values, are baked into our founding moment. Because for those who lived through the Revolution, this wartime experience was not distinct from nation building; it powerfully informed their vision for the nation they built.

Emerging out of this wartime trauma, the early republic ideal of domestic tranquility formed a critical pillar of the new nation, clearly signifying whose households, whose lives, whose rights the new government served to protect. Echoes of this patriarchal, inequitable vision of founding ideologies continue to resonate in contemporary laws about the rights of property owners and ongoing debates about the values that our country was founded upon. But the Revolution's domestic warfare shows us a messier, more complicated heritage that suggests that breaking down the guardrails erected at the founding is a first, vital step in the project of building an inclusive, equitable democracy in 2026.

Notes

This essay is derived from *The Home Front: Revolutionary Households, Military Occupation, and the Making of American Independence* (Omohundro Institute and the University of North Carolina Press, 2025).

1. Dan Zak, "The Gun-Toting McCloskeys Said They Feared Death. They Survived to Fight the Culture Wars," *Washington Post,* August 25, 2020.
2. For more on households, see William Cuddihy and B. Carmon Hardy, "A Man's House Was Not His Castle: Origins of the Fourth Amendment to the United States Constitution," *William and Mary Quarterly,* no. 3 (1980): 372–400; see also Stephanie McCurry, *Masters of Small Worlds: Yeoman Households, Gender Relations, and the Political Culture of the Antebellum South Carolina Low Country* (Oxford University Press, 1995); Carole Shammas, *A History of Household Government in America* (University of Virginia Press, 2002); and Holly Brewer, "The Transformation of Domestic Law," in *The Cambridge History of Law in America,* ed. Michael Grossberg and Christopher Tomlins (Cambridge University Press, 2008), 288–323.
3. John Dickinson, *Letters from a Farmer in Pennsylvania to the Inhabitants of the British Colonies,* ed. R. T. H. Halsey (Outlook, 1903), 137.
4. Declaration of Independence, 1776, National Archives and Records Administration (hereafter NARA).
5. Constitution of the United States, NARA.
6. "About Mount Vernon," https://www.mountvernon.org/about/; Debra Bruno, "If You Don't Have Time to Absorb Jefferson's Monticello, Head to Monroe's Highland," *Washington Post,* December 13, 2018.
7. Christian Barnes to Elizabeth Inman, [undated], Murray Robbins Family Papers, vol. 1, Massachusetts Historical Society (hereafter MHS).
8. "Andrew Eliot to Isaac Smith, Jr., Boston, June 19, 1775," *Proceedings of the Massachusetts Historical Society* 16 (1878): 288.
9. Elizabeth Lichtenstein Johnston, *Recollections of a Georgia Loyalist* (M. F. Mansfield, 1901), 63.
10. Elizabeth Drinker, *The Diary of Elizabeth Drinker,* ed. Elaine Forman Crane, vol. 1 (Northeastern University Press, 1991), 248.

11. Mary Gould Almy, "Cannonading of the French Fleet in Newport," August 7, 1778, Redwood Library and Athenaeum.
12. Mary Lucia Bull Guerard to Susannah Stoll Garvey, 1779, North American Women's Letters and Diaries, https://alexanderstreet.com/products/north-american-womens-letters-and-diaries.
13. John Jones to Polly Jones, October 7, 1779, in *Historical Collections of Georgia*, ed. George White (New York, 1855), 536.
14. Eliza Wilkinson, *Letters of Eliza Wilkinson, During the Invasion and Possession of Charlestown, S.C., by the British in the Revolutionary War*, ed. Caroline Gilman (New York, 1839), 88.
15. A[ndrew] Eliot to Rev. John Eliot, July 9, 1781, Eliot Family Papers, MHS.
16. General Court Martial (hereafter GCM) of John Ferne, Moses Abraham, Marcus Myers (New York, October 23, 1780), WO 71/92, 385, film 675, reel 14, David Library of the American Revolution (hereafter DLAR).
17. GCM of Lieut. John Cummings (New York, December 3–4, 1777), 30, WO 71/85, film 675, reel 9, DLAR.
18. Robert Gray, "Observations on the War in Carolina," ca, 1782, 7–10, South Carolina Historical Society.
19. Henry Drinker to Elizabeth Drinker, January 30, 1778, Drinker Letters, Haverford College Quaker and Special Collections.
20. Letter to George Washington, August 4, 1776, Sol Feinstone Collection, reel 3, 1737, DLAR.
21. *Pennsylvania Evening Post*, November 1, 1777.
22. H. Bancker to Everet Banker, May 9, 1783, Bancker Family Papers, New York Public Library.
23. *New-York Gazette, and Weekly Mercury*, June 30, 1777.
24. *Pennsylvania Packet*, July 16, 1778.
25. The best study of this is Jennifer L. Morgan, *Laboring Women: Reproduction and Gender in New World Slavery* (University of Pennsylvania Press, 2004).
26. *South Carolina and American General Gazette*, February 28, 1781.
27. William Matthews to Gideon White, April 26, 1782, White Family Papers, no. 130, reel 1, DLAR.
28. George Mason to George Washington, April 2, 1776, Founders Online.
29. For more on this, see Rosemarie Zagarri, *Revolutionary Backlash: Women and Politics in the Early American Republic* (University of Pennsylvania Press, 2007).

The Citizen-Soldier Is Dead. Long Live the Citizen-Soldier.

RICARDO A. HERRERA

Concluding an address to the New York Provincial Congress in 1775, George Washington wrote, "When we assumed the Soldier, we did not [lay aside the] Citizen."[1] Thus Washington touched upon one of the United States' foundational myths, the citizen-soldier—an idealized figure central to American memory, identity, and the founding story, then and now. Citizen-soldiers served the republic when called upon, and then set aside their weapons and trappings of war and picked up the implements of peace—much like the famed Roman general Lucius Quinctius Cincinnatus. Soldiering, like paying taxes and voting, was a fundamental element of virtuous republican citizenship, but it was not a vocation. Believers today argue that the citizen-soldier lives and have cast him in roles according to their sentiments and politics.[2]

In the American tradition, militiamen formed a semi-trained pool of part-time soldiers. Generally, men aged sixteen through sixty years of age embodied the militia. It represented a nascent universal military obligation in which nearly all free white men were to submit, as required by law; they were the community armed. They were "the people."[3] Laws required militiamen to muster and drill. Local elites most often filled the officers' ranks. In all cases, the militia existed by government sanction and acted in support of government, not in opposition to it. When called upon to provide quotas of soldiers, communities did not hesitate impressing into service men with the weakest, most tenuous, or troublesome ties to the community, those whose conduct transgressed norms, or those whose social or economic standing left them among the most vulnerable. Hence, the needs, desires, and demands of society and government overrode individual wishes. Personal liberty was not an absolute, yet men challenged or negotiated with authorities their terms and duration of active service and more. This contest between assertions of legal authority and personal rights, between communitarianism and individualism, between obligation and voluntarism, continues today. Its origins, however, antedate the United States.[4]

In the English Commonwealth tradition, writers like John Trenchard and Daniel Defoe pronounced the militia as a guardian of liberty. In the gendered conceptions of the age, thinkers conceived of liberty as feminine, and thus fragile, and always susceptible to domination by power and its propensity for establishing tyranny.[5] No institution better represented oppressive authority than a standing army under an absolute monarch. Hence, anti-army ideologues conceived of a virtuous people bearing arms in liberty's defense. They had but to reflect on fears of James II's standing army and his absolutist tendencies (not to mention his open Catholicism). Seemingly unconstrained by law and acting without regard to customs and traditions, an authoritarian ruler had it within his power to destroy liberty. In the wake of the Glorious Revolution, the Revolution Settlement firmly established parliamentary supremacy and gradually assuaged fears of a standing army. A peacetime army existed only with Parliament's consent, and civilian control of the military was a reality. With but often-scattered handfuls of regulars in the mainland colonies, the militia was the closest thing to an army that most colonists would ever see until the French and Indian War.[6]

Early American militias were the creations of their parent governments. Each regiment, each battalion, each company, and so on, was as particular to its home as its members were to their locales. Individual colonies and later states bore the responsibility for training and disciplining them. Arming was a different matter. Some militiamen bore private arms; others bore those issued by the Crown, colony, or state. Discipline had a dual meaning. It spoke to the good order and conduct of soldiers, much as it does today, but also to drill, the stuff of early-modern battle—marching, maintaining formation, and loading and firing a musket.

Early on the morning of April 19, 1775, Minutemen and British regulars exchanged fire on Lexington Green. The American War of Independence had begun.[7] When the war broke out, it was the military equivalent of a pickup game on the local basketball court. The colonies went to war against the mother country with the militias they had. Their funding, supply, discipline, leadership, experience, and overall quality varied widely, ranging from combat veterans of the French and Indian War to men more accustomed to mounting slave patrols. Each colony's militia was its parent society under arms. Each was distinctive in its social, cultural, economic, and political characteristics. The men shouldering arms were citizen-soldiers in the truest sense. They had temporarily left their homes and occupations to wage war on behalf of their beliefs, communities, and fellow townsmen. They were the American expression of "civic militarism," the notion that self-governing citizens had the primary responsibility for defending the republic, and that the best defenders were those who composed the body politic, hence, the citizen-soldier.[8]

Reality, however, intruded. Short-term soldiers would not do, so Congress acted swiftly On June 14, 1775, it adopted the militias laying siege to Boston as the Continental Army. The same reality that conceived the Continental Army briefly opened the door for free Black men to enlist in states' regiments and the Continental Line.[9] Their service and ensuing claims of rights and even citizenship, but also the obligations owed them for their service, remained contested ground until the twentieth century. Alongside men of color and volunteers came conscripts, paid substitutes, and enslaved substitutes.[10] Congress had unknowingly planted the seeds for the death of the citizen-soldier. It was a long, slow death to be sure, but a death it was. By creating the Continental Army, Congress had put into being a standing army whose discipline, loyalty, and long-term service, often distant from home, weakened or severed the close community bonds of the militias and squelched the citizen's exercise of his natural rights in favor of good order and discipline.[11]

With independence attained, the militias continued under the autonomous states of the Confederation and then the more unifying federal Constitution. The Continental Army shrank to fewer than one hundred soldiers. Still, the militia's charge remained, local defense and the support of government. The Articles of Confederation enjoined "every state . . . [to] keep up a well regulated and disciplined militia," armed and equipped at the public expense. The reality, of course, was different. Cash-poor and indebted from the war, most states failed to provide for their own common defense. Under the new Constitution, Congress assumed the notional responsibility for "organizing, arming, and disciplining, the Militia, and for governing such Part of them as may be employed in the Service of the United States." This Congress, too, failed to arm the militia. Still, the

Constitution charged these citizen-soldiers to "execute the Laws of the Union, suppress Insurrections and repel Invasions."[12]

Further legislation, including the Second Amendment and the militia acts of 1792 and 1795, reinforced the militia's role as an upholder of state order, not of opposition or resistance to it.[13] In the Second Militia Act of 1792, Congress established a universal military obligation for "each and every free able-bodied white male citizen of the respective States, resident therein, who is or shall be of age of eighteen years, and under the age of forty-five years (except as is herein after excepted)." These citizen-soldiers, Congress declared, "shall severally and respectively be enrolled in the militia." Congress also relieved the federal government of its responsibility to arm the militia and made that an individual responsibility. States like the Commonwealth of Massachusetts echoed federal legislation, when the General Court in 1793 ordered that all men between the ages of eighteen and forty-five be enrolled in the militia. The militia was to muster for "company discipline" (that is, drill) three days per year and annually on the first Tuesday of May for an "exact account of every mans arms and equipments."[14]

President Washington relied on the 1792 acts when he ordered into federal service the militias that cowed Pennsylvania's Whiskey Rebels into submission in 1794.[15] It was the second in a trio of uprisings against state and federal authority, of indebted Western yeomen against coastal creditors and elites—Shays's and Fries's Rebellions.[16] Plainly, the militia formed a bulwark of government and order, not resistance to it, or rebellion embodied. Why, indeed, would any constitution embed the right to overthrow or challenge the frame of government it established? Indeed, the authors of some fanciful and appallingly poor history have imposed their antistatist rhetoric upon the past so as to conjure a zombie-like creature that did not and does not exist. The National Rifle Association's Institute for Legislative Action divorces the militia obligation for bearing arms on behalf of government and argues for the ahistorical position that personal arms are for citizens "to protect themselves against the government." To argue such beggars the historical imagination. It exists in the realm of the most ridiculous and perfervid historical fantasy.[17]

Unrealized then, 1792 was a watershed moment in the militia's death, or as historian Richard Kohn puts it, "the murder of the militia system."[18] The 1792 militia acts came on the heels of two military disasters, the October 1790 defeat of Brigadier General Josiah Harmar's command and that of Major General Arthur St. Clair in November 1791.[19] The "losses were staggering," in the words of historian Colin G. Calloway. They stunned the Congress. Secretary of War Henry Knox "seized the opportunity provided by . . . defeat to challenge the nation's policy of relying upon a small cadre of regular soldiers backed by drafts of militiamen and backwoods volunteers for the conduct of frontier constabulary operations." Congress put aside republican ideology, concern over expense, and the belief in the efficacy of frontier militiamen to pass the militia acts of 1792 and then to enlarge the regular army.[20] Although the regular army's expansion was an expedient designed to quash Indian resistance in Ohio, the legislation was, in retrospect, the beginning of the end of militia primacy and the rise of a permanent standing army.[21] The citizen-soldier as originally envisioned was vanishing, and in his stead a deliberate institutional alternative arose.

The enrolled militia continued to exist, but even as the federal Constitution was turning thirteen, the states had begun weakening the institution. In 1800, the Massachusetts General Court declared "That every person who shall hereafter enlist into any volunteer corps (whether such person be exempt by this Act, from doing militia duty or not) shall be holden to do duty therein for the term of seven years, unless such person be sooner discharged."[22] Individual voluntarism had superseded community obligation.[23] The new republic was not quite a generation into its life, yet it was already shedding its military past.

By the time of the War of 1812, the states' militias were moribund, and little better than quaint paper notions. Their generally pathetic performance in this second contest with Britain confirmed as much.[24] Only, and but for a brief moment, did the militias continue as active organizations in Western states and territories where white encroachments onto Indian lands raised tensions and drove violence. In older, more settled states, the volunteer militia arose. Organized around shared ethnic, trade, socioeconomic, and other commonalities, these units were externally exclusive, but internally democratic. Members wrote their own constitutions, designed their uniforms, elected their officers, and determined admission into their ranks. By the 1820s, the explicit bond between citizen and soldier, however imperfectly expressed in the past, had broken. Universal military service was no longer a civic obligation but instead an unfair and unjust tax on the individual. Leather-apron men and shopkeepers alike could ill afford closing shop to participate in musters and drills, no matter how infrequent. Time away from business was business lost, profits unrealized, a limitation on personal economic advancement, and an imposition on the citizen.[25]

States' governors were happy to have the volunteer militia. They and volunteer fire companies performed vital civic functions maintaining public order and safety in the early republic. They also, to the dismay of many and the delight of others, exhibited some of the worst tribal traits of American society, including virulent nativism, anti-Catholicism, and racism. More than once, rival companies rioted, exchanged fire with one another in the streets, and traded volleys and individual rounds of musketry. Too often, the volunteer companies were the source of disorder, mayhem, and arson and were anything but servants of the common weal or safeguards of public order.[26]

As the revolutionary generation passed away, so too did the last of the citizen-soldiers. A standing army and volunteer militias had replaced them, and, much later, a professionalized National Guard had inherited the lineages of their states' militias.[27] In the wars that followed, volunteers, conscripts, and the federalized National Guard swelled the ranks of American armies. Like the mythic citizen-soldier, wartime volunteers enlisted and shouldered arms for a period and then most returned to civilian lives. They had volunteered for the myriad personal reasons, each soldier's motives unique unto himself. No matter, they had become soldiers for a season not a profession. Conscripts, on the other hand, whether willingly inducted or drafted against their will, also fit the mold. Like the enrolled militia that carried most men's names on its rolls, American conscripts served, and then the survivors returned to civilian callings.

One author, Sam Smith, has neatly encapsulated Americans' broader and more romanticized sentiments about the citizen-soldier. He contends that the women and men of the US Armed Forces "carry the mantle of both citizen and soldier," which on the surface is true. Smith argues that citizen-soldiers create a "balance between the martial and civic spheres," which is "essential to the perpetuation of representative democracy." Indeed, "One commitment [citizen or soldier] cannot outweigh the other." Drawing upon the story of Cincinnatus,[28] Smith argues that the "soldier must always be prepared to return to his home; [much as] the farmer must always be prepared to become a soldier."[29] Inspiring stuff, but it misses the mark widely. As of 2011, a mere "one half of one percent of the U.S. population" had served on active military duty since 2001. As of 2022, veterans constituted but 6 percent of the adult population. If citizenship and soldiering go hand in hand, then the postmortem is clear: The citizen-soldier is dead.[30]

To say that the citizen-soldier is dead is not to cast aspersions on the patriotism or good character of the professional soldiers, sailors, airmen, and marines of the regular and reserve armed forces. They are citizens or permanent residents of the United States, but they have chosen callings not envisioned for the citizen-soldier. They have voluntarily accepted and entered a professionalized and all-encompassing military culture that is distinct and separate from its parent society. Good citizens, permanent residents, and soldiers they are, but citizen-soldiers as originally envisioned they are not. Indeed, the Oregon National Guard suggests that its members are superior to the average citizen, a troubling proposition in a democracy. Its website states that "The Oregon National Guard is a Ready, Professional Militia dedicated to the highest quality service to our State, Nation, and Community." From the claim that "We are Soldiers, Airmen, Employees and Families adding value to America" and that its members are "Patriots leading the way into the Future," it can easily be inferred that other Oregonians and even their fellow Americans who are not in the National Guard are lesser citizens.[31]

Soldiering is no longer an obligation of citizenship, although Congress has declared "that in a free society the obligations and privileges of serving in the armed forces and the reserve components thereof should be shared generally, in accordance with a system of selection which is fair and just."[32] Registering for Selective Service, a legal requirement for "almost all male US citizens and male immigrants, who are 18 through 25," excludes women from this basic element of citizenship—military service on behalf of the republic—and in turn makes them second-class citizens. Title 10 of the US Code reinforces women's second-class status, even as it faintly echoes the Second Militia Act of 1792. It states, "The militia of the United States consists of all able-bodied males at least 17 years of age . . . under 45 years of age who are, or who have made a declaration of intention to become, citizens of the United States and of female citizens of the United States who are members of the National Guard."[33] This is not to demean the women who volunteer, but if the United States means to live up to the promise that "all men [and women] are created equal," then the country is falling short.[34]

The women and men of the armed forces embody some of the noblest and most praiseworthy attributes of American citizenship, but by embracing professional soldiering they have willingly forgone that which distinguished the citizen-soldier from the professional—the temporary, often involuntary, surrender of one's full rights for a season of soldiering and no more. They have subscribed to the code of the professional soldier. Today, in a world of near-instant communication and miscommunication, nuclear, biological, and chemical weapons, and so much more, this is only right and proper.

The citizen-soldier is long dead.[35] No good wishes, nostalgia, or hope will resurrect him. His time has passed, yet adherents of the myth refuse to allow the corpse a peaceful rest. Representative of symbolic American virtues and purported exceptionalism, this venerated figure deserves to be remembered for idealized and inspired service. While the citizen-soldier is dead, the image and the inspiration deserve to live. It is memory. As with all memories, images and inspirations suffuse history, and they become the stuff of heritage, the past idealized and raised to national allegory. Forfend the unhappy event that would require the United States to mobilize for war and call fully upon its people through conscription. It is long past time to bury, mourn, and celebrate this icon of American civic militarism.

Notes

The ideas expressed are those of the author and do not reflect the views of the United States government, the Department of Defense, the Department of the Army, or the United States Army War College.

1. George Washington, Address to the New York Provincial Congress, June 26, 1775, in *The Papers of George Washington: Revolutionary War Series*, vol. 1: *16 June–15 September 1775*, ed. W. W. Abbot (University of Virginia Press, 1985), 41.
2. Marcus Cunliffe, *Soldiers and Civilians: The Martial Spirit in America, 1775–1865* (Little, Brown, 1968), is a superb but often overlooked consideration of the American martial tradition. See Ricardo A. Herrera, *For Liberty and the Republic: The American Citizen as Soldier, 1775–1861* (New York University Press, 2015), for a cultural and intellectual study of soldiering and citizenship in the early republic.
3. Edmund S. Morgan, *Inventing the People: The Rise of Popular Sovereignty in England and America* (Norton, 1988).
4. See Michael D. Doubler, *Civilian in Peace, Soldier in War: The Army National Guard, 1636–2000* (University Press of Kansas, 2003). Greg Ablavasky, "Stanford's Greg Ablavsky on Law and the History of American Militias," *SLS Blog*, https://law.stanford.edu/2020/10/12/stanfords-greg-ablavsky

-on-law-and-the-history-of-american-militias/#:~:text=The%20militia%20was%20a%20long,men)%20were%20obligated%20to%20serve.

5. See David Wormsley, ed., *Writings on Standing Armies* (Liberty Fund, 2020), for a compendium of Commonwealth ideology.
6. An Act Declaring the Rights and Liberties of the Subject and Settling the Succession of the Crown, 1689, 1 W&M 2.c 2; Act of Toleration, 1689, 1 W&M c. 18; Triennial Acts, 1694, 6 & 7 W&M c. 2; Act of Settlement, 1701, 12 & 13 Will. 3 c. 2; Richard S. Dunn, "The Glorious Revolution and America," in *The Oxford History of the British Empire*, vol. 1: *The Origins of Empire: British Overseas Enterprise to the Close of the Seventeenth Century*, ed. Nicholas Canny and Wm. Roger Louis (Oxford University Press 1998), 445–66.
7. See David Hackett Fischer, *Paul Revere's Ride* (Oxford University Press, 1994).
8. Doyne Dawson, *The Origins of Western Warfare: Militarism and Morality in the Ancient World* (Westview, 1996), 4.
9. "An act for the more speedily completing the Quota of Troops [. . .]," May 20, 1777, in *The Statutes at Large; Being a Collection of All the Laws of Virginia from the First Session of the Legislature in the Year 1619*, ed. William Waller Hening (Richmond, 1821), 9:280; Judith L. Van Buskirk, *Standing in Their Own Light: African American Patriots in the American Revolution* (University of Oklahoma Press, 2017).
10. "An Act for speedily recruiting the Virginia Regiments [. . .]," May 20, 1777, in *Statutes at Large*, ed. Hening, 9:337–48; Robert A. Selig, "Black Soldiers in the Revolutionary War," https://www.americanrevolution.org/black-soldiers/.
11. See Michael A. McDonnell, *The Politics of War: Race, Class, and Conflict in Revolutionary Virginia* (University of North Carolina Press, 2007), for an incisive study of one state.
12. U.S. Art. of Conf., art. VI, cl. 4; U.S. Const., art. I, § 8; cl. 16, 15, amend. II; First Militia Act of 1792, Second Militia Act of 1792, 2d Cong., 1st sess. (May 1792); Militia Act of 1795, 3d Cong., 2d sess. (November 1794).
13. Eliga H. Gould, "Why the Second Amendment Protects a 'Well-Regulated Militia' but Not a Private Citizen Militia," *The Conversation*, June 14, 2021.
14. Second Militia Act of 1792, § 1; *Massachusetts, An Act for Regulating and Governing the Militia of the Commonwealth of Massachusetts* [. . .] (Boston, 1793), 381, 394–95.
15. See William Hogeland, *The Whiskey Rebellion: George Washington, Alexander Hamilton, and the Frontier Rebels Who Challenged America's Newfound Sovereignty* (Scribner, 2006).

16. Leonard L. Richards, *Shays's Rebellion: The American Revolution's Final Battle* (University of Pennsylvania Press, 2002); Paul Douglas Newman, *Fries's Rebellion: The Enduring Struggle for the American Revolution* (University of Pennsylvania Press, 2004).
17. Michael R. Rouland and Christian E. Fearer, "Calling Forth the Military: A Brief History of the Insurrection Act," *Joint Forces Quarterly* 99 (4th Quarter, 2020): 125–26; "Antigovernment Movement," Southern Poverty Law Center, https://www.splcenter.org/fighting-hate/extremist-files/ideology/antigovernment; Catrina Doxsee, "Examining Extremism: The Militia Movement," Center for International and Strategic Studies, https://www.csis.org/blogs/examining-extremism/examining-extremism-militia-movement; "What Is the Second Amendment And How Is It Defined[?]," NRA-ILA, https://www.nraila.org/what-is-the-second-amendment-and-how-is-it-defined/. The Declaration of Independence sanctions the right of revolution, but it is not a frame of government.
18. Richard Kohn, *Eagle and Sword: The Federalists and the Creation of the Military Establishment in America, 1783–1802* (Free Press, 1975), 128.
19. See Colin G. Calloway, *The Victory with No Name: The Native American Defeat of the First American Army* (Oxford University Press, 2015).
20. Andrew J. Birtle, "The Origins of the Legion of the United States," *Journal of Military History* 67, no. 4 (2003): 1255–56, 1257; Kohn, *The Eagle and the Sword,* 128–38. "Act for making farther and more effectual Provision for the protection of the Frontiers of the United States," 2d Cong., 1st sess., Chap. 9, March 5, 1792, in *Statutes at large of the United States, 1789–1873,* vol. 1, ed. Richard Peters (Boston, 1846), 241–43.
21. See William Hogeland, *Autumn of the Black Snake: The Creation of the U.S. Army and the Invasion That Opened the West* (Farrar, Straus and Giroux, 2017).
22. Commonwealth of Massachusetts, "An Act for regulating and governing the Militia of the Commonwealth of Massachusetts," (1800) § 3.
23. Peter Karsten, "The US Citizen-Soldier's Past, Present, and Likely Future," *Parameters* 31, no. 2 (2001): 61–62.
24. Robert Reinders, "Militia and Public Order in Nineteenth-Century America," *Journal of American Studies* 11, no. 1 (1977): 85–86.
25. Mark Pitcavage, "Ropes of Sand: Territorial Militias, 1801–1812," *Journal of the Early Republic* 31, no. 4 (1993): 481–500; John F. Kutolowski and Kathleen Smith Kutolowski, "Commissions and Canvasses: The Militia and Politics in Western New York, 1800–1845," *New York History* 63, no. 1 (1982): 5–38; Marilyn S. Blackwell and James M. Holway, "Reflections on Jacksonian Democracy and Militia Reform: The Waitsfield Militia Petition of 1836," *Vermont History* 55, no. 1 (1987): 5–15; Ricardo A. Herrera,

"Self-Governance and the American Citizen as Soldier, 1775–1861," *Journal of Military History* 65, no. 1 (2001): 21–52; Joseph J. Holmes, "The Decline of The Pennsylvania Militia: 1815–1870," *Western Pennsylvania Historical Magazine* 57, no. 2 (1974): 199–217.

26. Reinders, "Militia and Public Order," 82, 87–89. The literature on volunteer militia and fire companies is extensive. A small selection includes Amy S. Greenberg, *Cause for Alarm: The Volunteer Fire Department in the Nineteenth-Century City* (Princeton University Press, 1998); Jack Tager, *Boston Riots: Three Centuries of Social Violence* (Northeastern University Press, 2001); Daniel A. Cohen, "Passing the Torch: Boston Firemen, 'Tea Party' Patriots, and the Burning of the Charlestown Convent," *Journal of the Early Republic* 24, no. 4 (2004): 527–86; Ric Caric, "From Ordered Buckets to Honored Felons: Fire Companies and Cultural Transformation in Philadelphia, 1785–1850," *Pennsylvania History: A Journal of Mid-Atlantic Studies* 72, no. 2 (2005): 117–58; Lesley J. Gordon, "'Novices in Warfare': Elmer E. Ellsworth and Militia Reform on the Eve of the Civil War," *Journal of the Civil War Era* 11, no. 2 (2021): 194–223; Zachary M. Schrag, *The Fires of Philadelphia: Citizen-Soldiers, Nativists, and the 1844 Riots over the Soul of a Nation* (Pegasus, 2021).
27. Militia Act of 1903 (32 Stat. 775).
28. Rob Hardy, "Cincinnatus," in *The Digital Encyclopedia of George Washington*, ed. Anne Fertig and Alexandra Montgomery (Mount Vernon Ladies' Association, 2012–), https://www.mountvernon.org/library/digitalhistory/digital-encyclopedia/article/cincinnatus/.
29. Sam Smith, "The Citizen Soldier: Passion, Fury, Fidelity," March 28, 2016, updated February 7, 2024, American Battlefield Trust, https://www.battlefields.org/learn/articles/citizen-soldier.
30. Paul Taylor, ed., *The Military-Civilian Gap: War and Sacrifice in the Post-9/11 Era* (Pew Research Center, 2011), 2; Katherine Schaeffer, "The Changing Face of America's Veteran Population," Pew Research Center, November 8, 2023, https://www.pewresearch.org/short-reads/2023/11/08/the-changing-face-of-americas-veteran-population/#:~:text=The%20share%20of%20the%20U.S.,fell%20to%206%25%20in%202022.
31. Oregon National Guard, https://www.oregon.gov/omd/ong/pages/default.aspx. For more on military exceptionalism, see Susan Bryant, Brett Swaney, and Heidi Urben, "From Citizen Soldier to Secular Saint: The Societal Implications of Military Exceptionalism," *Texas National Security Review* 4, no. 2 (2021): 9–24.
32. Military Selective Service Act, 50 U.S.C. App. 451, sec. 451, (c).
33. Linda K. Kerber, *No Constitutional Right to Be Ladies: Women and the Obligations of Citizenship* (Hill & Wang, 1998), 221–302; Title 10, U.S. Code, Chap. 12, § 246.

34. "Who Needs to Register," Selective Service System, https://www.sss.gov/register/who-needs-to-register/; Thomas Jefferson, et al., July 4, 1776, Declaration of Independence.
35. For a counterargument, see Ronald R. Krebs, "The Citizen-Soldier Tradition in the United States: Has Its Demise Been Greatly Exaggerated?" *Armed Forces & Society* 36, no. 1 (2009): 153–74.

PART FIVE

Remembering the Revolution

The Irrelevance of the American Revolution

MICHAEL A. MCDONNELL

In 1967 the multiple Grammy Award–winner Ray Charles released "Here We Go Again." It would become one of his most commercially successful songs. Originally a country song, it also contains gospel influences, and Charles infused it with a soulfulness drawn from the Southern blues tradition. It was, perhaps, a quintessentially American song that achieved worldwide success. The original and later versions—most notably a duet with Norah Jones in 2004 that earned two Grammy Awards—have been heard drifting across the shores of all three countries I've lived in over the last fifty years or so, including Wales, Canada, and now Australia.

As we approach the 250th anniversary of the Declaration of Independence, the song's resigned lyrics resonate again for reasons other than the lost loves of my youth: "Here we go again / The phone will ring again / I'll be her fool again / One more time." Perhaps amplified this time by the waters that again distance me from the United States—and the gloomy domestic and international political outlook—the resigned heartbreak is about the continued focus on 1776 as a moment that can (still) save the nation, and the world. US politicians on all sides invoke it constantly: If only we could realize the true meaning of the Revolution, all would be well. And historians inevitably get drawn into this debate by arguing themselves about which side is interpreting the founding—and the so-called founding fathers—correctly.[1]

Meanwhile, the world burns. As the anniversary approaches, many of us feel we live in a world once again turned upside down. We are besieged by reports of genocide in one settler colonial state, continued violence in others, ongoing refugee crises in Europe and Asia, tensions between leading powers that threaten new wars, deadly citizen protests within nations over growing inequalities, and deep divisions across many political societies—including the United States, where many have begun to wonder out loud if the country is on the eve of another civil war. In his pamphlet *The Crisis,* Thomas Paine caught the mood of December 1776 in phrases that might feel familiar to us today: "These are the times that try men's souls," he intoned, while he concluded his first essay with the gloomy words, "Look on this picture and weep over it!"[2]

Paine's essay reveals a great deal about the reality of the American War of Independence and the lessons it might have for today's troubles. But his words have usually been reduced to inspirational sound bites—a rallying cry for patriots in the American Revolution, a crucial moment in the founding of a nation, and a call to arms today. Barack Obama quoted *The Crisis* in his 2009 inaugural speech: "Let it be told to the future world . . . that in the depth of winter, when nothing but hope and virtue could survive . . . that the city and the country, alarmed at one common danger, came forth to meet [it]." And Obama concluded his address by echoing Paine's words: "Let it be said by our children's children that when we were tested we refused to let this journey end, that we did not turn back nor did we falter; and with eyes fixed on the horizon and God's grace upon us, we carried forth that great gift of freedom and delivered it safely to future generations."[3]

Even at the relatively new and much-lauded Museum of the American Revolution, we don't get past the first lines of Paine's pamphlet: "These are the times that try men's souls. The summer soldier and the sunshine patriot will, in this crisis, shrink from the service of their country; but he that stands by it now, deserves the love and thanks of man and woman. Tyranny, like hell, is not easily conquered; yet we have this consolation with us, that the harder the conflict, the more glorious the triumph." His words, the exhibition notes, "stirred Americans to regroup, re-enlist, and fight again." We are urged to "Read aloud the opening words" of his pamphlet to be similarly energized.[4] While Obama and the museum invoke Paine as a call for citizens to fight inequality and injustices and to be active citizens, it is worth remembering that right-wing militias also routinely cite Paine to add legitimacy and urgency to their more literal call to arms to overthrow perceived government overreach or tyranny.[5]

The superficial use of Paine in so many contexts today points to a number of tensions that continue—and will continue—to derail efforts to learn from the past as we approach the anniversary of the American Revolution. The most important of these is the weight the era bears as a moment in which a nation was created—a nation that endures today. That weight immediately yokes and subordinates historical events of the era to civics lessons. Despite massive social, cultural, and political changes in the intervening years, any discussion of the nature of civil society today seems to begin—and sometimes end—with the Revolution. Instead of examining and dissecting the law, civil codes, the operation of government, and the political roles, rights, and obligations of citizens today, we immediately turn to the Revolution to look for what these were, not what they should or could have been.

Because we do so, we also cannot escape from a narrative historical account that is inevitably linear and teleological—where the most important and pressing issue is to explain how the nation came to be rather than to dwell on the complexities and divisions of the past. We cite Paine to illustrate how difficult it was to achieve independence, and to inspire to action today, but we do not pause long to reflect on why his words were needed in the first place—and then why they were preserved at all. A selective reading of Paine "fits" the narrative we need to understand the creation of a nation.

And that narrative, of course, was first articulated by politicians embroiled in a civil uprising against a lawfully constituted government that would today be called an insurgency—or worse. The so-called founding fathers spun a tale of a legally justified rebellion from the start, well aware that if their case was not persuasive, their necks were on the line. That tale was of a unified citizenry revolting against a tyrannical government. It allowed only limited dissent, few complexities, and no contradictions. It was built on and sustained by the exclusion of the majority of the population of the continent at that time—Native Americans, enslaved Africans, women, unpropertied men, and loyalists. Despite those exclusions, that story was amplified and expanded by those in favor of a national government and echoed by the first generation of nationalist historians and echoed again and again down to today—almost verbatim. It has been a compelling story of the creation of a nation.[6]

It has been particularly compelling precisely because it lacks complexity and contradictions and instead favors the enunciation of ill-defined, elastic, but noble ideals that can be interpreted by everyone, for whatever purposes—as they were by the founders themselves in the exclusions they assumed. Equality, liberty, the pursuit of happiness. Who could possibly argue with those ideals as the basis of a nation? But instead of interrogating what they meant at the time and what political purposes they were put to by diverse groups of people, we are too often focused on them as ideals rather than contested ideas. We are thus stuck in endless arguments about how best to uphold so-called American founding values of liberty and equality, where everyone along the political spectrum from the Far Right to the Far Left simply invokes rather than interrogates the American Revolution—without examining the historical context.

Historians often recognize the contested nature of the ideas, and their contradictions, but we also struggle to escape this paradigm. We get sucked into the general story and can only debate its relative merits. We recognize complexity, but we still need to narrate the creation of the nation. We can question the limits of the Revolution, but we rarely question the event itself. We accept the founding fathers' version of events, and then debate the contours. We strive mightily to make it an inclusive story, but we are beholden to it. We focus on different ideals and debate the degree to which they measured up to reality at the time, but we find it difficult to tell the story without them. We rarely entertain other possibilities—other political and social arrangements that might even have made for a more inclusive, less unequal society.

We even try to tell a more expansive story of an unfinished Revolution still in the making, but after 250 years that feels a little hollow, and echoes the empty rhetoric of politicians. Some have dared to suggest alternative national stories and themes, but the fate of the 1619 Project alone suggests that those alternate tellings will always fall before the sacred altar of the American Revolution.[7] We are, effectively, stuck in a paradigm fabricated by the founders. It is hard to think of another example of a single historical era having as great a hold on the historical and public imagination as the American Revolution has had—apart from China, perhaps? If, as many argue, the founding fathers were geniuses, this was their true legacy. A common question these days is, What would the founders think? What would they think of this inability to move beyond this moment? I suspect they'd be weeping, or having a good laugh.

If we shed the framework of a triumphal story of the Revolution as the birth of a nation, what would we see? Historians have uncovered a lot over the past decades, and a great deal that does not fit into the stories we tell about the creation of the nation—so they don't make much of a dent in the national collective consciousness. We know now, for example, that the passage of the Stamp Act in 1764 had little to do with despotic government, and a great deal to do with international events. The extraordinary costs of the first global war in history, the Seven Years' War, almost crippled Britain and forced reforms. But the colonists participated in and benefited from this war as eagerly as did Britain—only they were not willing to shoulder the costs of the victory. Equally costly was the war that has come to be known as Pontiac's—one of the largest pan-Indian uprisings in North America—starting in 1763. Sovereign and independent Native peoples tried to stem the tide of colonial settlement. They were largely successful, and helped trigger the Revolution because colonists chafed under the restrictions of new imperial reforms introduced to appease Native peoples. They were only successful, of course, until aggrieved settlers launched a new war of conquest between 1774 and 1795. That, too, was part of the story of the Revolution.[8]

Historians have also noted that the consequences of the Seven Years' War were far-reaching and affected many colonists differently. Some suffered mightily from a postwar economic depression; others grew rich on the back of freer trade within the expanded British Empire, land speculation, and the labor of others. Convict servants flooded the Chesapeake, and colonists also imported captive and enslaved Africans in rapidly expanding numbers—the last quarter of the eighteenth century might have been an era in which Jefferson penned the phrase that all men were created equal, but it was also the era in which the Atlantic slave trade peaked. Against this backdrop, colonial assemblies trained a new pool of elites in the not-so-subtle arts of politics, and new imperial legislation was one of many different causes of contention and growing factionalism in these bodies—as politicians tried to outdo themselves to emulate Parliament and claim *English* rights. This aspect of the anglicization of the colonies was only the most ironic manifestation of the rage for empire—and the desire of colonists to replicate rather than separate from Britain in the decade before the American Revolution.

Those politics grew more heated over the years, as a relatively small group of hotheaded pamphleteers increasingly demonized their opponents, used the threat of crowd action, and spun a tale of persecution in the partisan public newspapers in which many were invested. That crafted story drew on racialized language and stoked white colonial fears of insurrectionary slaves in their midst and bloodthirsty Indians on their flanks. At the same time, pamphleteers channelled a host of disparate social and economic grievances into a papered-over kaleidoscopic coalition with vague promises of popular rights. If this sounds familiar to readers today, we would do well to remember that the colonists largely stumbled into outright war with Britain—with even many of the most militant critics of Parliament uncertain that separation from Britain was desirable, even after blood had been shed. It was, by then, too late. The only thing patriot leaders could do by late 1775 was cry unity and do what they could to retain their own power when declaring independence.[9]

The shaky foundations of the patriot cause better explains Thomas Paine's *The Crisis*, written about six months after the Declaration of Independence. Any enthusiasm for the conflict with Britain had been exposed as limited and had petered out quickly. The Continental Army was disintegrating and had been chased out of New York and across New Jersey. A panic ran through the country, Paine noted. But it was not just that the summer soldiers had gone home. The cause was hardly unified. Thousands of colonists wanted to stay loyal to the Crown; thousands more simply wanted to stay out of the conflict. Paine wailed about both groups—the Tories, and those determined "to stand the matter out"—but those parts of his pamphlet are rarely cited. In the end, the "city and the country" were not in fact "alarmed at one common danger" and did not "c[o]me forth to meet [it]," as Obama imagined. Instead, Washington got lucky at Trenton and then ensured he would never again be so embarrassed. He pressed the states to introduce conscription and called on Congress to make an unholy alliance with Catholic France—the nation he himself had warred against alongside the British officers he desperately emulated only fifteen years earlier.

The Revolutionary War did not create a magical "band of brothers," as Washington put it, and as countless textbooks and now the Museum of the American Revolution have echoed. Had the colonists been as united as modern pundits claim, the war would have been over in a matter of months. Instead, historians have uncovered a traditional eighteenth-century war fought by professional armies, many of whom were drafted, which quickly became an international conflict that dragged on for years. Yet there were differences in this war. For one thing, at least 20 percent of the population was enslaved, with Black majorities predominating in some areas. While patriots used the fear of slave insurrections to try to mobilize their neighbors, many stayed at home precisely because of their fears. Enslaved Africans themselves sought freedom behind British lines in extraordinary numbers. They also served as substitutes for their white owners in patriot lines—but only after extracting promises of freedom in return. By the end of the war, some desperate patriots were proposing arming their enslaved population en masse to fight the British; others proposed to offer confiscated slaves belonging to loyalists to poorer neighbors if they would serve in the army.[10]

The war many white colonists waged against Native Americans in the West and enslaved people in their midst was further complicated by it being a true civil war. Tens of thousands of people joined British auxiliary forces or lent support to the British army and navy. Many paid a heavy price for their loyalty as some seventy thousand people were driven out of the colonies—including thousands of enslaved Africans who were forced to leave with their owners, thousands more formerly enslaved Africans who sought liberty *from* their patriot owners, and tens of thousands more whose property was confiscated in the name of liberty and who were hounded out of their homes by their neighbors and sometimes their own families. On a per capita basis, this would be the equivalent of some seven million refugees today. They became international exiles—and many of them were lucky enough to become settler colonists in new lands such as the colonies that would become Canada, Australia, and Sierra Leone. It was a desperate, chaotic, bloody, and divisive civil war that dragged on for eight years and in which more people were killed by diseases ravaging the continent than in combat. Indeed, even a conservative estimate of thirty thousand deaths on the eastern seaboard would again mean the per capita equivalent of some three million people dying in a conflict on American shores today. The destructive conflagration only came to a halt because Britain could not sustain an international war any longer in the face of French support for the newly independent states. In other words, the new United States was dependent on others for its independence.[11]

It was a hollow victory for so-called patriots. Bereft of British trade, the postwar period ushered in what historians are now calling the First Great Depression, and most people just wanted to be left alone in the wake of the conflict. But many states were still at war with Native peoples on their borders, and many creditors were keen to get their debts paid back by impoverished neighbors and claim Western lands they had speculated on. Depending on their legislative composition, different states passed new tax and debt laws—some that hit debtors hard, others that disadvantaged creditors. More progressive radicals wanted greater representation in their new state governments, while nationalist-minded men yearned for less democracy and a more centralized government capable of enforcing tax laws and circumventing the power of individual states. The result was the counterrevolutionary coup of the federal Constitutional Convention, an extralegal gathering that had no popular mandate to create a new government, but they did it anyway—and got it ratified in the face of widespread opposition. A powerful federal union and centralized government emerged from it that looked and acted remarkably like the British government that most thought they had been fighting against. It curbed the more democratic elements of the state constitutions and ensured economic prosperity by allowing the continuation of slavery for another seventy years—until an even greater Civil War brought it down—and creating a military powerful enough to continue a war of conquest of Native American lands that arguably continues to today.[12]

Historians have known most of these details for years now, and we are still digging up more contradictions and further complexities. But we have not changed the main contours of the story much at all. This is partly our fault. There is money to be made, after all, in climbing on the founding fathers' bandwagon. Other well-intentioned historians want to expand the story. Those on the left, for example, want to "reclaim" the founding and just make it a more inclusive story—to add more voices and stir. They focus on and emphasize the ideal of equality—even as conservative detractors emphasize liberty. But they are still telling the story the same way. It has proved too compelling to do otherwise. And perhaps too dangerous to try hard to overturn it armed merely with different stories and alternative perspectives. In the hypernationalist and exceptionalist frameworks that the founders created and politicians on the left and right parrot today, questioning the founding was and is akin to treason. It is Washington, after all. It is the Constitution. It is the nation.

And it is certainly true that the messy, contradictory, complex, bloody, divisive, and grubby historical details of the period between 1763 and 1789 don't make for a soothing civics story about national origins. The historical realities do not elevate Washington, Jefferson, and Madison into demigods; they give the lie to founding ideals of equality and liberty, and they expose the startling inequalities on which the United States was based from the start. Those facts force us to see that the United States was simply another settler colony born of European conquest and unchecked imperialism—albeit one of the more "successful" settler colonies in its ruthless and unapologetic theft of Native lands.[13] They might even help us better understand the more elemental forces behind the production of knowledge and the writing of history once we acknowledge that history is, indeed, most often written by the "winners." Indeed, they force us to confront the fact that the fabricated nation was created and ruled by wealthy elites, predicated on a massive expulsion of refugees, a civil war, on the wealth that enslaved labor and stolen Indigenous lands created, and doomed to be riven by extraordinary and lasting divisions that could not be papered over in 1860, and cannot today. The history written by the winners is looking increasingly unconvincing, especially since the number of "winners" seems to be diminishing. Of course, it has always looked unconvincingly thin to those outside this exclusive group. It was not and is not a pretty story. But, then again, it might be a story that better explains the mess we're in today—and it might also offer us important and more general lessons in how to deal with a world on fire. But it is not a story that is easy to sell.

Instead, we cling to hope. In the absence of an appetite for a public deep dive into the paradoxes and contradictions, the violence and divisions, and the global consequences and meanings of the Revolutionary Era, we cling to the audacity of hope instead. Indeed, it is almost as if we keep the Revolution especially off-limits when thinking about the messiness of the world today. It is the one historical place into which Americans can retreat—and cling to whatever mythical version of the past they want as a refuge from the seemingly far more troublesome and complicated times we face today. Obama enjoined us to choose our better history, not to grapple with it: "With hope and virtue, let us brave once more the icy currents, and endure what storms may come." We continue to ignore or bypass or simplify the past in order to hope for a better future. At the Museum of the American Revolution, we are urged to follow in the footsteps of Ben Franklin—to look resolutely forward and see the creation of the new nation as the rising of a new sun. And to think about the "promise of equality."

It is certainly alluring. The hopefulness of a new start. A do-over. Is that what people mean by the American Dream? Even as a foreigner I often cannot resist. I'll keep teaching American history. I'll keep writing about American history. I'll keep accepting invitations to reflect on the American Revolution. Because there's always a glimmer of hope that it might be useful in some way. That this history might help us understand our current predicaments. But that hope is now resigned, tempered by experience—and Ray Charles comes to mind more often than he should. Charles's life was entwined in complicated ways with the unfolding history of the post–Second World War period in American history. His own life story was messy and complex, and he endured much. Yet he remained hopeful, just. Two months after his death in 2003, another version of "Here We Go Again" was released that betrayed this knowing resignation to hope: "I've been there before / And I'll try it again / But any fool knows that there's no way to win."

Notes

1. Andrew M. Schocket's *Fighting over the Founders: How We Remember the American Revolution* (New York University Press, 2015) is probably the best single-volume treatment of the different ways in which the Revolution is invoked by so many for diverse and often contradictory reasons. Compare Michael D. Hattem, *The Memory of '76: The Revolution in American History* (Yale University Press, 2024).
2. "The American crisis (No. 1) By the author of Common sense. [Boston] Sold opposite the court house Queen Street [1776]," http://hdl.loc.gov/loc.rbc/rbpe.03902300.
3. Barack H. Obama, "Inaugural Address," January 20, 2009, https://obamawhitehouse.archives.gov/blog/2009/01/21/president-barack-obamas-inaugural-address.
4. In the exhibition *The Darkest Hour,* Museum of the American Revolution, Philadelphia, https://www.amrevmuseum.org/virtual-museum-tour.
5. Clare Corbould and Michael A. McDonnell, "Why the Alt-Right Believes Another American Revolution Is Coming," *The Conversation,* January 15, 2021.
6. See, for example, Robert G. Parkinson, *The Common Cause: Creating Race and Nation in the American Revolution* (University of North Carolina Press, 2016), for the fabrication of this story by the newspapers at the time, and Michael D. Hattem, *Past and Prologue: Politics and Memory in the American Revolution* (Yale University Press, 2020), for the reinforcement and amplification of this story in the early republic by a small cabal of nationalist historians and archivists; and Michael A. McDonnell, "War Stories: Remembering and Forgetting the American Revolution," in *The American Revolution Reborn,* ed. Patrick Spero and Michael Zuckerman (University of Pennsylvania Press, 2016), 9–28.
7. See "The 1619 Project," *New York Times,* August 14, 2019; "The 1619 Project and the Long Battle over US History," *New York Times,* November 12, 2021; and David Waldstreicher, "The Hidden Stakes of the 1619 Controversy," *Boston Review,* January 24, 2020.

8. Woody Holton, *Forced Founders: Indians, Debtors, Slaves, and the Making of the American Revolution in Virginia* (University of North Carolina Press, 1999); Michael A. McDonnell, *Masters of Empire: Great Lakes Indians and the Making of America* (Macmillan, 2016). The literature on the history of the Revolution is immense. Here I will cite only one or two for each topic for the sake of brevity—and an entrée into the literature.
9. Parkinson, *Common Cause;* Marjoleine Kars, *Breaking Loose Together: The Regulator Rebellion in Pre-Revolutionary North Carolina* (University of North Carolina Press, 2002); Holton, *Forced Founders.*
10. Sylvia R. Frey, *Water from the Rock: Black Resistance in a Revolutionary Age* (Princeton University Press, 1991); Michael A. McDonnell, *The Politics of War: Race, Class, and Conflict in Revolutionary Virginia* (University of North Carolina Press, 2007).
11. Colin G. Calloway, *The American Revolution in Indian Country: Crisis and Diversity in Native American Communities* (Cambridge University Press, 1995); McDonnell, "War Stories."
12. Woody Holton, *Unruly Americans and the Origins of the Constitution* (Macmillan, 2007); Ned Blackhawk, *The Rediscovery of America: Native Peoples and the Unmaking of US History* (Yale University Press, 2023).
13. James Belich, *Replenishing the Earth: The Settler Revolution and the Rise of the Angloworld* (Oxford University Press, 2009).

The Ethos of Revolution

Past and Present

JOANNE B. FREEMAN

Revolutions are messy things. They involve upset, conflict, and transformation—sometimes for better, sometimes for worse. They are violent, unpredictable, and fueled by force. Even the abstract ideas and ideals that spawn and bolster them are often a messy mix of purposes. However unified in message they may seem, revolutions rest on the impulses and urges, needs and yearnings, hopes and fears of individuals with a sense of injustice, however defined.

For all of these reasons, cohesion and endurance don't come naturally to revolutions, which themselves embody change.[1] To channel that change, revolutionaries deploy a blend of persuasion and force: declaring their cause into existence in print; empowering it with proclamations and declarations; and forcing it into being with threats, oaths, and loyalty tests.

The American Revolution was no exception. It was bitter and often brutal, dividing families, destroying property, stoking violence, and taking lives and livelihoods. The bonds of society were under attack, and there was no telling how things would end. Not surprisingly, by the war's close, between sixty thousand and eighty thousand loyalists had left their homes and fled to friendlier climes.[2] In terms of today's population, more than three million patriot soldiers were killed.[3]

The passage of 250 years has all but erased that roiling instability. Yet it's impossible to understand the Revolution without it. Extreme contingencies infused the revolutionary ethos; *anything* could happen. Even the framing and ratification of the Constitution brought no easy answers, not even for the men who did the framing; their fears are palpable in their writings. "We are in a wilderness without a single footstep to guide us," wrote "Father of the Constitution" James Madison as the new government launched in 1789. George Washington was all too aware that he was "on untrodden ground."[4]

This is not the Revolution that Americans remember. There is an inevitability to America's origins narrative, an assumption that "right"—of course—prevailed. Of course there was a war. Of course independence was declared. Of course the colonists won. Of course they came together as a nation.

This storybook view of the American Revolution is hardly new; in some ways, the revolutionaries themselves invented it. They knew that their success relied on the support of both a national and international audience, so they accentuated—even exaggerated—the positive. Providence and the laws of nature were on their side, they argued. They were fighting against injustice and tyranny to birth a new world order grounded on a new understanding of the rights of man; once unleashed, American ideals would transform the world.

It's a powerful story, though it wasn't just a story. Revolutionary Americans high and low sincerely believed in their cause as they defined it—*when* they defined it. And there was the rub, because ideals are strongest when they're undefined, conveniently amorphous enough to bridge divides without demanding compromise. Thus the colonies' sluggishness with slavery. It's not that the founding generation somehow couldn't grapple with the internal paradox of fighting for freedom while enslaving people. For the most part, they chose not to. They wanted the strength and breadth of hazy ideals to unite and fuel their cause.

But hazy ideals alone do not a nation make. And as posterity minded as they were, the framers and founders felt that keenly. They created new governments even as they were trying to topple old ones. They well knew that political processes would make or break their efforts, particularly with the war's end and the waning of its *rage militaire*.

They also knew that with the passage of time, an idealistic origins story with few roots in hard realities would do the nation more harm than good. History taught that republics were fragile. They survive only with the continued efforts and watchfulness of their citizens. The new American nation would not go of itself. A fairytale founding denied that basic truth. A New World Order brought to life by superhuman luminaries and unfailingly stoic patriots would be a one-time miracle with a beginning and an end that could not be repeated, hard work be damned.

Thus John Adams's fears as he witnessed the embalming of the Revolution within his lifetime. He could see it in the countless letters he received, often from strangers, asking him to recount the nation's founding miracles. "I ought not to object to your Reverence for your Fathers as you call them . . . much less can I be displeased at your numbring me among them," he told one such correspondent in 1811:

> But to tell you a very great secret, as far as I am capable of comparing the Merit of the different Periods, I have no reason to believe that We were better than you are. We had as many poor Creatures and selfish Beings, in proportion among us as you have among you: nor were there then more enlightened Men, or in greater Number in proportion than there are now.[5]

He said the same when correspondents compared America's current government with its founding equivalent and found it sorely wanting. "I Say We do not make more mistakes now than We did in 1774. 5. 6. 7. 8. 9. 80. 81. 82. 83," he wrote in 1812. "It was patched and piebald Policy then, as it is now, ever was, and ever will be world without End."[6] He put things more plainly in a letter to his friend Benjamin Rush the next year:

> You and I and our contemporaries have no Right to reproach the present government or the present generation. We blundered at Lexington at Bunkers Hill, in Rhode Island, New York, Long Island, Staten Island Haerlem Heights, Fort Washington, Fort Lee, Brandy Wine, Germantown Monmouth South Carolina, Virginia, Canada! Where indeed did We not blunder? except Saratoga and York where our Tryumphs redeemed all former disgraces.[7]

Even the Revolution's most seemingly sacred moment was no exception to this rule. Asked whether everyone in the Second Continental Congress wholeheartedly signed on to the Declaration of Independence, Adams denied it:

> They who were then Members all Signed it, and as I could not See their hearts, it would be hard for me to Say that they did not approve it: but as far as I could penetrate, the intricate internal foldings of their Souls, I then believed, and have not Since altered my opinion, that there were

> Several who Signed with regret, and Several others with many doubts and much lukewarmness.[8]

Why was this important? Because Adams and his cohort knew that their awareness of the Revolution's extreme contingencies had carried them through many a crisis. Had they not grasped that key reality—that the Revolution could fall to ruin at any given moment—they would not have recognized or risen to the crises of their times. The same would hold true for future generations, they assumed. The fragile republic would topple and fall if Americans didn't own the simple fact of its contingency—that it might fail and fall.

Over the course of centuries, Americans have not only lost touch with that message, but they've come to believe its precise opposite. American exceptionalism preaches that the United States is better and truer to its ideals than the rest of the world. Our nation can't fail, it argues, an idea so powerful that it is part of America's national identity—at least, as understood by Americans. The right wing's ongoing assault on democracy has shaken that fundamental faith for many; it *can* happen here. Indeed, it's already happening. But even with the threat of authoritarianism looming large, for many Americans, exceptionalism lives on, with hazy American ideals at its core.

Those enduring revolutionary ideals have served the United States well over the centuries. They are a national mantra of sorts, a touchstone of national purpose, a shared set of goals, however contested or neglected they may be. They've been righteous vehicles of change, enabling marginalized peoples to claim their rights. In point and purpose, they define us—at least, in the American imaginary.

Thus the symbolic importance of celebrating July Fourth, the day that the Second Continental Congress adopted the Declaration of Independence and had it printed, rooting America's revolutionary ideals in a historical event and committing them to paper.[9] Thomas Jefferson said as much in 1826 in his last letter: "[F]or ourselves let the annual return of this day, for ever refresh our recollections of these rights and an undiminished devotion to them."[10] John Adams predicted the same for July 2, the day that Congress voted for independence:

> The Second Day of July 1776, will be the most memorable Epocha, in the History of America.—I am apt to believe that it will be celebrated,

> by succeeding Generations, as the great anniversary Festival. It ought to be commemorated, as the Day of Deliverance by solemn Acts of Devotion to God Almighty. It ought to be solemnized with Pomp and Parade, with Shews, Games, Sports, Guns, Bells, Bonfires and Illuminations from one End of this Continent to the other from this Time forward forever more.[11]

For these revolutionaries and forever after, July Fourth would be a "great anniversary" that reinforced the nation's founding principles.

That symbolic importance becomes all the more powerful during landmark anniversaries. Nationally sponsored checkpoints of patriotism, they drive home the power of America's ideals with extravagant displays of money, pomp, and circumstance that cast a spotlight on the nation's founding principles, and in so doing, invite people to question them. They are national reckoning times with work to do.[12]

Which brings us to the celebration of American independence in 2026, its semiquincentennial, a moment when there is a *lot* of reckoning to do. Fundamental ideals are at risk, constitutional structures are being eroded, our willingness as a people to join as a nation is being assailed. America's democratic spirit and structures are under attack. The crisis is real, the contingencies extreme. At this time of high stakes and hard choices, what we do matters.

On that count, the ethos of the American Revolution has much to say. A sincere belief in a flawed and all-too-human founding—a visceral grasp of the fact that our nation never has—and never will—go of itself is essential. The contingency-framed ethos of revolution teaches that lofty ideals alone are not enough. They need defending by clear-eyed people who see the crisis at hand. For this reason and more, our semiquincentennial must be more than "pomp and parade." It must convey the value and fragility of what we stand to lose.

Of course, there is no single Revolution frozen in time. Different peoples in different eras have celebrated it in different ways, revealing much about themselves in the process.[13] The centennial celebration in 1876, eleven years after the Civil War, focused on reconciliation with the hope that remembrance of the Revolution would remind Americans of their common ties. Almost unavoidably, this campaign for unity exposed the deep fissures at the heart of American nationhood, highlighting the demands and challenges raised by women, Black Americans, and immigrants arriving in unprecedented numbers.

The bicentennial celebration was no different. Given the shadow of the Cold War, the 1960s-induced clash between traditional values and social consciousness, and the national disillusionment of the Vietnam War, the bicentennial seemed like a golden opportunity to unite the nation with a glitzy blast of patriotism. Government agencies and large corporations took on the challenge, blanketing the country with red, white, and blue symbolism and display. The bicentennial had work to do.

I received that message loud and clear. Fourteen years old in 1976, I was the perfect age to own that message. Teenaged me wasn't primed to pick up subtleties. But the bicentennial wasn't about subtleties. It was a clarion call of patriotism intended to unite and inspire a nation at war with itself.

Throughout the bicentennial, that message was loud and clear. Democracy, liberty, freedom, and rights: These ideals were celebrated though not defined, a free-floating haze of American glories. That said, there *were* important interventions that themselves defined the times. The multiculturalism of a changing America had an impact. Marginalized groups wove their stories into America's founding narrative throughout the bicentennial, introducing many Americans to the complexities of inclusion and exclusion during the Revolution and beyond, offering a more mature understanding of the Revolution—and the nation—in the process.[14]

Also reflective of the times was the onslaught of bicentennial merchandising. The overflowing abundance of bicentennial "stuff" was a tribute of sorts to America's ever-grasping corporate powers that be. There were "Bicentennial Minutes" on CBS that aired nightly beginning in July 1974, which were just what they sound like: minute-long snippets about events and peoples two hundred years past, narrated by a celebrity and sponsored by a large corporation that advertised itself at their close. And the countless knickknacks of nationhood! Mini Liberty Bells! Fake quill pens! I had them all, and I wasn't alone. Buying them during the bicentennial seemed like an act of patriotism. Radical historian Jesse Lemisch and his students at SUNY/Buffalo commemorated the crass commercialization of the moment by amassing a collection of "Bicentennial Schlock," its contents ranging from plastic bags, sugar packets, cereal boxes, a pair of stuffed mice in bicentennial clothing, and "The All-American Novelty Condom." "A tribute to disposable patriotism," the *New York Times* quipped.[15]

The "Freedom Train" offered a more heroic message. A twenty-six-car train with twelve display cars that traveled around the nation between April 1975 and December 1976, it placed visitors on a conveyor belt that moved them past a string of historical objects and manuscripts behind glass, car after car, at an unshifting pace: George Washington's personal copy of the Constitution, Thomas Edison's first working light bulb, a lunar rover, John F. Kennedy's rocking chair, Hank Aaron's baseball bat, a dress worn by Judy Garland in *The Wizard of Oz.*[16] A flash of recognition, then you moved along. The Freedom Train offered a quick and breezy view of American history, studded by material proof of alleged greatness.

I probably saw the Freedom Train in Tarrytown, New York, in August 1976; it's the closest it came to Yorktown Heights, my home. Forty-four years later, I have vague memories of the semi-darkened train cars; I don't remember what I saw, but I remember my excitement at the chance to see it. According to a *New York Times* review, what I saw "fell somewhere in the middle-American terrain bounded by the Fourth of July, a county fair, a branch library in Dubuque and a technically sophisticated science and history exhibit."[17] Such was much of the bicentennial. And in some ways that was fitting. A hodgepodge of Americana, it gave the bicentennial's high-flying historical narrative some human roots, however glitzy.

The movie *1776* achieved something similar. A musical recounting of the creation of the Declaration of Independence released in 1972, it was based on a Tony Award–winning Broadway musical of the same name. Featuring an antiwar song and a musical attack on "cool conservative men," it had political resonance. There's a reason why President Richard Nixon allegedly demanded that the song "Cool, Cool Considerate Men" be cut from the film.[18]

But *1776* wasn't primarily political. Like *Hamilton,* it set founding-era history to music, humanizing, romanticizing, simplifying, and humorizing historical figures in the process. In a sense, it humanized patriotism. More than one early American historian in my cohort has privately told me that it stirred their interest in the period. For them, as for me, *1776* achieved the seemingly impossible. It made the Revolution human. For that reason, much like *Hamilton,* it gained and has retained a small but fervent fan base. If I poke fun at it, students protest.

Ironically, despite such excess, my most meaningful bicentennial moment was its most fleeting. On July 4, 1776, bells around the nation rang at 2:00 p.m. EST in tribute to the Second Continental Congress's adoption of the Declaration of Independence. According to the American Revolution Bicentennial Administration, the time marked "exactly 200 years from the precise moment that the Liberty Bell proclaimed the independence of the new nation"—a story invented by writer George Lippard in 1847.[19] It's somehow fitting that the alleged peak moment of the bicentennial's peak day was fictitious. But it was a good story, and I fell for it. People all over the United States were joining to celebrate their history as a nation at that precise moment. And just like that, "the nation" took on new meaning for me. I hadn't yet envisioned the United States in quite that way—as a huge geographic national whole. The bicentennial gave me a sense of a broad national something. It enabled me to envision a national "us."

Fifty years later, we're at a very different place, with little if any sense of a broad national "us." While all time is contingent—people live looking forward in time, not knowing what's to come—we are living in a state of extreme contingency. Democracy is imperiled, right here, right now. Can it survive ongoing attempts by the powers that be to undermine it? We don't know.

It has taken years for many Americans to grasp this ugly reality. Even now, with fundamental rights seemingly up for grabs, people deny it. The weighty constant of American exceptionalism has blinded people to the high-stake risks of our times. Yet big questions with sweeping implications loom. Do Americans share national ideals? Do they understand, know, or even value them? Some Americans, for example—on the left and right—naysay democracy in its entirety. In 2022, I tweeted out what seemed like a simple statement: "I think that a lot of people don't understand what it means to lose democracy." To my surprise, many people on the right said they were ready for something better, and many people on the left denied that we'd ever had democracy at all.[20] It's hardly surprising that this lapse in political ideals has made violence seem possible, even probable. You can see the spirit of our time in a recent burst of historical scholarship focused on the place of violence and bloodshed in our national origins.[21]

How should we reckon with the American Revolution during a national identity crisis? What kind of origins story should we—can we—tell? Pure celebration seems wrong; it takes success for granted, and we should not, *must* not. Some self-reflection is essential, but at a time when some deny the existence or even the desirability of democracy, that's hard to do.

The American Revolution holds partial answers. We are living at a time of extreme contingency when great change is possible, for better and worse. On this count, the American Revolution speaks loud and clear. There is no preordained outcome. We don't know how this struggle will end, and the outcome could be revolutionary in ways good or bad. The roiling instabilities of extreme contingency are the ethos of our time.

To move ahead—to embrace diversity and tolerance—to defend and better democracy—we must understand that. We must accept the high stakes at hand. As the revolutionaries themselves lived and knew, an awareness of extreme contingencies can be a trigger for action. We can't adapt to the crises at hand without grasping the contingencies of the here and now.

There's more than doom and gloom to this challenge. Contingencies offer a chance for positive change. The revolutionary generation knew this heart and soul. They believed that they were being given a chance to better their nation and their world. Of course, they failed that task in countless ways. But the chance for positive change stands before us. We can live up to our responsibilities as American citizens, and defend, bolster, and improve American democracy. Or we can turn a blind eye to the current moment and veer toward despotism. Such is the seemingly inconceivable truth of our time.

America at 250 is immersed in a battle over democracy with unknown outcomes. And true to the spirit of the Revolution, we will be missing the moment if we don't use this anniversary to truly reckon with who we are, what we've been, and where we're headed. As John Adams suggested, American citizens can make or break their nation. Only by owning the contingencies of the moment will we be able to rise to the demands of our times with our eyes open. Only then will the semiquincentennial be a time of informed patriotism—not blind idolatry but, rather, a time to take stock, acknowledge our failures as well as our successes, and go forward in wisdom and strength as a democratic nation.

Notes

1. John Demos argues that the word "revolution" took on a new meaning during the American Revolution, "which began in a spirit of restoration, or reengaging principles and structures supposedly forgotten (or abandoned, or subverted)"—the original cyclical concept of revolution—but "came to

embrace the novelty of what was happening" (Demos, *Circles and Lines: The Shape of Life in Early America* [Harvard University Press, 2004], 46–47).

2. See, for example, Kathleen DuVal, *Independence Lost: Lives on the Edge of the American Revolution* (Random House, 2015); Maya Jasanoff, *Liberty's Exiles: American Loyalists in the Revolutionary World* (Knopf, 2011); Serena Zabin, *The Boston Massacre: A Family History* (Mariner, 2020); and, on a broader level, Alan Taylor, *American Revolutions: A Continental History, 1750–1804* (Norton, 2016).
3. Holger Hoock, *Scars of Independence: America's Violent Birth* (Crown, 2017).
4. James Madison to James Madison Sr., July 5, 1789; George Washington to Catharine Sawbridge Macaulay Graham, January 9, 1790, both in Founders Online.
5. Adams to Josiah Quincy III, February 9, 1811, Founders Online.
6. Adams to Benjamin Rush, August 17, 1812, Founders Online.
7. Adams to Rush, February 23, 1813, Founders Online.
8. Adams to William Plumer, March 28, 1813, Founders Online.
9. See, for example, Len Travers, *Celebrating the Fourth: Independence Day and the Rites of Nationalism in the Early Republic* (University of Massachusetts Press, 1999).
10. Jefferson to Roger Chew Weightman, June 24, 1826, Founders Online.
11. John Adams to Abigail Adams, July 3, 1776, Founders Online.
12. On the near-spiritual importance of the Declaration of Independence in American memory, see Pauline Maier's *American Scripture: Making the Declaration of Independence* (Vintage, 1998).
13. Michael Hattem's *The Memory of '76* offers a wonderfully nuanced account of how the Revolution has been conceived over time, and its implications (Hattem, *The Memory of '76: The Revolution in American History* [Yale University Press, 2024]).
14. Hattem, *The Memory of '76*, 235–65.
15. "In Memoriam," *Perspectives on History*, December 3, 2018; "'Bicentennial Schlock' Spoofs Tradition," *New York Times*, October 11, 1976.
16. John Kelly, "In 1975 and '76, an Artifact-Filled Choo-Choo Chugged Around the U.S.," *Washington Post*, May 25, 2019.
17. Wayne King, "Freedom Train Starts on Bicentennial Tour of Nation," *New York Times*, April 2, 1975.
18. Ferdinand Lewis, "Heated Debate About 'Cool' Cut," *Los Angeles Times*, September 7, 2001. Nixon had demanded that the song be cut from the play when it was performed at the White House, though the cast held firm. The film's producer, Jack Warner, a friend and supporter of Nixon, cut the song from the film when it finished shooting and director Peter Hunt was

on his honeymoon and unaware. When the DVD and video versions of a new director's cut were released in 2002, the song was restored.

19. *Bicentennial Times* (American Revolution Bicentennial Administration), 3 (April 1976), 1, 3. The legend of the bell ringing on July 4, 1776, seems to have started with an 1847 newspaper story (John R. Vile, "George Lippard," The Liberty Bell and Its Legacy: An Encyclopedia of an American Icon in U.S. History and Culture [ABC-Clio, 2020], 141–44; Gary Nash, *The Liberty Bell* [Yale University Press, 2011]). For a reprinting of the original story as printed in the Philadelphia *Saturday Courier,* see "Fourth of July 1776!," *Wisconsin Argus* (Madison), July 20, 1847. The Bicentennial Administration's source for their 2:00 p.m. ring-time is unknown.
20. As of August 14, 2024, three million people have seen my tweet; thousands responded. https://x.com/jbf1755/status/1478007059790671877.
21. For example, recent years have seen the publication of Hoock, *Scars of Independence;* Rob Parkinson, *The Common Cause: Creating Race and Nation in the American Revolution* (Omohundro Institute of Early American History and the University of North Carolina Press, 2016); Patrick Griffin, Robert G. Ingram, Peter S. Onuf, and Brian Schoen, eds., *Between Sovereignty and Anarchy: The Politics of Violence in the American Revolutionary Era* (University of Virginia Press, 2015); and T. Cole Jones, *Captives of Liberty: Prisoners of War and the Politics of Vengeance in the American Revolution* (University of Pennsylvania Press, 2019).

The American Revolution in France
(1976–2026)

BERTRAND VAN RUYMBEKE

"TODAY, A majority of French people are so proud of their revolution that they forget there were illustrious previous revolutions before 1789. Either because they do not know of their existence or because they think revolutionary and Napoleonic expansion made them possible, as propagated by textbooks and the press, stamped with French-centered complacency apparently irradicable."[1] So did Annie Jourdan, an Amsterdam-based French historian, so well capture the overwhelming position the French Revolution has held in French schools, teachings, press, general knowledge, culture, and imagination. In France, the French Revolution is *the* benchmark to measure how revolutionary were all other revolutions worldwide and the quintessence and epicenter of eighteenth-century revolutions.

This being said, the American Revolution holds a special place in French collective memory, even if it is primarily due to France's direct military, diplomatic, and financial involvement in the Revolutionary War. As French maritime historian Olivier Chaline observed, Louis XVI's decision to assist the American patriots—still referred to in French as "insurgents"—and fight Great Britain on a global scale may have been ill-advised (as his minister of finances, Anne-Robert-Jacques Turgot, warned in April 1776) because it accelerated the monarchy's financial ruin and led, in part, to the French Revolution, but it was a positive decision for posterity, and of course, one might add, for the United States.[2] Thanks to Louis XVI and his chief diplomat, the Comte de Vergennes, the architect of the 1778 Franco-American alliance, France can proudly boast of having decisively helped the United States to achieve its independence. Contemporary French politicians comfortably and ceaselessly contend that France has been the United States' oldest ally and friend. In the mind of the French people and its leaders, France can therefore claim to enjoy a special relationship with the United States based on its decisive assistance when America needed a strong ally to fight for its independence.

Since the 1980s, D-Day anniversaries have always been a high point in the celebration of this Franco-American friendship, attended by the French and American presidents and other high-profile politicians and public servants. On June 6 particularly—but anytime, anywhere when applicable to international events, in fact—speeches uniformly emphasize this "oldest friendship" and "oldest alliance" sealed in wartime heroism and sacrifice. I happened to attend the fortieth anniversary of D-Day in 1984 as an undergraduate student in Anglo-American studies at the University of Caen, Normandy. I accompanied a veteran and his wife, both from South Carolina, to Omaha Beach and to the American military cemetery at Colleville-sur-Mer, near Bayeux. It was quite an experience for a student of United States history. I was moved by hearing personal anecdotes and seeing World War II veterans mourn the loss of their comrades—especially so since my own father had landed in Provence in August 1944 and fought for the liberation of Toulon, an action for which he won an American Silver Star. As I realized that day, France's relation to the United States was not only of personal interest to me but of national interest. And this interest is rooted in the American Revolution.

Lafayette and Franklin

Yet, what do French citizens actually know about the American Revolution 250 years later? More than ever, I would say, but still not much. Most French people know that there were thirteen colonies—but not the names of them all—which rebelled against Great Britain and that France helped them achieve their independence. The latter fact is the most important, of course. Two historical figures stand out in French memory and imagination when the American Revolution, or rather the birth of the United States, comes up in public remarks: the Marquis de Lafayette and Benjamin Franklin. Some members of the French public can also identify George Washington as a general, and perhaps also as the first US president, and Thomas Jefferson, because of his Francophilia and, to a lesser extent, the 1995 movie *Jefferson in Paris*. But few would know that he was the main author of the Declaration of Independence. Everyone knows, however, that the Fourth of July is known as Independence Day, in part because of Hollywood's influence in Europe. Other founders, such as John Adams, who, after all, also lived in Paris, remain totally unknown.

The images of Lafayette and Franklin are very different. Lafayette was the object of an episode of a very popular TV history show in France, *Secrets d'histoire* (History's secrets), which aired in 2012. This show usually depicts the eventful and sumptuous lives of French kings and queens in Versailles, so Lafayette as a subject was a noteworthy departure. He was also the subject of an award-winning biography written by a retired journalist from the French newspaper of record, *Le Monde*.[3] We love historical biographies as a nation, with some of them leading bestseller lists for weeks on end, so this 2019 book introduced Lafayette to even more people.

However, Lafayette has a checkered image in France, and, ironically, it is his popularity in the United States that intrigues French people. While he was the young, idealistic, and—most importantly—rich young man who left France to fight for American independence, he was also the general who turned his back on the French Revolution and joined ranks with the Austrians in 1792. This choice has kept him from having an important, and positive, place in French textbooks. Lafayette's image in France is therefore not at all comparable to the one he enjoys in the United States.

By the way, was there a France before 1789? One may wonder when considering that our flag, our anthem, our national motto, and many of our national symbols and references are rooted in the French Revolution. Even if we do love our chateaux and cathedrals, Lafayette was a nobleman, and we have a difficult relationship with nobility because of the Revolution and the related hated issue of privilege, aristocratic or not.

Franklin, however, can boast of a very positive—even if a bit fuzzy—image in France. He is most famous for having invented the lighting rod; in other words, people here know him more as a scientist than a diplomat. In 2006, on the occasion of the tercentenary of his birth, the Musée Carnavalet, a museum devoted to the history of Paris, staged a very successful exhibit titled *Benjamin Franklin: An American in Paris, 1776–1785*.[4] The title is standard, always used for Americans who have enjoyed living in Paris, from Franklin down to Ernest Hemingway. But the exhibit put Franklin on the map of French public consciousness, as it were. Just recently, in 2024, the Apple TV series *Franklin* elevated him even further. It received excellent reviews in the French press and was a tremendous success for a show airing on a paid channel. This series, a Franco-American coproduction, emphasized the Franco-American alliance of 1778 and the arduous and uncertain negotiations that led to it, bringing into public focus the birth of the special relationship between France and the United States.

The Influence of the Bicentennial

In 1955, historians Robert Palmer and Jacques Godechot read a joint paper in French titled "The Problem of Atlantic History in the 18th and 19th Centuries" at the annual International Congress of Historians in Rome. As Palmer reminisced thirty-five years later, their paper "met with what was to me a surprisingly cool reception." "We were accused, then and later, of being apologists for NATO and the newfangled idea of an Atlantic community," he explained. The reason was that "a certain French national self-image was offended. We were thought to downgrade the importance or uniqueness of the French Revolution by diluting it into a vague general international disturbance."[5] In 1950s, neither French historians nor the wider public were ready to compare the French Revolution to other eighteenth-century upheavals. Only the French, Russian, and Chinese counted as "true" revolutions. According to France's leading historian at that time, Albert Soboul, the American Revolution was "narrowly bourgeois and conservative."[6]

The American bicentennial in 1976, however, changed the historical field and led to the gradual emergence of generations of Americanists. It also suddenly brought the American Revolution to the attention of the French public. That year, historians André Kaspi and Élise Marienstras, who had, in a very unusual move for their time, devoted their careers solely to the study of American history, published two influential books on the American founding.[7] Kaspi is a famous French intellectual on American topics, who often appears on TV. His works are very much read by the public at large.

Aside from Kaspi's and Marienstras's landmark books, the bicentennial also prompted two history journals, *Annales de Bretagne et des pays de l'Ouest* and, most importantly, *Annales Historiques de la Révolution Française*, to publish issues entirely devoted to the American Revolution.[8] The American Revolution's grand entrance in the prestigious *Annales Historiques de la Révolution Française* in particular must have seemed to Godechot a triumph of sorts twenty-one years after his paper with Palmer failed to gain recognition in Rome. In the issue's introduction, he stated pointedly: "Do we need to insist on the numerous ties that united the American and French Revolutions? That the creation of the United States was to have a profound influence on the rest of America, on all of Europe, and in particular on France, was perceived at the very moment of its triumph."[9]

The 1976 bicentennial has had an even deeper impact on French historical scholarship and academia through the *agrégation*, the upper-level nationwide exam that every teacher and professor in secondary or higher education has to pass. In 1977, the topic in *civilisation*, a discipline within the Anglo-American studies track just created by ministerial thinkers and incorporated into the *agrégation* program, was "The American Revolution (1763–1789): Political, Social, and Economic Conflicts." It needs to be stressed that the selection of a question for the *agrégation* attracts nationwide attention among students, scholars, professors, and even publishers, as books and textbooks appear in great number to prepare budding instructors for this exam.[10] Any topic that becomes part of this exam will then also be taught at the secondary level. In other words, after the bicentennial, the American Revolution started to appear in French textbooks, alongside—albeit covered in far fewer pages—the French Revolution. At long last, after 1977, generations of French school pupils were finally taught some information about the American Revolution.

A New School of Americanists Emerges

In the wake of this momentous addition to the *agrégation* program, new professors specializing in American history, society, arts, culture, or politics emerged, who became quite a large community of Americanists. In fact, when I was an undergraduate at Caen in the early 1980s, my professor in American civilization, Jean-Pierre Fichou, had been instrumental in putting American studies on the map and inspired me to embark on my career.[11]

This new community of Americanists organized the Association Française des Études Américaines (AFEA) in 1976, the year of the bicentennial. It is now one of the largest societies of Americanists in Europe. Starting in the late 1980s, new generations of scholars, of which I am a part, specialized in the history and culture of the United States, and our numbers have increased decade after decade. Even if the majority of my colleagues work on the twentieth and twenty-first centuries, the number of books on the American Revolution has grown expansively. A recent survey based on the catalogue of the Bibliothèque Nationale shows that if one monograph was published on the topic in the 1950s and none in the 1960s, seven were in the 1970s, eleven in the 1980s, eighteen in the 1990s, and thirty-seven in the 2000s.[12] Among these, Bernard Cottret's 2004 widely successful trade book on the American Revolution cast as a "quest for happiness" familiarized a wide French readership with the details of the American founding. This book appeared at a crucial juncture, when tensions between France and the United States were at an all-time high due to the war in Iraq, which France ostensibly opposed.[13]

In addition, France's own bicentennial in 1989 gave a boost to publications on the American Revolution; the French public at that point became eager to know more about "the other revolution," creating a market opportunity for publishers, who could now draw on newly trained French academics specializing in American studies as authors. Training and public demand created a nice synergy that led to an unprecedented surge of publications on the American founding period.

The Twenty-First Century: The American Revolution as a Field

Since the 1990s, the American Revolution has become a field of its own in France. In 2004 the *agrégation*, this time in history, had a question on revolts and revolutions from 1773 to 1802 that included revolutions in the Americas. Whereas in 1977 the American Revolution as a topic was limited to the field of Anglo-American studies, twenty-seven years later it became a topic for historians, an important institutional and academic distinction in the French educational system. In fact, it was not the inclusion of the American Revolution that surprised anyone but the exclusion of the birth of the Haitian Republic.

Excluding the Haitian Revolution seemed to perpetuate the old-fashioned, narrow focus on the United States and western Europe as the essence of the revolutionary Atlantic. It did not take into account all the recent works that had already by then shown how intricate, complex, and influential the Haitian Revolution was. This omission also seemed astonishing in the context of the anniversary of the birth of the Haitian Republic (1804–2004). Finally, since this exam is meant to train future professors, what image of the field would it give them?

After 2004, the American Revolution became the subject of various comparative publications on revolutions, textbooks included. There followed a repetition of 1977, but even more prominently now, given the high status of history as a discipline in France. In addition, in 2004, the French state journal *La Documentation Française* also published an issue on the origins of American democracy, which explored events, documents, and issues such as the Revolutionary War, the Declaration of Independence, the federal Constitution of 1787, US territorial growth, slavery and its abolition, and the Civil War.[14] Considerations of the American Revolution had gone mainstream.

Since then, the number of French publications on the American Revolution and the birth of the United States has not abated and is still growing. In 2016, on the occasion of the 240th anniversary of 1776, the *Annales Historiques de la Révolution Française* published a special issue entitled "Independences in the Atlantic World ca. 1763–ca. 1829," featuring interviews with historians Jack Rakove, Manuel Covo, and Clément Thibaud, who discussed US, Haitian, and Latin American revolutions and independence movements in comparative contexts.[15] This publication established both the American Revolution and Atlantic history as fully recognized objects of studies in French academia. That same year I organized an interdisciplinary conference at my institution, Université Paris 8, on the American Revolution, which led to the publication of an edited volume and a special issue of the French history magazine *Historia*.[16] *Historia* is one of the top two most popular magazines in history, available in every bookstand in the streets, in airports, and in train stations in France.

An important sign that the American Revolution is a vibrant interdisciplinary field in France is the number of dissertations in history, civilization, political science, political philosophy, and law that have been defended since the early 2000s on its various aspects. No longer do these projects need to focus exclusively on its relation to France and to the French Revolution. I happened to have trained four doctoral students in that field since 2015 at University Paris 8, and I have currently five more working on the American Revolution and the early republic. Four other dissertations on the American Revolution have been defended at Aix-en-Provence, Besançon, and the Sorbonne since 2019. Finally, the *Revue Française d'Études Américaines*, the main journal for French Americanists, published a special issue in 2022 in English on the American Revolution and Europe, featuring articles by French, Italian, Dutch, and German historians and literary scholars.[17] Additionally, the American Revolution is again on the program of the *agrégation* for the 2026 session ("*La révolution américaine, 1763–1783*"). With 2026 on the horizon, the French academy has fully embraced the study of the American Revolution, and it is now our task to translate our knowledge to the wider French public.

America at 250 in France: New Perspectives

Now that the American Revolution has been solidly established as a research field, and given the thorough Americanization of French culture, politics, and way of life, the 250th anniversary of 1776 will undoubtedly lead to a—shall we say, well-deserved and long-overdue—flurry of academic conferences, television programs, exhibits, and publications. Founded in 2021, the French-led European consortium "AMERICA 2026" (America, Europe, Revolutions, Independence, and Commemorations in the Atlantic World) that I coordinate has organized an average of two topical conferences per year in France and in Europe for the past few years. Originally financed by a grant from the American Philosophical Society and now principally funded by the French state agency L'Agence Nationale de la Recherche (ANR), AMERICA 2026 features French and American, as well as British, Dutch, Irish, Italian, German, and Hungarian stakeholders.

We will hold a summer school for American and French college students in Strasbourg in June 2026 and an exhibit at the Musée du Nouveau Monde in La Rochelle in the summer of 2026, which will feature a series of public talks intended to spread our knowledge to the wider French citizenry. We are also building an unprecedented online corpus of European published sources on the American Revolution (EPSAR) from 1763 to 1800, have developed pedagogical programs for teachers to assist them in teaching the American Revolution in French high schools, and will hold a final international conference in Paris in the fall of 2026. Members of AMERICA 2026 have already and will continue to publish journal issues in French and in English as well as a first-ever companion to the American Revolution in French equally geared toward scholars and general readers, produce contributed volumes, and put together special issues of history magazines.

Born out of an intention to launch a conversation between European Americanists and American scholars of early and revolutionary America, this program also is intended to bring to public attention American trends in research designed to shine a light on the histories of women, Indigenous societies, and slavery. In addition, the *Annales Historiques de la Révolution Française*—the French landmark historical journal on revolutions to this day—will publish a new dossier on the American Revolution in 2026. I also know of several trade books on the American Revolution as well as biographies of Jefferson, Franklin, Beaumarchais, and Washington that are currently in preparation.

The upcoming publications by French historians and the activities of AMERICA 2026 will no doubt bring new international perspectives to what has become a vibrant field. Never before has the American Revolution been the object of so much attention from French academics, learned societies, publishers, and also French society at large. It is my hope that over the next few years, French citizens will come to appreciate the many factors that led to American independence and think about the American Revolution as more than simply an event that led to the ruin of the French state as a result of France's military intervention in a prelude to our Revolution. I also hope that all these conferences and publishing activities will mean that members of the French public will come to associate more historical phenomena and actors with the early United States, beyond Lafayette, the questionable aristocrat, and Franklin, the American inventor.

Notes

1. Annie Jourdan, *La Révolution, une exception française?*, new ed. (2004; Flammarion, 2006), 279.
2. Olivier Chaline, Philippe Bénichon and Charles-Philippe de Vergennes, eds., *La France et l'indépendance américaine* (Presses de l'Université Paris-Sorbonne, 2008), 20.
3. Laurent Zecchini, *Lafayette* (Fayard, 2019).
4. Miriam Simon, ed., *Benjamin Franklin, un Américain à Paris (1776–1785)* (Paris Musées, 2007).
5. Jacques Godechot and Robert Palmer, "Le problème de l'Atlantique du XVIIIe au XXe siècle," *Relazioni del X Congresso Internazionale di Scienze Storiche* (Rome, 1955), vol. 5, *Storia Contemporanea* (Sansoni, 1955), 175–239."American Historians Remember Jacques Godechot," *French Historical Studies* 16, no. 4 (1990): 883.
6. Albert Soboul, *La révolution française* (Éditions des Sciences Sociales, 1948, with multiple revised editions since), quoted in Ghislain Potriquet, "How the American Revolution Earned Its *Indépendance*," in *Remembering Early Modern Revolutions: England, North America, France and Haiti*, ed. Edward Vallance (Routledge, 2018), 99.

7. André Kaspi, *L'indépendance américaine, 1763–1789* (Gallimard, 1976); Élise Marienstras, *Les mythes fondateurs de la nation américaine* (Maspéro, 1976).
8. "De l'Armorique à l'Amérique de l'indépendance," special issue, *Annales de Bretagne et des pays de l'Ouest* 84, no. 3 (1977); Jean Meyer, "La Bretagne et la guerre d'Indépendance américaine," ibid., 183–202; Jean-Louis Debauve, "Un Américain en Bretagne: Séjours dans l'Ouest de John Paul Jones (1778–1780)," ibid., 203–21.
9. "Pour le Deuxième Centenaire de la Déclaration d'Indépendance des Etats-Unis (4 juillet 1776)," special issue, *Annales Historiques de la Révolution Française* 48, no. 226 (1976); Jacques Godechot, "Le Bicentenaire de la Révolution américaine," ibid., 481.
10. On the copy of Merrill Jensen, *The Articles of Confederation: An Interpretation of the Social-Constitutional History of the American Revolution, 1774–1781* (1970), held by the Sorbonne Library, is still written in pencil "Agrégation 1977." Students use the Sorbonne Library to prepare for the exam, and the library holds on-site all the books that they may need.
11. Jean-Pierre Fichou, *Enseigner la civilisation* (Presses Universitaires de France, 1979).
12. Ghislain Potriquet, "How the American Revolution Earned Its *Indépendance*," 96.
13. Bernard Cottret, *La Révolution américaine: La quête du bonheur, 1763–1787* (Perrin, 2004).
14. Marie-Jeanne Rossignol, Dany Bataille, and François Bonjour, eds., *La documentation photographique: Aux Origines de la démocratie américaine*, no .8038 (La Documentation Française, 2004).
15. Marc Belissa, Manuel Covo, Jack Rakove, Clément Thibaud, and Bertrand Van Ruymbeke, eds., "Les indépendances dans l'espace atlantique, v.1763–v.1829," special issue, *Annales Historiques de la Révolution Française* 384, no. 2 (2016): 167–98.
16. Bertrand Van Ruymbeke, Brigitte Félix, and Audrey Fogels, eds., *L'Indépendance des États-Unis: Héritage et interprétations. Arts, lettres, politique (1776–2016)* (Les Perséides, 2021); special issue, *Historia* (2021).
17. Carine Lounissi and Bertrand Van Ruymbeke, eds., "The American Revolution and Europe: New Transnational Perspectives," special issue, *Revue Française d'Études Américaines* 173 (December 2022).

Echoes of the Revolutionary Era

ANDREW M. DAVENPORT

In often inexplicable and entirely unpredictable ways, echoes of the Revolutionary Era continue to reverberate in the present. Over the years I've worked as a historian at the Thomas Jefferson Foundation, which owns and operates Monticello as a museum, I've received innumerable calls, emails, and letters from Americans all over the country who relate how US history has influenced their lives. Memorable communications include the person who professed to "channel Jefferson's spirit" or the woman who claimed that, "in one of my previous lives," she was Harriet Hemings, daughter of Jefferson and Sally Hemings. Some reverberations from the past ring truer than others, but an openness to listen is a crucial skill set for a historian, especially for me and my colleagues at Monticello's Getting Word African American Oral History Project. Since 1993, Getting Word—its name was inspired by how Black families "get word" to younger generations about their ancestral past—has researched Jefferson's enslaved families and collected oral histories with hundreds of their descendants.[1] Recently, no echo from the past has proven more significant to Getting Word than a March 2023 note sent to our website by a graduate student. Jennifer Williams wrote that she'd met James Clark, a then eighty-two-year-old US Army veteran and retired welder, who is a descendant of the Fossett family who were enslaved at Monticello.

> Hello, I'm a public history student at Northern Kentucky, working with Mr. James Clark, a man whom I believe to be descended from the Fossett family. He grew up in the Fossett home in Cincinnati and has family photos and other resources. We are interested in learning more

about the Fossetts' time at Monticello, and we may have important documents that might help flesh out their story.[2]

I wish I could say that I immediately saw Williams's message, but it languished in our spam folder for four months until an eagle-eyed colleague fished it out and alerted me.[3] Relieved that the note didn't come from Jefferson's ghost and excited that it was aligned with my research into Monticello's enslaved families, I asked Williams to call at her convenience. Still, I hoped she'd hurry. "Family photos" and "important documents" are essential ingredients in my blend of catnip.

The Fossett family of Monticello were revolutionary in every sense of the word. Joseph Fossett was born in Governor Jefferson's household in Richmond, Virginia, in November 1780, at a pivotal moment during the Revolutionary War.[4] Fossett's mother, Mary Hemings—the oldest sister of Sally Hemings—was an enslaved domestic; his father was likely William Fossett, a white craftsman at Monticello.[5] Fossett was barely two months old when the British invaded Richmond in January 1781. Isaac Granger, who was five years old at the time and, like Fossett, enslaved in the governor's household, dictated his memories of the raid to an interviewer in 1847. "When the British was expected," Granger said, "old master kept the spy-glass & git up by the sky-light window to the top of the palace looking towards Williamsburg."[6] From Jefferson's rooftop vantage it was impossible to tell if the distant soldiers were enemies, but "that moment they fired every body knew it was the British," Granger remembered, and "in ten minutes not a white man was to be seen in Richmond." There was "a monstrous hollering & screaming of women & children"; it "seemed like the day of judgment was come."

The principal author of the Declaration of Independence escaped judgment day, but several of his enslaved people, including the young Granger and Fossett, were captured and forced to Yorktown as prisoners of war.[7] Months passed before the Americans, allied with the French, defeated the British on the Virginia coast. "Old master was mightly pleased to see his people come back safe & sound," Granger reflected, "although 'all men by nature are free & equal.'" Granger's ironic reference to the natural rights rhetoric of the founding era is reflected in three other extant memoirs of men—including the 1898 recollection of Fossett's son Peter—who were born enslaved by Jefferson. Each recollection gestures to Jefferson as a lover of liberty and enslaver of men and hints that among the keenest interpreters of Jefferson's noblest ideals were the people he held as property.[8]

The Revolution initially brought about a shift in whites' views on slavery. Jefferson himself recognized this. "I think a change already perceptible, since the origin of the present revolution," he wrote in 1781.[9] "The spirit of the master is abating, that of the slave rising from the dust, his condition mollifying, the way I hope preparing, under the auspices of heaven, for a total emancipation, and that this is disposed, in the order of events, to be with the consent of the masters, rather than by their extirpation." After the Revolution, Jefferson informally freed Granger's father; he also legally freed two of Fossett's uncles and sold his mother, Mary Hemings, to Thomas Bell, the white father of two of her children, who permitted her to live like a free woman.[10] Granger and Fossett, each of whom learned metalwork in the nailery at Monticello and became talented blacksmiths, would have had some reason to believe that they, too, could one day be free.[11]

However, one of the terms of the Treaty of Paris to end the Revolution in 1783 proved ruinous for indebted Virginians like Jefferson. The fourth article of the treaty declared "that Creditors on either Side shall meet with no lawful Impediment to the Recovery of the full Value in Sterling Money of all bona fide Debts heretofore contracted."[12] That spelled disaster for Jefferson, who'd inherited substantial debts from his father-in-law and was never able to recover.[13] However, the calamity of Jefferson's debts was most brutally experienced by the families he enslaved. Between 1784 and 1794, he "alienated" 161 people by sale or gift.[14] In 1797, he gifted Granger as a wedding present to his daughter and her husband.[15] Few documents survive, but Granger returned to Albemarle County in another transaction before he was again forced away in the early 1820s, likely to Petersburg, Virginia, where he eventually lived.[16]

One example from Jefferson's presidency demonstrates how Black families feared separation. Joseph Fossett had recently married Edith Hern, who was sent to the President's House to serve as a cook. Fossett remained at Monticello, 120 miles distant from his wife. One day in the summer of 1806, Fossett learned something so startling that he departed from Monticello for Washington to see her immediately. Jefferson sent a slave catcher after him, writing to a white servant in Washington that, "We know [Joseph Fossett] has taken the road towards Washington, & probably will be there before the bearer. He may possibly trump up some story to be taken care of at the President's house till he can make up his mind which way to go; or perhaps he may make himself know [*sic*] to Edy only, as he was formerly connected with her."[17] But Annette Gordon-Reed notes that the Fossetts were only "formerly connected" insofar as Jefferson had disconnected them; they were very much still together.[18] Jefferson believed Fossett would flee to freedom and probably attempt to bring his wife with him. Fossett was captured while he calmly left the front door of the President's House, not exactly behavior associated with one intent on secrecy.[19] The precise issue has never been identified, but family separation was doubtless at the core of it all. Jefferson did not sell Fossett, though he did spend one night in jail as punishment. Many other enslaved people were not nearly as fortunate. From 1776 to 1865, more than one million African Americans were forced from the Upper South to the Deep South.[20]

The clearest example of how Jefferson's debts affected Black families is the auctions after his 1826 death on the fiftieth anniversary of the adoption of the Declaration of Independence.[21] The freedom Fossett longed for was granted to him and four other men by the terms of Jefferson's will, but approximately two hundred other enslaved people, including Fossett's wife and seven of their children, were sold to try to repay Jefferson's debts in January 1827.[22]

Williams, the graduate student from Northern Kentucky University, couldn't have known it when she reached out, but I'd spent years trying to piece together what happened to enslaved families, including the Fossetts, in the wake of the auctions from Jefferson's estate. I follow harrowing clues left in archives to learn what I can of how Black families were affected by Jefferson's debt, and how they tried to resist the worst effects. One buyer at the sale at Jefferson's Poplar Forest plantation retreat, near Lynchburg, Virginia, demanded a refund for a fourteen-year-old girl named Janetta, one of ten siblings auctioned. An overseer had burned her from her right shoulder to her foot, grievously so on her breasts. "The unhappy creature" could no longer use several fingers, her owner wrote to the executor of Jefferson's estate.[23] But Janetta declared she "would rather die than return" to the plantation, where she "would not find her mother, brothers, & sisters," who'd been sold as she had. Records of people who were sold as children, like Janetta and her siblings, or the youngest Fossetts, are the likeliest to be located for they may have lived until the 1870 Census, the first to list all Black Americans by name. But Janetta probably did not live until then. Her burns caused an infection on her breasts that likely led to an early death. For such devastating reasons, the auctions present stories of haunting absence and sudden glimpses of presence.

By the summer of 2023, I'd given up hope that Williams would call back. I cursed the algorithm that had sent her initial note to the spam folder. Then, in July, as I was leading a meeting with my Getting Word colleagues, Williams finally called. What Williams shared with me caused my eyes to go wide. My colleagues motioned to me to ensure that I was OK. I placed the call on speakerphone, and we listened in rapt attention as Williams described how she met Mr. Clark, as she referred to him, at a jazz club in Cincinnati. Williams had taken an evening off from studying to visit Caffé Vivace, in the Walnut Hills neighborhood. Unbeknownst to her, Mr. Clark was a regular—his photo hangs on one of the walls near pictures of Louis Armstrong, Duke Ellington, and Billie Holiday. He is locally famous for his incredible wealth of knowledge of jazz and had recently begun to bring into the bar historic papers he'd found in his attic.

By bringing documents into Caffé Vivace, Mr. Clark did not want to show off; he wanted someone to listen to his family's oral tradition of descent from Monticello. He was thrilled to learn Williams was an aspiring historian, and she was captivated by the documents, which included Fossett's son Peter's manumission papers from 1850 and an 1858 letter to Fossett from his daughter Martha. In the intervening months, Williams had pored over research to learn about the Fossett family. Based upon Williams's story, I understood that Mr. Clark stewarded the only privately owned manumission papers of someone born enslaved at Monticello and the only letter exchanged between Jefferson's former slaves. I immediately ran down the stairs and into a colleague's office to relate the news. "What are you still doing here?!" he exclaimed. My colleague implored me to brush up on my knowledge of jazz and book a flight to Cincinnati. Three weeks later, I met Williams, Mr. Clark, and two of his sons in Walnut Hills.

Mr. Clark announced his arrival by pulling his candy-apple-red Mercedes sedan into a handicapped spot outside the Walnut Hills library. I watched as he exited the car, one impossibly long, denimed leg at a time. He was tall, light-complected, and lean. "You the one from Monticello?" Mr. Clark asked me in his raspy southern Ohio drawl. "You must be legit!"[24] I'd seen photographs of some of his Fossett ancestors and searched his face for signs of them. It's a privilege to meet the descendants of the enslaved families I study, and time often feels like it collapses in on itself when we are in conversation. As I turned to meet one of Mr. Clark's sons, I was stunned to see his resemblance to Peter Fossett. Soon, I was holding the Clarks' ancestor's free papers, reading them in the library's private room Williams reserved for us. "Know all men by these presents," I read aloud,

> that I John Vowles of the County of Albemarle have emancipated and set free, & do by these presents emancipate & set free & discharge forever from all manner of servitude my negro man slave Peter, about thirty years of age The said Peter is a mulatto. In witness where of I do hereunto set my hand & seal this 25th day of January 1850.[25]

I imagined that Fossett kept the papers in his breast pocket and patted the record many times daily to ensure it was still there. Late in life, Fossett told a newspaper reporter that when he was enslaved, he'd "wanted to get free or die in the attempt."[26] How desperately he wished to be free! And here were the very papers that enabled Fossett to reunite with his parents—who'd purchased and freed several of their children and grandchildren in Charlottesville before moving to Cincinnati around 1840—in the city where I now sat transfixed in the presence of his descendants.[27]

Although the Fossett surname was not listed, it was clearly Peter's original manumission record. From prior research, I knew that Vowles, a white man, was an ally of the extended Fossett family; he'd witnessed the will of one of their relatives.[28] Vowles likely acted as a proxy for the Fossetts and purchased Peter with their savings. Fortunately, Vowles did; the notorious slave trader Silas Omohundro also signed Fossett's manumission record. Fossett may have been held in Omohundro's jail, at risk of being sold South, before being freed.

Then Williams took out the 1858 letter to Joseph Fossett from his daughter Martha.

"Is this *the* letter?" I asked.

"This is *the* letter," Williams responded.

Martha Fossett was sold from Monticello in 1827 and attempted to escape six months later, only to be recaptured and sold to New Orleans.[29] She was freed there, adopted the surname Jefferson, amassed a small fortune, and migrated to Gold Rush–era San Francisco.[30] In this letter, she observed that she'd recently given five hundred dollars—equivalent to about twenty thousand dollars in 2024—to the family.[31] "I am getting tired of being asked for money," she wrote to her father. Her candidness was extraordinary but recognizable for anyone who has supported relatives financially. It was not the first time she'd sent some of her savings from San Francisco to her relatives in Ohio.

"This is the only record that we know about—only thanks to you all," I said to Mr. Clark, his sons, and Williams, "of a letter between formerly enslaved people from Monticello. Letters between enslaved people are very rare. A letter between a daughter and a father, separated by 2,500 miles in 1858? Even rarer."

I shared with the group that I believed Martha Fossett Jefferson couldn't read or write. In all the legal documents I'd come across of her life, she always made her mark—an "X" in place of a signature. She likely dictated this letter to someone she trusted.

"That's funny," the retired welder Mr. Clark reflected. "I can't read or write, but put a blueprint in front of me—I can tell you in detail and build whatever you want built."

I read the letter aloud to the group. Mr. Clark's sons had never seen the letter before, let alone heard it read. They were gobsmacked. We half joked that Mr. Clark had better check his attic to see what other rare documents he had in there.

For the rest of the evening, at dinner at a barbecue joint or while listening to jazz at Caffé Vivace, Mr. Clark must have introduced me to a hundred people. "He's from Monticello," Mr. Clark said, nodding to me with evident pride. "Came to talk to me about my people, who were slaves there before coming to Cincinnati." I sensed that many of the people I met had heard Mr. Clark's story before but hadn't believed him. I made it a point to affirm Mr. Clark's history to the jazz heads I met.

Mr. Clark impressed me with his coolness, savviness, and humor; Williams impressed me with her authenticity, research skills, and attentiveness. Mr. Clark was right to trust her to reach out to Monticello in the first place. She knew he wanted his questions answered, and she could help. I treated Mr. Clark and Williams to drinks at the café as we took in the music. When the show ended, I prepared to take the bus back to my hotel, but Mr. Clark insisted on driving me. He wanted to show me some of the sights in his neighborhood. I relished the opportunity as I figured it'd be a long time before I could make a return visit. My wife was seven months pregnant, and I didn't foresee doing much traveling after the birth of our son.

I opened the passenger side door of Mr. Clark's Mercedes only to find a 24-ounce Miller Genuine Draft in a brown paper bag in the cupholder, an empty beer can in the footwell, and a golf club in the front seat. *Mr. Clark really is an eccentric,* I thought to myself. I asked if he did much golfing.

"Golf?" Mr. Clark laughed. "That club's there in case I gotta slap a motherfucker if they try to take my shit!" He put the key in the ignition, and jazz came over the speakers, nearly drowning out my laughter. Mr. Clark lit a cigarillo and drove us to nearby Eden Park.

"Before I went into the Army, me and my girl used to come down here at night. . . . The ducks like to splash around over here," Mr. Clark noted as we drove past a pond. "When I was coming up, whites was moving out of here. Now they're fighting to get back in. Getting ready to pull in right here, and we gonna get out for a minute so you can see."

We stood at the overlook, seemingly hundreds of feet above the city.

"And that's the mighty O-hi-o," Mr. Clark intoned. The moonlit river coursed below us.

"So narrow here," I said. "That's all that separated people from free state and slave state."

Mr. Clark's Fossett ancestors were Underground Railroad activists. I knew they'd helped escort enslaved people, perhaps some across the Ohio River, to freedom.

"And that water is deep, too. I used to fish over in there, and those sinkers would go forty or fifty feet deep. Yep. And that's Newport, Kentucky, just beyond. Liquor's cheaper in Kentucky," he winked.

Mr. Clark never missed the chance to slip in a joke. I laughed so hard during portions of our day together that the recordings are occasionally inaudible.

Before Mr. Clark dropped me off back at my hotel downtown, I begged him to look for more "old stuff" in his attic. He mentioned having some expensive dishware. I wondered if it belonged to the Fossetts, who were famous caterers in Cincinnati in the post–Civil War period, but I didn't have the time to examine them. I had to return home to Charlottesville.

Back at my office, I regaled my colleagues with stories of my adventure with Mr. Clark and Williams. I noted how Mr. Clark, although he could not read nor write, rightly held his sons in high esteem. "I'm proud of both of them. They got their education," Mr. Clark said. One son is a librarian; the other works in food service as their ancestors did. But the echoes of the past didn't stop there. Mr. Clark himself was a metalworker, just like Joseph and Peter Fossett. As they had fought for their and others' freedom during slavery, so did Mr. Clark, who served in the US Army in the mid-twentieth century. As I consider these striking coincidences, I remember what my late colleague Aurelia Crawford often said: "Monticello constantly reveals itself." Of course, every revelation also unveils new aspects of the national experience. Every American story makes this nation what it is. The 250th is a chance to consider how we build upon the foundations laid by those who came before us, including those like the Fossett family, whose experiences have only recently received historians' attention. Next time echoes of the Revolutionary Era reach me, I'll be prepared. I've already adjusted the setting on our website's spam folder.

Notes

I'd like to thank my colleague Brandon Dillard for his help with this essay.

1. To learn more about the Getting Word African American Oral History Project, visit gettingword.monticello.org. See also Andrew M. Davenport, "Putting Enslaved Families' Stories Back in the Monticello Narrative," SmithsonianMag.com, June 14, 2018; and Niya Bates, "'Monticello Is a Black Space': The Getting Word Project and the Future of African American History at Monticello," in *Segregation and Resistance in the Landscapes of the Americas*, ed. Eric Avila and Thaisa Way (Dumbarton Oaks, 2023), 347–73.
2. This note has been edited for clarity (author's personal files).
3. Thanks to Auriana Woods for locating Williams's note.
4. Monticello Enslaved Community Database, https://www.monticello.org/enslaveddb/.
5. Annette Gordon-Reed, *The Hemingses of Monticello: An American Family* (Norton, 2008), 126.
6. For a digitized transcript of the recollections of Granger (also known as Isaac Jefferson, or Isaac Granger Jefferson), see https://encyclopediavirginia.org/primary-documents/life-of-isaac-jefferson-of-petersburg-virginia-blacksmith-by-isaac-jefferson-1847/.
7. Gordon-Reed, *The Hemingses of Monticello*, 136–37.
8. Andrew M. Davenport, "Mourning at Monticello," in *Mourning the Presidents: Loss and Legacy in American Culture*, ed. Lindsay Chervinsky and Matthew Costello (University of Virginia Press, 2023), 42.
9. *Notes on the State of Virginia*, in Jefferson, *Writings*, ed. Peterson (Library of America, 1984) 289.
10. In his 1847 recollection, Granger said his father "got his freedom," but there is no extant record. For the manumission of Fossett's relatives, see Gordon-Reed, *The Hemingses of Monticello*, 115, 317.

11. Gordon-Reed, *The Hemingses of Monticello*, 510.
12. Treaty of Paris; 9/3/1783; Perfected Treaties, 1778–1945; General Records of the United States Government, Record Group 11; National Archives Building, Washington, DC. For a transcript, see https://www.archives.gov/milestone-documents/treaty-of-paris#:~:text=This%20treaty%2C%20signed%20on%20September,States%20as%20an%20independent%20nation.
13. For Jefferson and debt, see Herbert Sloan, *Principle and Interest: Thomas Jefferson and the Problem of Debt* (Oxford University Press, 1995).
14. Lucia Stanton, *"Those Who Labor for My Happiness": Slavery at Thomas Jefferson's Monticello* (University of Virginia Press, 2012), 4.
15. "Isaac Granger Jefferson," Thomas Jefferson Encyclopedia, https://www.monticello.org/research-education/thomas-jefferson-encyclopedia/isaac-granger-jefferson/.
16. "Isaac Granger Jefferson."
17. Thomas Jefferson to Joseph Dougherty, July 31, 1806, Founders Online.
18. Gordon-Reed, *The Hemingses of Monticello*, 573.
19. Joseph Dougherty to Thomas Jefferson, August 3, 1806, Founders Online.
20. Steven Deyle, *Carry Me Back: The Domestic Slave Trade in American Life* (Oxford University Press, 2006), 4.
21. Andrew M. Davenport, "'We Were Scattered': The African American Diaspora from Monticello, 1826–1900" (PhD diss., Georgetown University, 2024).
22. Davenport, "Mourning at Monticello," 33.
23. Peter Leuba to Thomas Jefferson Randolph, January 11, 1827, Randolph Family Papers, University of Virginia.
24. All quotes (some of which have been edited for clarity and brevity) from this trip to Cincinnati are from the author's personal files or James Clark Jr., oral history interview, August 21, 2023, Getting Word Project Archive.
25. [John] Vowles to Peter [Fossett], deed of emancipation, private collection.
26. *New York World*, January 30, 1898.
27. *Cincinnati Directory for 1843*, 393.
28. Critta Bowles, will, Albemarle County Will Book, 20:144
29. *Virginia Advocate*, August 25, 1827; William Boswell, vol. 15, Act 479, May 14, 1831, New Orleans Notarial Archives.
30. New Orleans (LA) Office of the Mayor, "Register of free colored persons entitled to remain in the state," 1840–64, 4 vols., vol. 1, "1840–1856," p. 42; *San Francisco Examiner*, August 14, 1896.
31. Martha (Fossett) Jefferson to Joseph Fossett, March 19, 1858, private collection.

Epilogue

A Case for Redemption

PATRICK GRIFFIN

I KNOW EXACTLY where I was fifty years ago. On July 4, 1976, I sat along the Jersey City side of the Hudson River to watch Operation Sail. I only learned recently that watching as well, at the exact spot I took in the spectacle, was someone else who has written an essay in this volume. Brendan McConville's father, an ironworker in Jersey City, told him this would be the ideal vantage point from which to see it all. My father worked as a machinist at the Colgate Palmolive plant, right where the bleachers were set up. An immigrant from Ireland and an operator, he had no problem scoring tickets. I remember the anticipation. We had been preparing for this day for a year at St. John's Grade School.

I had good reason to be excited. We, Jersey City's working class, felt, for once, that we belonged. We had a prime spot in what we knew to be a national celebration. And for the son of Irish immigrants, there was much to celebrate. My father loved this country. It gave him something an impoverished West Cork never could: dignity and the ability to support his family. He and my mother, also an immigrant, came over to large extended families that unabashedly considered themselves American. They fought in the nation's wars, they voted in its elections, they embraced its culture. All without tugging a forelock and without apology. They belonged. So, we were ready for the tall ships.

Ship after ship made its way into the harbor, under the Verrazzano, and up the Hudson. For a kid, unfortunately, the whole thing turned out to be a bit underwhelming. Soon, we were broiling in the sun. We couldn't wait for it to end. The tall ships, alas, had too much to live up to. To add to my malaise, I got soaked in a thunderstorm making my way home. But bored or not, wet or not, we had no doubt this moment was ours.

I appreciate now, though I did not then, the undercurrents of that momentous albeit anticlimactic event. My first real memories of politics involved the Vietnam War on the evening news, POWs coming home, rallies and protests, and tales of Watergate. The Cold War consensus had come undone, and the 1950s were gone for good. Cities had burned. African Americans had marched for their rights. Working-class whites, some from my neighborhood, contested what Blacks hoped to achieve. The New Deal seemed a thing of the distant past. The era of heavy industrialization had ended. Nineteen seventy-six was not so much a reckoning with these more fundamental issues as it was a hopeful attempt to revive a nation that had just taken a pounding. Nineteen seventy-six was America's true *Rocky* moment, and it's no mistake that that film came out that year. The question that hung over everyone's heads, the great unspoken issue, was how or if America could get off the mat after being knocked down.

No doubt, much of this sentiment is bound up in nostalgia. Surely 1976 was tied to the pain of perceived loss and a hope to return home—what the etymology of the word *nostalgia* suggests. Many wanted to revert to what they took to be a normal state of affairs, when men and women could make it on working-class jobs, when the United States strode as a colossus in the world after the Second World War, when everything seemed just a little more peaceful and orderly. No doubt, lots of people were hearkening back to a lost world, seen through rose-tinted glasses, that we know now to have been a postwar bubble. After the war, Americans had lived during an exceptional period of peace and prosperity, even if they did not appreciate it at the time. Then it all seemed to burst. Maybe we could reclaim an imagined past. Maybe we could go back to the way things had been, even if this was illusory and rooted in a mythic conception of what the nation was. Perhaps the nation could get off the canvas. For kids like me in Jersey City and more precisely their parents, 1976 meant all of this. All this being said, the tone for the country, in general, was one of celebration. A small chorus of voices contested this rosy interpretation, some even offering "alternative" bicentennials, and all was more complicated than a young boy could appreciate; but, even so, most of those contesting official interpretations argued that excluded groups should be incorporated into a national story most lauded.[1]

Scholars saw things a bit more critically. Americanists of all stripes still thought that the Revolution mattered, that it had to stand as the center of civic life, and for national aspiration, but that we as a society had not measured up. A few believed that we had fulfilled its promise, if only imperfectly. Others argued we had failed. For both, the principles of 1776 served as a measuring stick. Whatever the interpretation, they came to these conclusions after a generation or so of probing work on the Revolution when some had expanded the cast of characters beyond the founders. As a rule, historians embraced a set of tropes that spoke to the messiness, to the incomplete nature of the American experiment: hypocrisy; failure; ambivalence; contradiction; paradox. Edmund Morgan's testimony to the meaning of 1976, *American Slavery, American Freedom*, seemed to capture that zeitgeist of the scholarly mind perfectly.

Even if all assumed we still had to center discussion on the principles of 1776, most historians knew the foundational ideal was rooted in myth. But they had accepted that we as a people had to order and organize ourselves by something. All nations, of course, did and do so. These, as a rule, harken back to foundational moments. National-origin myths comprise part of the bargain for diverse people, with different hopes and dreams and worldviews, to live together in peace. In this vein, scholars and the public saw eye-to-eye, even if the latter wanted to celebrate while the former hoped to understand.

We have moved a long way from this vision as we commemorate—and certainly do not celebrate—the 250th anniversary of American independence. As a primary-source document that captures our moment, this collection makes clear that we now have what we could call the "disenchanted revolution." The national experiment has at best gone awry or at worst was ill-conceived to begin with. We are considering today what that Revolution meant and means in the wake of George Floyd and #Me-Too. We have limped through MAGA and Trump, Part 1. We have managed financial crashes and the retreat of American power abroad. We confronted searing debates about migration and about climate change. Not to mention COVID-19 and January 6. All seems dark. Some would even question whether 1776 has any utility or meaning at all. The nation can't be fixed. Perhaps it should not be.

This is quite a shift in our understanding of 1776. Since the early nineteenth century, Americans held to a very different idea of the American Revolution and what it implied for civic life. The founding had been understood throughout our sometimes patchy history as premised on the hope of redemption. Life, liberty, and the pursuit of happiness were not abstractions but represented principles that could and should organize national aspirations. Many, of course, were left out. In fact, the rights that the Declaration proffered were won for some at the expense of many. Today we know and acknowledge this to be the case. Nonetheless, those on the outside pushed to become incorporated into the story. Their perseverance in the face of hatred and injustice and their belief in progress, despite the vile attitudes of many, now inspire us. Their sacrifice has made them every bit as critical to the American story as the so-called founders. Perhaps even more so. Men and women fought and died for this simple but powerful narrative. All of these people deserve to be honored.[2]

Of course, all of this loss and sacrifice was based on pious myth. But does that make it any less meaningful? The myth animated the nation in the nineteenth and twentieth centuries. It inspired abolitionism, Seneca Falls, the sacrifices in the Civil War, the struggle of the working classes in the nineteenth century. It underscored what the children of immigrants in its cities subscribed to and what the champions of the civil rights movement gestured to as they demanded equality. No doubt, it served almost as a religious ideal that shaped American exceptionalism. But the myth has achieved so much more. It ennobled suffering. It made sacrifice meaningful. It gave struggle direction.

It was most fully articulated by Frederick Douglass, perhaps now our greatest founder. He appreciated that 1776 was premised on redemption, and that was the only thing that could save the nation. This was his creed.

The simple narrative most subscribed to, whether celebrating or offering alternative visions, has splintered and frayed. Some would abandon it altogether. No doubt, some of this has to do with the fact that ideas of redemption appear to come from another time. Maybe we need a new foundation, as what we have had for generations is now clearly fundamentally flawed and irredeemable. Perhaps we need a fresh start beyond the hypocrisy and repeated failures to live up to the mythic conception of who we are.

I would urge us to reconsider. Getting rid of foundational myths makes for sobering work. This sort of fundamental change, as we know from all the fine recent work on the American Revolution, does not come without violence, and fear, and uncertainty. Reckonings that remake society root and branch are awful to contemplate, as these essays collectively make clear. New foundational myths only come at a great cost.

Seventeen seventy-six may be a myth, and it may disappoint and even disquiet. Seventeen seventy-six, though, always assumes a more enlightened and just way. It suggests we can strive to be better. It's not a vision for puritans. That's easy. Just get rid of the offending ideas and all will be well. Alas, things never work out that way. Seventeen seventy-six offers hope. Hope is hard, but it compels us to resist nihilism. Redemption recognizes grim realities and painful exclusions; however, it offers a way to sustain a social order that can rectify wrongs. Of course, we can and never will fully realize what 1776 can ideally mean. The only way to do that would be to fix the human condition, and those sorts of experiments do not end well.

I doubt we will recapture the nostalgia of 1976 in 2026. Things don't appear so simple today. And that's all to the good. Nostalgia tries to recapture what never was so we can justify not addressing the problems that are. But redemption does not follow the 1976 model. Redemption offers something deeper that has a moral core. This myth offers both belonging and healing, just as it encourages us to see things as they are, to recognize shortcomings and failures. Redemption demands humility, at both the national and personal level. And it has taken this nation through some of its darkest moments and has been championed by some of our most courageous men and women. So many have laid down their lives for it. All in the hope that we as a people could be better. That, above all, makes it compelling. The 1776 ideal is not perfect. But that's the point.

Notes

1. Michael Hattem, *The Memory of '76: The Revolution in American History* (Yale University Press, 2024).
2. See Annette Gordon-Reed, "Kamala Harris Earned Her Place in History," *New York Times,* August 22, 2024.

ACKNOWLEDGMENTS

This volume originated in a conversation between myself, Patrick Griffin, and Nadine Zimmerli about what might be done to make a meaningful contribution to the discourse around the semiquincentennial of the American Declaration of Independence. We expected that there would be a lot of noise around the anniversary—though we did not anticipate the possibility of UFC bouts at the White House—and sought to create something that might shed some light on its significance. Patrick and Nadine are very much intellectual progenitors of this project, and I'm grateful to them, as well as Christa Dierksheide and Eliga Gould (who coedit the series in which it appears) for their support and friendship. Leslie Greene Bowman, president emerita of the Thomas Jefferson Foundation, saw the value of this project and offered the Foundation's support for the workshop during which we crafted this volume. Caitlin Lawrence did a wonderful job organizing that workshop. This volume differs from most contributed academic collections in style and substance. It was also produced under unique circumstances—a hard deadline. We wanted it be available in advance of the July 2026 anniversary, which meant that contributors as well as colleagues at the University of Virginia Press had to work at a pace unusual for a contributed volume. I'm grateful for the professionalism and good humor with which all involved responded to deadlines and my occasional chiding email messages. Although this volume was produced with an eye on the 2026 anniversary, I believe that its value will endure beyond that date. That is what Patrick, Nadine, and I envisioned when we first discussed it. We want this to be something that can read profitably after the fireworks (literal and metaphorical) are forgotten.

CONTRIBUTORS

Allison Bigelow is Associate Professor in the Department of Romance Languages and Literatures at the University of Notre Dame and the author of *Mining Language: Racial Thinking, Indigenous Knowledge, and Colonial Metallurgy in the Early Modern Iberian World.* She and Teresa Pollak cochaired the Presidential Committee on the George Rogers Clark Statue at the University of Virginia.

T. H. Breen is William Smith Mason Professor of American History Emeritus at Northwestern University. His most recent book is *The American Revolution on Trial: A New Nation Confronts the Burden of Independence.*

Katherine Carté is Professor of History at Southern Methodist University. Her latest book is *Religion and the American Revolution: An Imperial History.*

Lindsay M. Chervinsky is Executive Director of the George Washington Presidential Library at Mount Vernon. Most recently, she is the author of *Making the Presidency: John Adams and the Precedents That Forged the Republic.*

Francis D. Cogliano is Professor of American History at the University of Edinburgh. He is the author of *A Revolutionary Friendship: Washington, Jefferson, and the American Republic* and *Thomas Jefferson Survives* with Peter S. Onuf. He is the cohost of *The Whiskey Rebellion* podcast.

Marlene L. Daut is Professor of French, African American Studies, and History at Yale University. Her most recent book is *The First and Last King of Haiti: The Rise and Fall of Henry Christophe.*

Andrew M. Davenport is Vice President for Research and Saunders Director of the Robert H. Smith International Center for Jefferson Studies at Monticello.

Christa Dierksheide is the Brockman Foundation Jefferson Scholars Foundation Professor at the University of Virginia, where she directs the Center for the Study of the Age of Jefferson. Her most recent book, coauthored with Nicholas Guyatt, is *Jefferson's Wolf: The Struggle to End Slavery in the Founding Era.*

Lauren Duval is Assistant Professor of History at the University of Oklahoma. She is the author of *The Home Front: Revolutionary Households, Military Occupation, and the Making of American Independence.*

Joanne B. Freeman, Alan Boles Class of 1929 Professor of History and American Studies at Yale University, is the author of *Affairs of Honor: National Politics in the New Republic* and editor of *Alexander Hamilton: Writings* and *The Essential Hamilton.* Her most recent book is *The Field of Blood: Violence in Congress and the Road to Civil War.* She hosts the weekly webcast *History Matters.*

Annette Gordon-Reed is Carl M. Loeb University Professor at Harvard University and the author or editor of several books. She won the Pulitzer Prize in History for *The Hemingses of Monticello: An American Family.*

Eliga H. Gould is Professor of History at the University of New Hampshire. He is the author of *Among the Powers of the Earth: The American Revolution and the Making of a New World Empire* and is currently writing a book on the Anglo-American Treaty of Paris that ended the Revolutionary War.

Patrick Griffin is Madden-Hennebry Family Professor of History at the University of Notre Dame and a fellow of St Edmund's College, Cambridge. His latest book, *Prizefighter: Yankee Sullivan and the Hands That Built the Modern World,* is forthcoming.

Nicholas Guyatt is Professor of North American History at the University of Cambridge. He is most recently the author, with Christa Dierksheide, of *Jefferson's Wolf: The Struggle to End Slavery in the Founding Era.*

Ricardo A. Herrera is Professor of Military History, retired, at the US Army War College. He is the author of *Feeding Washington's Army: Surviving the Valley Forge Winter of 1778* and *For Liberty and the Republic: The American Citizen as Soldier, 1775–1861.*

Woody Holton is Professor of History at the University of South Carolina. His most recent book is *Liberty Is Sweet: The Hidden History of the American Revolution.*

Brendan McConville is Professor of History at Boston University and Head of the David Center for the American Revolution at the American Philosophical Society. His most recent book is *The Brethren: A Story of Faith and Conspiracy in Revolutionary America,* and he is cohost of the radio program *The Historians.*

Michael A. McDonnell is Professor of American History at the University of Sydney. He has published widely on the American Revolution and Native American history, and he is currently finishing a book on Revolutionary Era memoirs.

Peter S. Onuf is Thomas Jefferson Memorial Foundation Professor of History Emeritus at the University of Virginia. His most recent book is *Jefferson and the Virginians: Democracy, Constitutions, and Empire.*

Robert G. Parkinson is Professor of History at Binghamton University and the author of *Heart of American Darkness: Bewilderment and Horror on the Early Frontier.* His book on the grievances of the Declaration of Independence is forthcoming.

Teresa R. Pollak is an enrolled citizen of the Monacan Indian Nation. She sits on many committees as a Tribal representative and speaks to classes and the general public about the history of the Monacan Nation.

John A. Ragosta, former Interim Director of the International Center for Jefferson Studies at Monticello, has taught at the University of Virginia, George Washington University, Hamilton, Oberlin, and Randolph Colleges. His most recent book is *For the People, For the Country: Patrick Henry's Final Political Battle.*

Bertrand Van Ruymbeke is Professor of American History at Université Paris 8, France. He is an elected member of the American Philosophical Society and the principal investigator of the program AMERICA 2026 (www.america2026.eu). His most recent book is *1776, L'année américaine.*

Rosemarie Zagarri is Distinguished University Professor and Professor of History at George Mason University. Her most recent book is *Revolutionary Backlash: Women and Politics in the Early American Republic.*

INDEX

Aaron, Hank, 226
abolition. *See under* slavery
Adams, Abigail, 174
Adams, John: common cause and, 61, 163; creation of state governments and, 131; family of, 174; fears and apprehensions of, 125, 154, 222–23; and interpretation of law, 64; July Second and, 223–24; presidency of, 156; views on religion, 166–68; views on slavery, 67
African Americans. *See* Black Americans
Age of Revolutions, 68
Aitken, Robert Ingersoll, 94
Allston, Lynnette, 93
Almy, Mary Gould, 186–87
amendments, constitutional, 151, 155–58; Eleventh, 155; Fifteenth, 157–58; First, 144, 168; Fourteenth, 157–58; Nineteenth, 158; Second, 159, 183, 197; Thirteenth, 75, 157
AMERICA 2026, 238–39
American Civil War, 41, 75, 157–58, 216, 254
American exceptionalism, 109, 201, 216; ideals of, 223, 227, 254; Jefferson and, 31–32; and uniqueness of the revolution, 113, 119
American experience, 3, 6–7, 163, 249; of war, 184–87, 191
American experiment, 13–14, 16, 31, 130, 253
Americanists, 234–37, 253
American Philosophical Society, 238
"American Revolution (1763–1789), The," 235
American Revolution Bicentennial Administration, 227
"Americans Are Beautiful" (Ford), 47–48
American Slavery, American Freedom (Morgan), 253
Anglo-Americans, 102–6, 185–86
Anglo-American studies, 232, 235, 236
Annales de Bretagne et des pays de l'Ouest (journal), 234
Annales Historiques de la Révolution Française (journal), 234–35, 237, 238
anti-Catholicism, 146, 199
antisemitism, 73
Appalachian settlement, 50
Arnold, Benedict, 54
Articles of Confederation, 151–53; militia creation and, 196; religion and, 167–68; replacement of, 15; rights of enslavers and, 40; structure of, 39
Ashley, John, 36
Association Française des Études Américaines (AFEA), 235
authoritarianism, 153, 195, 223
authority of government: Congress, 128, 131–32, 152; Parliament, 123–24; provincial institutions and, 129; religion and, 143; resistance to imperial reform and, 102, 105–6; slave trade legislation and, 69; Stamp Act Congress, 127. *See also* sovereignty

Bacon's Rebellion, 49
Bailyn, Bernard, 112
Balfour, Lawrie, 77
Baltimore, 117
Bancker, Hannah, 189
Baptist religion, 140–41, 145, 167
Barnes, Christian, 186
Bastille, 29
Bates, Berke, 89

Battles: Bunker Hill, 65, 67, 119, 186, 222; Gettysburg, 157, 175; Great Bridge, 138; Lexington and Concord, 65, 117, 129, 163, 222; Saratoga, 141, 222
Bell, Thomas, 243
Bellah, Robert, 170
Benjamin Franklin: An American in Paris, 1776–1785 (exhibit), 233
Bernard, Francis, 126
Bibliothèque Nationale, 236
bicentennial (1976): celebration of, 1, 3, 47, 225, 251–52; impact on French scholarship, 234–35; messaging of, 3, 225, 227; nostalgia and, 255; partisanship and, 3–4, 225; President Ford's address, 47, 58
Bicentennial Minutes, 1, 8
Biden, Joe, 5, 122
Bigelow, Allison, 90
Bill of Rights, 155
Bishop's Controversy, 139
Black Americans: civil rights of, 75, 158, 252, 254; 1870 census, 244; family separation and, 243–44; identity and culture of, 48; immigration of, 48; loyalists, 38, 53; oral histories of, 241; rights of, 18, 34, 48, 87, 113; role in the Revolution, 69, 178; segregation and, 75, 87, 170; violence against, 140, 187; voting rights of, 37; women, 174. *See also* racism; slavery
Black Lives Matter, 183
Bland, Robert, 82
Boston: imperial occupation of, 17, 186; slave trade in, 39–40; tensions with Britain, 127–29
Boston Massacre, 127
Boston Tea Party, 117, 128
boycott, 65, 127–29
Brink, Brandon, 87–88
Britain. *See* British Empire
British East India Company, 124
British Empire, 25–26; defeat of, 242; England, 41, 62–63, 116; hostility toward, 40, 65–66, 127, 130; imperial policy of, 119; and inclusion of North America, 49, 104–5, 123–24; military of, 56, 127–29, 186–87; protest of, 51, 124, 150; Scotland, 41; separation from, 25–27, 52, 123, 232; slavery and, 63, 189–90; Stamp Act, 125–26, 213; tensions with, 101, 119, 130–31, 139. *See also* Parliament
British Labor Party, 18
Brown v. Board of Education, 149n34
Bryant, Zyahna, 74
Bunker Hill, Battle of, 65, 67, 119, 186, 222
Burr, Aaron, 156
Burrows, Edwin G., 175
Busby, Virginia, 89
Butler, Mary Middleton, 33–36, 38–39, 40–42
Butler, Pierce, 33, 38–41

Caffé Vivace, 245, 247
Calloway, Colin G., 198
Calvinism, 18
Campbell, William, 66
Canada, 129, 139, 179, 215, 222
capitalism, 3, 18, 86
Capitol police, 122
Caribbean, the, 49–52, 178
Carleton, Sir Guy, 33, 38, 69
Carrington, Edward, 154
Catholicism, 137, 139, 146, 164, 199
Cavalier Daily (newspaper), 77
centennial (1876), 224–25
Chaline, Olivier, 231
Chanlatte, Juste, 80
Charles, Ray, 209, 217–18
Charleston (Charlestown), 33, 39, 66, 176, 186–87
Charlottesville, 72–74, 86–87, 117, 246
Charter of 1691, 130
Chemerinsky, Erwin, 22n1
Cheroenhaka-Nottoway (tribe), 92
Cherokee (tribe), 92
Chesterfield, 140, 142
Chickahominy (tribe), 92
Chinese Revolution, 18, 234
Chisolm v. Georgia, 155

Christianity, 142–43, 145, 165, 168–70, 254
Christian nation, 142–43, 145
Chronicles of America, 94
Church of England, 138, 139, 140–42, 165, 167
church-state, 14–15
Cincinnati, 241, 245–48
Cincinnatus, Lucius Quinctius, 194, 199
citizenship: barriers to, 7; birthright, 157; legal definition of, 157–58; responsibilities of, 26, 194; restrictions and exclusions of, 52, 146, 156, 200; rights, 39, 52, 146, 156–58, 196
citizen-soldier, 194, 196, 198–201
City Beautiful movement, 87
civic life, 19, 253
civic militarism, 196, 201
civil rights, 75, 158, 252, 254
Civil Rights Act, 158
civil uprising, 211
Civil War, 41, 75, 157–58, 216, 254
Clark, George Rogers, 85–86, 88–90, 92, 94–95
Clark, James, 241, 245–48
Clark, William, 86
class, 6–7; privileges of, 191; solidarity, 109; tensions, 124; upper and middle, 187; working, 18, 252, 254
climate change, 34, 253
Clinton, Henry, 69
Coercive Acts, 126–28
Cold War: ideology, 159; lasting influence of, 3, 5, 6, 252; religious unity during, 170–71
Collett, John, 65
colonialism, 109; rights of colonists, 49–51, 101–2, 105, 124, 127; settler, 86, 92–93, 216; slave-based empire and, 35, 49–51, 56
committees of correspondence, 125, 127–29
common cause, 109, 114, 128, 141; dedication to, 105; fear and, 61; by persuasion and force, 220
Common Cause, The (Parkinson), 62
Common Sense (Paine), 13, 106–7, 117, 164
Comte de Vergennes, 231
Confederation Congress, 55
Congress: authority of, 131, 152; Confederation, 55; Declaration of Independence and, 67–68; duties of, 122, 156; equality and, 35; French alliance with, 214; House of Representatives, 40, 123, 153, 155–56; military service and, 196; religion and, 165–66; Senate, 153, 155; slavery and, 40–41. *See also* Continental Congress
Connecticut, 139, 165
Connecticut Journal, 41
conscription and recruitment of soldiers, 142, 176–80, 196–201, 214; enslaved and Native peoples, 65–66, 69, 177, 189, 214–15
Constitution: colonial, 102, 103; compromise and, 153–54; creation and framing of, 150–54, 216, 220–21; drawing inspiration from, 157; military and, 196–97, 216; modern interpretation of, 75–76, 145, 158–59; preamble to, 184; ratification of, 220–21; religion and, 145, 168, 172n10; slavery and, 41, 154, 157, 216; structure of government and, 106–7, 224; three-fifth clause, 39, 75; transition of power and, 123. *See also* amendments, constitutional; state constitutions
Constitutional Convention, 40, 150, 153–55, 216
Continental Army: actions of, 176, 186, 214; Black members of, 35, 196; command of, 123, 129; creation of, 65, 196; infectious disease and, 175–76
Continental Association, 65, 128
Continental Congress: authority of, 130–32, 188; First, 16, 65, 128; institution building and, 125; legality of, 128; loyalty to King George III, 101; and national day of fasting, 165; religion and, 167; Second, 129–32, 222–23, 226–27
Continental Line, 196

contract theory, 16
Cottret, Bernard, 236
Court of the King's Bench, 62
COVID-19, 85, 253
Covo, Manuel, 237
Crawford, Aurelia, 249
creole constitutionalism, 102
creole identity, 102, 103–4
Crisis, The (Paine), 210, 214
Crisis, The (publication), 112, 114–20
critical interpretation of the Revolution, 5, 13, 21, 253–55
Crouch, Charles, 118–19
Crown Point, 179–80
Cruise O'Brien, Conor, *The Long Affair,* 29
Crusard, John, 188
Cuffe, John, 37, 39
Cuffe, Paul, 37, 39
Cullen, Jay, 89
Culpeper, 138, 140, 143
Culpeper Minutemen, 138
culture wars, 4, 16
Cushing, Judge, 40
Customs House, 127

Dartmouth (Massachusetts), 37
Daughters of Liberty, 124
D-Day, 232
Deane, Silas, 167
debt and debtor laws, 19, 215
Declaration of Independence, 7; circularity of, 106; congressional consensus and, 222–23; as a declaration of war, 109; draft of, 52, 68–69; goals of, 35, 102, 108; groups excluded from, 254; Jefferson and, 25–26, 52, 67–69, 76–78, 109; passage by Congress, 132, 222–23, 226–27; principals of, 78, 80, 102, 109, 151–53; purpose of, 15, 151–52; slavery and, 41, 52, 67, 158; 250th anniversary of, 2–3
Declaration of Rights, 36
Defoe, Daniel, 195
Delaware (tribe), 88
democracy, 192, 225; attacks on, 123, 159, 224, 227, 228; defense of, 7, 228; origins of, 237; promises and principles of, 91, 123; representative, 199, 215–16
Democratic-Republicans, 123, 156
Denmark, 41
deportation, 56–57, 215
depression, economic, 213, 215
Dessalines, Jean-Jacques, 80
Dickinson, John, *Letters from a Farmer in Pennsylvania,* 63, 184
disenchanted revolution, 253
dissolution of government, 16–17, 130
diversity, 48, 164, 170, 228
Documentation Française, La, 237
Douglass, Frederick, 75, 158, 254; "What to the Slave Is the Fourth of July?," 75
draft. *See* conscription and recruitment of soldiers
Dred Scott v. Sanford, 63
Drinker, Elizabeth, 186
Drinker, Henry, 188
Dunmore, Lord, 65–66, 68, 126, 177–78.
Dunmore's Proclamation, 4, 52, 69, 130, 189; limitations of, 66
Dutty, Boukman, 79
dysentery, 174, 175, 178, 180–81n3

Eastern Chickahominy (tribe), 92
Edison, Thomas, 226
Educated in Tyranny (McInnis and Nelson), 74
education, 4–5, 13, 93–94; of enslaved children, 55; in France, 235–39; free, 78; school choice and, 149n34; study of the American Revolution, 237, 238
1870 census, 244
Electoral College, 40, 123, 154, 156
Eleventh Amendment, 155
Eliot, Andrew, Jr., 187
emancipation. *See under* enslaved persons
Embargo Act of 1807, 31
England, 41, 62–63, 116. *See also* British Empire
English civil wars, 16

English Country ideology, 18
Enlightenment, 24, 26, 143, 146, 147
enslaved persons: emancipation of, 36, 38, 53–57, 66, 243–46; military service and enlistment bounties of, 177, 181n10, 189–90, 214–15; narratives of, 158; revolts and pursuit of freedom of, 13, 15, 81, 130, 189; runaway, 65–66, 69, 81, 178, 246; vengeance of, 190
Essex Gazette, 118
Ethiopian Regiment, 177–78

Federal Convention, 40, 150, 153–55, 216
Federalists, 30, 123, 155, 156, 169
Fenn, Elizabeth, 179
Ferguson, Victoria, 93
Fichou, Jean-Pierre, 235
Fields, James Alex, 73
Fifteenth Amendment, 157–58
First Amendment, 144, 168
First Continental Congress, 16, 65, 128
First Great Awakening, 139
First Great Depression, 215
First World War, 2
Florida, 34, 66
Floyd, George, 4, 253
Ford, Gerald R., 47–48, 58; "Americans Are Beautiful," 47–48
Fort Johnston, 65
Fort Sackville, 86, 88
Fossett, Joseph, 242–44, 246, 248
Fossett, Peter, 242, 245–46, 248
Fossett, William, 242
Fossett family, 241–42, 245–46, 248
founders: and consensus building, 211, 220; and the Constitution, 170, 172n10; criticism of, 14, 112–13; Douglass, 254; interpretations of, 14, 209, 212, 216; spirit of improvisation and improvement, 150–51, 158–59; values and intentions of, 109, 139, 183–85, 221
Fourteenth Amendment, 157–58
Fourth of July, 158, 223–24, 226, 233
fragility, 168, 171, 190, 195, 221–24
framers. *See* founders
France: education in, 235; free-soil jurisdiction of, 41; Haitian independence from, 79–80; involvement in Revolutionary War, 129, 215, 231–33; knowledge of the American Revolution, 234, 237, 238–39; Seven Years' War, 26, 101; tensions between United States and, 236. *See also* French Revolution
Franco-American alliance, 139, 214–15, 231–32, 234, 242
Franklin (television series), 233–34
Franklin, Benjamin, 24, 217; common cause and, 61; image in France, 232–34, 239; *Observations Concerning the Increase of Mankind*, 49; political involvement of, 167; views on race, 51, 56
freedom: antislavery legislation and, 55; defense of, 69, 114, 157; Dunmore's Proclamation and, 4, 52, 177; enslaved people's attempts to gain, 13, 64, 214–15, 248; as a founding principle, 113, 158, 210, 221, 225; in Haiti, 80–81; property and, 191; Providence of, 38; restrictions on, 124; of speech, 169; utopic, 20. *See also* religious freedom
Freedom Train, 226
Freeman, Elizabeth (Mum Bett), 36
Freeman's Journal, 36
free speech, 73, 169
French and Indian War, 123–24, 195–96
French Revolution, 133, 231, 233–35, 237; Jefferson's response to, 29; and the perfect citizen, 18
Fries's Rebellion, 197
Fristoe, William, 139–40

Garland, Judy, 226
gender, 7, 185, 191
General Assessment, 143–45
Gentleman's Magazine, 116
geographic scope, 6
George III, 53; criticism of, 114–15; loyalty to, 101; and tensions with colonies, 51, 55, 68, 103
Georgia, 15, 37–38, 51, 176–77

Getting Word African American Oral History Project, 241, 245
Gettysburg, Battle of, 157, 175
global dominance, 13
Global War on Terrorism, 3, 7, 61, 236
Glorious Revolution of 1688–89, 16, 103–4, 124, 195
Godechot, Jacques, 234–35; "The Problems of Atlantic History in the 18th and 19th Centuries," 234
Gordon, Bethany, 87
Gordon-Reed, Annette, 243–44
Granger, Isaac, 242–43, 249n10
Gray, Robert, 188
Great Bridge, Battle of, 138
Great Britain. *See* British Empire
Great Negro Cause, 62
Green, Thomas, 117
Greene, Jack P., 112
Greene, Nathanael, 178
Grégoire, Henri, 56
Guerard, Benjamin, 40
Guerard, Mary Lucia Bull, 187

Haiti, 41, 51, 79–81, 236
Haitian Revolution, 51, 79–81, 133, 236–37
Hale, Grace, 87
Hall, Samuel, 118
Hamilton (musical), 226
Hamilton, Alexander, 34, 51
Hamond, Andrew Snape, 178
Hancock, John, 40, 178
Hannah-Jones, Nikole, 4, 8n7
Hanover Presbytery, 141, 143
Harmar, Josiah, 197
Harris, Joseph, 66
Harrop, Scott, 78
Hartford, 116
Harvie, John, 23
Hasford, Samuel, 40
Hattem, Michael, 3
Hawley, Joseph, 129
Haynes, Lemuel, "Liberty Further Extended," 35
Heinecke, Walt, 90
Hemings, Harriet, 241
Hemings, Mary, 242–43
Hemings, Sally, 79, 81, 241–42
Henderson, Archibald, 86
Henry, Patrick, 16–17, 52–53, 142, 179
Hern, Edith, 243–44
Heyer, Heather, 73, 89
Historia (magazine), 237
hope: for the future, 210, 217–18; for improvement, 20–21, 150, 255; of redemption, 254–55; for unity, 224; utopic, 19
House of Burgesses, 25, 64, 125–26
House of Commons, 115, 124, 126, 128
House of Lords, 115, 118, 124, 126, 128
House of Representatives, 40, 123, 153, 155–56
Hughes, Mary, 90
human nature, 15, 17–20, 52, 153
Hutchinson, Thomas, 64, 126, 130
hypocrisy: of the American experiment, 253; religious, 35; of revolutionary leaders, 14; rhetoric of, 39; of slavery, 28, 35, 37–42, 51–53

ideals and principles: of equality, 212, 216–17, 254; founding, 35, 216, 253, 255; fundamental, 113, 123, 223–24; national, 211–12, 221, 223–25, 227; of the Revolution, 6, 19–20, 220–21, 223
identity politics, 14, 18
Illinois, 94
immigration and immigrants, 254; criticism of, 57–58, 61; European settlement, 49–50, 54, 57; hostility toward, 58, 169–70, 253; praise of, 47–48; racism toward, 56, 58; and replacement of Black people, 48–49, 56–57; rights of, 49, 54, 58
Imperial Constitution of Haiti, 80
imperial crisis, 49–50, 101, 105–6, 108–9, 129
imperialism, 124, 216
Independence Day, 158, 223–24, 226, 233
Independence Hall, 152

"Independences in the Atlantic World ca. 1763–ca. 1829," 237
India, 124
Indiana, 86, 94
Indigenous peoples. *See* Native Americans
inequality, 3, 53, 185, 210, 216
infectious disease, 180, 215; in British prisons, 175; climate and, 177; dysentery, 174, 175, 178, 180–81n3; inoculation and, 24, 179; malaria, 175–76, 178–79; respiratory illness, 180n3; smallpox, 24, 174–75, 177–79; soldiers and, 175–76, 189, 215; Tidewater fevers, 177; typhoid fever, 175; typhus, 178; yellow fever, 175–76
injustices, 220–21, 254; contemporary, 3, 183; of government overreach, 124, 210; of slavery, 28, 158
institution building, 123, 125, 129, 150–51
insurrection of January 6, 2021, 122–23, 133, 253
International Congress of Historians, 234
international tension, 2, 213–14
Iraq War, 3, 7, 61, 236
Islam, 164

Jackson, Thomas "Stonewall," 85
James II, 195
Jay, John, 17
Jefferson, Lucy Elizabeth, 54
Jefferson, Martha, 54
Jefferson, Martha (Fossett), 245–46
Jefferson, Peter, 23
Jefferson, Thomas: American exceptionalism and, 31–32; aspirations of, 48; common cause and, 61; debt of, 243–44; Declaration of Independence and, 25–26, 52, 67–69, 76–78, 109; democratic constitutionalism and, 108; early life and education of, 23–25; Francophilia of, 232–33; July Fourth and, 223; modern opinion of, 5, 14, 216; *Notes on the State of Virginia*, 28, 55–56, 57, 81; philosophies of, 23–25, 28–32, 51–52, 107, 130; political involvement of, 26–27, 54–55, 156; Poplar Forest, 244; presidency of, 30, 76, 156, 243–44; and slave ownership, 24–25, 56, 76–77, 79, 241–44; *A Summary View of the Rights of British America*, 25, 51–52, 64; views on immigration and race, 49, 56–58; views on religion, 27, 31, 142–43, 144, 147; views on slavery, 28, 35, 54–58, 64, 80–81. *See also* Monticello
Jefferson Council, 74, 77
Jefferson in Paris, 232
Jeremiah, Thomas, 66
Jernigan, Kasey, 94
Jersey City, 251–52
Jim Crow era, 86–87
Johnston, Elizabeth, 186
Jourdan, Annie, 231
Judaism, 164
July Fourth, 158, 223–24, 226, 233

Kaspi, André, 234–35
Kennedy, John F., 226
Kentish Gazette, 116
Kenton, Simon, 94
Kentucky, 94
Kercheval, Samuel, 107
King George III. *See* George III
King Philip's War, 88
Knott, Katherine, 85
Knox, Henry, 198
Kohn, Richard, 197
Kristol, Irving, 47–48
Ku Klux Klan (KKK), 72–73

Lafayette, Marquis de, 55, 232–33, 239
L'Agence Nationale de la Recherche (ANR), 238
land control and ownership, 19, 31, 49–50, 184–85, 190–92; speculation, 50, 213, 215; theft, 74, 86, 88, 96, 216–17. *See also* property
"Last Dying Speech of the Crisis, The," 116
Laurens, Henry, 34–35, 41–42; *South Carolina Protest Against Slavery, A*, 41

Laurens, John, 34, 41, 177
law of coverture, 33
Lee, Arthur, 50
Lee, Richard Henry, 142
Lee, Robert E., 73–74, 85
left, the (liberals), 18, 183, 212, 227; interpretation of the Revolution, 3–7, 14, 216
legacy of the Revolution, 158, 185; diversity, 48; improvement, 150–51, 157, 159; rejection of, 4, 14; suspicion of power, 17; unity and common identity, 3, 7; utopianism, 15
legislatures, colonial, 124–25, 129
Leland, John, 143–44
Lemisch, Jesse, 1, 225
Lenape (tribe), 86, 88, 92
Leslie, Alexander, 39
Letters from a Farmer in Pennsylvania (Dickinson), 63, 184
Lewis and Clark expedition, 85
Lexington and Concord, Battles of, 65, 117, 129, 163, 195
Lexington Green, 195
liberty, 35, 61, 104, 119, 225; defense of, 7, 195; empire of, 108; founding principle of, 113, 188, 212, 216, 254; paradox of, 74–75; religious, 141–42, 167; right to, 36; slavery and, 64–65, 69, 79–80, 215
"Liberty and Peace" (Wheatley), 35
Liberty Bell, 227
"Liberty Further Extended" (Haynes), 35
"Liberty Poles," 126
"Liberty Trees," 126
Lincoln, Abraham, 157, 164
Lippard, George, 227
Lloyd, Rachel, 90
Locke, John, 16
London, 51, 52, 62, 114
Long Affair, The (O'Brien), 29
Lopez, Anthony Guy, 90
Lost Cause, 86, 169–70
Louisiana purchase, 31
Louis XVI, 231–32
Lunsford, Lewis, 145
Madison, James, 31, 140, 216, 221; Constitution and, 39, 155; religious freedom and, 139, 143–44, 146
MAGA, 253
malaria, 175–76, 178–79
Manhattan. *See* New York City
Mansfield, Lord, 41, 62–63
manumission law, 54, 56–57
manumission papers, 245–46
Marbois, François, 55
marginalized groups: contributions to the Revolution, 3, 6, 225; exclusion of, 7, 18, 20
Marienstras, Élise, 234
Martin, Josiah, 65
Marxism, 3, 14
Maryland, 37, 177
Maryland Gazette and Baltimore Advertiser, 117
Mason, George, 50, 191
Massachusetts, 15, 36–37, 126–28, 165, 197–98; Assembly, 126; dysentery epidemic in, 174–75; General Court, 64, 198; slavery and, 36, 39–41, 64
Mattaponi (tribe), 92
Matthews, William, 190
McBride, Spencer, 165
McClanahan, William, 138
McCloskey, Mark, 183
McCloskey, Patricia, 183
McDonald, Kevin, 89
McInnis, Maurie D., *Educated in Tyranny*, 74, 76, 81
McIntire, Paul Goodloe, 86
McIntosh, Lachlan, 176–77
Memorial and Remonstrance Against Religious Assessments, 144
Memorial to Enslaved Laborers, 76–78
#Me-Too, 253
Miami (tribe), 88
Middle Passage, 57
Middleton, Thomas, 34
migration. *See* immigration and immigrants
militia, colonial, 65, 129, 141, 163, 194–98

militia acts of 1792, 198
Mingo (tribe), 88
Mink, Alexander, 88
Miranda, Lin-Manuel, 34
Monacan (tribe), 74, 92, 95–96
Moncrief, James, 33–34
Monde, Le, 233
Monroe, James, 31
Monticello, 31, 54, 56; construction of, 27–28; as a museum, 47–48, 185, 241; slavery and, 79, 241–43, 245–47; Thomas Jefferson Foundation, 241
Monument Lab (Mellon Foundation), 91
monuments: to enslaved laborers, 76–78; messaging of, 87, 90–91; removal of, 74, 85–86, 89, 95
more perfect union, 105, 150–53, 157, 159
Morgan, Daniel, 141
Morgan, Edmund, *American Slavery, American Freedom*, 253
Mormonism, 144
Morris, Gouverneur, 154
Morristown, 175
Mother Emmanuel Church, 87
motivations, founding, 6, 209; creation of a new nation, 48; fear, 67, 185; liberty, rights, and justice, 61, 63, 113–14, 212; progress, 24–25, 26, 28–29, 31–32, 254; property, 185; representation, 125
Mount Rushmore, 5
Mount Vernon, 53, 56, 123, 185
Musée Carnavalet, 233
Musée du Nouveau Monde, 238
Museum of the American Revolution, 210, 214, 217
myths, foundational, 4, 194, 217, 253–55

Nansemond (tribe), 92
national day of fasting, 165
National Guard, 199–200
national identity, 102, 107, 109, 223, 249; and excluded groups, 53, 252, 254; and legacy of the Revolution, 7
nationalism, 16, 215–16
National Rifle Association's Institute for Legislative Action, 197
nation building, 104, 191–92, 211, 213, 216
nationhood and national origins, 105, 107
Native Americans: citizenship and sovereignty, 96, 213; defense and theft of own land, 19–20, 74, 176, 198, 215–16; depictions on monuments, 85–86; exclusion of, 113, 211; Proclamation Line and, 50; and relationship with the British Empire, 69, 86, 88; rights of, 39, 87, 113, 156; as a threat to independence, 53, 61, 69, 124–25, 133n7; violence toward, 88, 198; women, 174. *See also* tribes, Native American
Native American Student Union, 89–90
Native Nations, 86–88, 96, 186
nativism, 199
NATO, 234
natural law, 16
natural rights: independence and, 16, 109; limit of, 196; race and, 37, 74–75, 242
Negro Seamen's Acts, 54
Nelson, Lewis, 89
Newbern, 65, 116
New England, 40, 65, 128, 138–39, 169
New England Historic Genealogical Society (NEHGS), 175
New Hampshire, 117, 119, 139
New-Hampshire Gazette, 119
New Jersey, 64, 125, 175, 214
New Jim Crow, 75
New London, 116
New-London Gazette, 117–18
New Palace Yard, 112, 115
Newport, 116, 186
New World Order, 221
New York City, 69, 116–17, 186
New York State, 38, 41, 155, 214, 222; Provincial Congress, 194
New York State Rifle & Pistol Association, Inc. v. Bruen, 159
New York Times, 225, 226
New York Times Magazine, 4, 8n7
9/11 attacks, 7, 61, 163–64

Nineteenth Amendment, 158
Nixon, Richard, 3, 226
Norfolk, 66, 138
North Carolina, 37, 176–77
Norwich, 116
Notes on the State of Virginia (Jefferson), 28, 55–56, 57, 81
Nottoway (tribe), 92
Nova Scotia, 38

Obama, Barack, 61, 210, 214, 217
"Observations Concerning the Increase of Mankind" (Franklin), 49
Occaneechi-Saponi (tribe), 92
O'Connor, Sandra Day, 146
Ohio, 50, 94, 198, 245–46
Ojibwe (tribe), 88
Omohundro, Silas, 246
Operation Sail, 1, 251
optimism, 19, 24–25, 26
oral histories, 241, 245
Oregon, 200
originalism, 159
Otis, James, 50, 51, 64
Ottawa (tribe), 86, 88
outrage, 51, 67, 69, 124–25, 127
Owen, Kenneth, 125

Paine, Thomas, 51, 164, 210–11, 214; *Common Sense*, 13, 106–7, 117, 164; *The Crisis*, 210, 214
Palmer, Robert, 234–35; "The Problems of Atlantic History in the 18th and 19th Centuries," 234
Pamunkey (tribe), 92
Paris, 27, 29, 55, 233, 238
Parkinson, Robert, 53; *The Common Cause*, 62
Parliament, 103–5, 116, 123–25, 127–28, 195
partisanship, 2–5, 123, 163, 167, 213
patriarchal society, 184, 188, 191–92
Patriot Act, 61
patriotism, 142, 200, 224, 225–26, 228; in education, 5; and interpretation of the Revolution, 3, 113, 225
Pauley, George, 40
Pauley, Jack, 40
Pawley, Anthony, 39–40
Pawley, Percival, 39–40
Peckham, Howard H., 175
Pendleton, Edmund, 54
Pennsylvania, 36, 41, 50, 55, 169
Pennsylvania Evening Post, 118
Pew Research Center, 164
Philadelphia, 36, 116–17, 128–29, 152, 186
Philipsburg Proclamation, 189
Phillips, Jack, 40
Pinckney, Thomas, 156
Pleasants, Robert, 52–53
Plumer, William Swan, 145
Pocock, J. G. A., 112
polarization, 163–64, 171
political opinion and philosophy, 15–16, 117, 165, 237
Pollak, Teresa, 90, 93
Pontiac's War, 213
Poplar Forest, 244
population transfer and removal, 49, 55–56, 57–58
Portsmouth, 117, 119
postliberal, 14
Powell, Lewis, 47
Presbyterianism, 140–41, 143, 165
presentism, 21, 254
presidency, 122–23, 153, 156–57; Adams, 156; Jefferson, 30, 76, 156, 243–44; Washington, 197
Priestly, Joseph, 30
principles. *See* ideals and principles
"Problem of Atlantic History in the 18th and 19th Centuries, The" (Palmer, Godechot), 234
Proclamation Line, 50
progress, 113, 254; American exceptionalism and, 31–32; Enlightenment and, 26; inevitable, 24–25; of political and military mobilization, 108; skepticism of, 28–29
propaganda, 53, 66; political, 67, 116, 124; social and economic grievances and,

214; use of race and fear, 61, 67, 69, 70, 213
property: acquisition of, 20; castle doctrine and, 183–84; as central to the Revolution, 185–86, 188, 190–91; rights, 33, 183–84, 188, 191–92; sense of security and, 187; slavery and, 34, 40, 53; of women, 33. *See also* land control and ownership
protest: against British repression, 51, 117, 124, 126–28, 150; racial justice, 4, 89, 183; religious, 144, 169; against white supremacy, 72–73
Protestantism, 139, 164, 166, 169–70
Province of Freedom, 38
provincial assemblies, 103, 125, 129
provincial congresses, 103, 125, 129
provincial conventions, 103, 125, 129
Provision for the Protection of the Frontiers of the United States, 198
Punch (magazine), 2
Puritanism, 40, 138
Putnam, G. P., 41–42

Quakerism, 64, 138, 167, 188
Quebec, 179
Quebec Act, 139

race and identity, 6–7, 20, 48, 124
Racial Integrity Act, 87
racism: carceral system and, 75; immigration and, 56, 58; Jefferson and, 56, 76; in militias, 199; for political goals, 61–62; population transfer and, 49, 56, 57; segregation and, 75, 87, 170; slavery and, 34, 41, 75; symbols of, 73, 86; white nationalists and, 73. *See also* white supremacy
Ragsdale, Bruce, 50
Raimond, Julien, 80
Rakove, Jack, 237
Ramsay, David, 53, 56
Randolph, Edmund, 139, 142
Rappahannock (tribe), 92
Raucher, Alice, 89
regicide, 115
Rehnquist, William, 145
rejection of heritage, 4–5, 13–14, 22n1
relevance of the Revolution, 3, 6, 13, 15–16, 217
religion: Baptist, 140–41, 145, 167; Catholic, 137, 139, 146, 164, 199; Christian, 142–43, 145, 165, 168–70, 254; Church of England, 138, 139, 140–42, 165, 167; church-state and, 14–15; criticism of, 137–38; disputes and violence, 140, 146; dissent and, 139–40, 144; Islam, 164; Judaism, 164; Mormon, 144; Presbyterian, 140–41, 143, 165; Protestant, 139, 164, 166, 169–70; public, 167, 169–70; Puritan, 40, 138; Quaker, 64, 138, 167, 188; slavery and, 35, 169; taxation and, 139, 146–47; unity and, 165. *See also* separation of church and state
religious freedom, 78, 137–38, 142–47, 168–69; absence of national church, 26–27, 166; and support of the war, 140–41, 144, 146
Religious Right, 170
replacement theory. *See* population transfer and removal
representation: in government, 125, 129, 131–32, 153, 215; taxation and, 37; three-fifth clause, 75, 154; virtual, 103
republican government, 28–29, 57, 120, 130; establishment of, 7, 26, 102, 106; principals of, 13, 108, 143, 198
respiratory illness, 180n3
Revolutionary War, 210, 214–15; beginnings of, 65, 103, 131, 195, 213; civilian casualties of, 175, 186–87; experience of, 184–87, 191; French involvement in, 231; infectious disease and, 175–76, 189, 215; military casualties of, 220; property and, 33; rebellious nature of, 101–2, 107, 123, 197, 211; slavery and, 33, 54–56, 67, 69, 214; and support of dissenters, 141, 144, 146; violence and terror of, 184–85, 187, 189–90, 215. *See also* Battles
Revolution of 1800, 30

Revolution Settlement, 195
Revue Française d'Études Américaines, 237
Reynolds v. United States, 144
Richmond, 54, 242
right, the (conservatives), 18, 170, 183, 212, 227; challenges to democracy and, 223; interpretation of the Revolution and, 3–4, 7, 14, 216; tradcons and, 14
rights, 17–18; of Black Americans, 18, 34, 48, 87, 113; citizenship, 39, 52, 146, 156–58, 196; civil, 75, 158, 252, 254; of colonists, 49–51, 101–2, 105, 124, 127; equal, 35–36, 52, 105, 113, 141; government benefit, 143; immigrant, 49, 54, 58; legal, 146; marriage, 139, 141–42, 174; of Native Americans, 39, 87, 113, 156; property, 33, 183–84, 188, 191–92; religious, 139–41, 146, 147, 169; speech, 169; voting, 36–37, 39, 75, 87, 156; of women, 125, 156, 158, 174, 200–201. *See also* natural rights
Roach, Beth, 93
Rodney, Caesar, 131
Roosevelt, Franklin D., 47, 123
Roosevelt, Theodore, 94
Royal Exchange, 115
rule of law, 16, 123, 131, 133
Rush, Benjamin, 53, 64–65, 222
Russell, Zac, 90, 92
Russian Revolution, 18, 234

Sacajawea, 85, 87
Saint-Domingue. *See* Haiti
Salem witch trials, 138
Saratoga, Battle of, 141, 222
Savannah, 186–87
Scalia, Antonin, 145
Schmidt, Jalane, 90
Schuyler, Philip, 179
science, 24–25
Scotland, 41. *See also* British Empire
Seabury, Samuel, 165
Second Amendment, 159, 183, 197
Second Continental Congress, 129–32, 222–23, 226–27
Second Militia Act, 197, 200
Second World War, 232, 252
Secrets d'histoire, 233
segregation, 75, 87, 170
self-improvement, 19, 24–25
self-perception, national, 16
Sellar, W. C., 2
semiquincentennial (2026): celebration of, 5, 224; in France, 238; reflection of, 150, 224, 228, 249, 253–55
Senate, 153, 155
Seneca Falls, 254
separation of church and state, 138, 142, 144–47, 166, 169; *Brown v. Board of Education,* 149n34
settler colonialism, 86, 92–93, 216
1776 (film), 226
1776 Commission, 4–5, 9n11
Seven Years' War, 26, 50, 101, 175, 213
shadow government, 129
Shadwell, 23
Sharp, Granville, 53, 63, 65
Shawnee (tribe), 88
Shays's Rebellion, 197
Sheffield Declaration, 36
Shenandoah Valley, 141
Short, William, 29
Shoshone (tribe), 85
Sierra Leone, 38, 41
Simpson, Leanne, 92
Sinatra, Frank, 170
1619 Project, 4, 5, 8n7, 9n11, 212
slavery: abolition of, 36, 39, 52–55, 79–81, 254; "benevolent" slaveholding, 56, 86; criticism of, 34, 41, 53, 64–65, 80; hypocrisy of, 28, 35, 37–42, 51–53; legality and legislation of, 36, 39–41, 50–52, 62–63; manumission law and papers, 54, 56–57, 245–46; paradox of, 20, 74–75, 221; religion and, 35, 169; Thirteenth Amendment and, 75, 157; as a threat to independence, 49, 52, 56, 124–25; Underground Railroad and, 248; University of Virginia and, 76. *See also* enslaved persons; slave trade

slave trade: abolition and legislation against, 36, 52, 54–55, 69; criticism of, 64, 68, 69–70; economic and commercial reliance on, 62–63; peak of, 57, 213; restrictions and taxation of, 50–51, 64
smallpox, 24, 174–75, 177–79
Smith, Elizabeth Quincy, 174
Smith, Margaret Bayard, 27
Smith, Sam, 199
Smith, Samuel Stanhope, 56
Soboul, Albert, 234
social mobility, 18, 20
Solomon, Samantha, 90
Somerset, James, 62–63
Somerset v. Steuart, 41, 62–64
Sons of Liberty, 124, 126
South Carolina, 33–35, 40, 51, 54; citizenship and voting rights in, 37, 39; infectious disease in, 176–77
South Carolina Gazette and Country Journal, 118–19
South Carolina Protest Against Slavery, A (Laurens), 41
sovereignty, 17, 92, 96, 107, 108; popular, 16, 104, 106
Spirit of '76, 15, 30
Stamp Act, 125–28, 213
Stamp Act Congress, 126–28
state constitutions, 102, 106, 131; abolition and, 54; bill of rights in, 36; democratic elements of, 106, 216; prohibitions of, 146–47; rewriting of, 15, 151
Statute for Religious Freedom, 144
St. Clair, Arthur, 197–98
Steuart, Charles, 62–63
Stiles, Ezra, 165
Stuart, John, 66–67
suffrage. *See* voting
Sugar Act, 50
Sullivan, Teresa, 77
Summary View of the Rights of British America, A (Jefferson), 25, 51–52, 64
Summer of Hate, 72, 81
Supreme Court: *Brown v. Board of Education,* 149n34; *Chisolm v. Georgia,* 155; *Dred Scott v. Sanford,* 63; *New York State Rifle & Pistol Association, Inc. v. Bruen,* 159; religion and, 145–47, 169; *Reynolds v. United States,* 144; and use of racial data in admissions decisions, 96
suspicion of power, 17

tall ships, 1, 251–52
taxation, 103, 105, 129–30; authority and legality of, 123–24, 152, 215–16; without consent, 63, 101; relief from, 37; religion and, 139, 140–42, 146–47; slave trade and, 51, 64; Stamp Act, 125–28, 213
Tea Act, 127–28
technology, 14, 16, 24–25
tensions, 114, 119, 125–27, 130–31, 139; international, 2, 210, 236; race, class, and ethnic, 124
1066 and All That (Sellar and Yeatman), 2
Thibaud, Clément, 237
thirteen colonies, 6, 62, 123–24
Thirteenth Amendment, 75, 157
Thomas, Clarence, 145–46, 149n34, 159
Thomas Jefferson Foundation, 47, 241, 257
three-fifths clause (compromise), 39, 40, 75, 154
Ticonderoga, 179
Tidewater fevers, 177
Title 10, 200
Toryism, 24, 167, 214
Townshend Acts, 126–27
trade, 123, 187, 213, 215. *See also* slave trade
transition of power, 20, 122–23, 131–33, 156
trauma: generational, 93; theory, 89, 93; wartime, 55, 191
treason, 216
Treaty of Paris, 35, 152, 243
Treaty of Tripoli, 168
Trenchard, John, 195
tribes, Native American: Cheroenhaka-Nottoway, 92; Cherokee, 92; Chickahominy, 92; Delaware, 88; Eastern Chickahominy, 92; Lenape, 86, 88, 92; Mattaponi, 92; Miami, 88; Mingo, 88; Monacan, 74, 92, 95–96; Nansemond, 92;

tribes (*continued*)
Nottoway, 92; Occaneechi-Saponi, 92; Ojibwe, 88; Ottawa, 86, 88; Pamunkey, 92; Rappahannock, 92; Shawnee, 88; Shoshone, 85; Upper Mattaponi, 92; Wampanoag Confederation, 88; Wyandot, 88
Truman, Harry, 47
Trump, Donald J., 4–5, 77, 122, 133, 253
Tucker, St. John, 80
Turgot, Anne-Robert-Jacques, 231
typhoid fever, 175
typhus, 178
Tyrannicide, 39–40
tyranny: British, 118, 132, 141; fight against, 221; government overreach and, 143, 210–11; slavery and, 28, 50–51, 69, 81; of a standing army, 195

Uncle Tom's Cabin (Stowe), 158
Underground Railroad, 248
union of states, 39, 107, 152–53, 157
United States Semiquincentennial Commission, 5
unity: damage to, 253–54; national, 224–25, 227–28; political, 163–64, 171; through religion, 167–68, 170; during the Revolution, 68, 127, 211, 214
University of Virginia, 85–87, 92; Black students and staff, 78–79, 82; Clark statue, 85–87, 89, 91–92, 94–95; *Memorial to Enslaved Laborers*, 76, 78; slavery and, 76, 78, 81; white supremacist rallies and, 73–74
unrest, current, 217; distrust of government and, 17; hypocrisy and, 34; instability and, 209–10, 224, 228; international tension and, 2, 209–10; partisanship and, 2, 4, 146, 209–10; racism and, 58; violence and, 210, 227
Upper Mattaponi (tribe), 92
utopianism, 15, 18, 19–20, 21, 28

Valley Forge, 47
Vietnam War, 3, 225, 252
Vincennes (film), 94
Vincennes (Indiana), 86, 88
violence, colonial, 120, 133; armed resistance and, 49, 114; militia and, 198–99; mob, 122–24, 132; racial, 140; religious, 140; slave revolts and, 130
Virginia: anti-slave-trade legislation, 51–52, 55–56, 64; Bacon's Rebellion, 49; Culpeper Minutemen, 138; immigration and, 56–57; manumission law and, 56–57; Native American tribes of, 90, 95; religion and, 139, 142, 144, 145; resistance to Parliament in, 125–26; slavery and, 4, 50, 51–52, 54–57, 66; suffrage laws and, 37
Virginia Gazette, 117, 141
voting, 26, 123, 156; rights, 36–37, 39, 75, 87, 156
Vowles, John, 246

Waccamaw Neck, 39
Walker, Quock, 40
Wallace, Caleb, 141
Wall Street Journal, 22n1
Walnut Hills, 245
Wampanoag Confederation, 88
War of 1812, 198
War of Independence. *See* Revolutionary War
Washington, George: command of Continental Army, 65, 129, 176, 179–80; Constitutional Convention and, 153; fears and apprehensions of, 221; land ownership and settlement, 50, 53; modern opinion of, 5, 216; presidency of, 197; retirement of, 123; revolutionary proclamations of, 17; and slave ownership, 49–50, 53, 56, 66, 81; and soldiers and militias, 194, 197, 214. *See also* Mount Vernon
Washington Post, 122
Watergate, 3, 252
wealth: gap, 75, 213; from slavery, 50, 63, 213, 217
Wedderburn, Alexander, 115

Wesley, John, 167
West Indies, 63
Westminster, 37, 51, 112, 115, 119
"What to the Slave Is the Fourth of July?" (Douglass), 75
Wheatley, Phillis, 35–36; "Liberty and Peace," 35
Whigs, 103, 177–78
Whiskey Rebels, 197
White House Task Force on Celebrating America's 250th Anniversary ("Task Force 250"), 5
white supremacy, 41, 72–74, 86–87, 89, 91. *See also* racism
whitewashing history, 93–94, 142
Wilkinson, Eliza, 187
William & Mary, 23, 25
Williams, Jennifer, 241–42, 244–47
Williams, Roger, 138–39
Williamsburg, 25, 65, 116, 242
Wilson, Barbara Brown, 90
Winthrop, John, 40
women: exclusion of, 54, 113; infectious disease and, 175, 179; labor of, 189; marriage and, 174; military employment of, 179, 189, 200; rights of, 125, 156, 158, 174, 200–201; violence against, 187, 189
Wood, Gordon, 8n7
Wood, Karenne, 90–91
World War I, 2
World War II, 232, 252
Wuthnow, Robert, 164
Wyandot (tribe), 88
Wythe, George, 25, 54

Yale University, 94
Yeatman, R. J., 2
yellow fever, 175–76
Yorktown, 54, 176, 242

Zenger Club, 41

The Revolutionary Age

The American Revolution on Trial: A New Nation Confronts the Burden of Independence
T. H. Breen

The Global Age of Revolutions: A History from 1650 to Today
Bryan A. Banks and Cindy Ermus, editors

Barbary Entanglements: Realizing American Independence on the World Stage
John M. Chamberlin

The Course of Human Events: The Declaration of Independence and the Historical Origins of the United States
Steven Sarson

Napoleon in America: Bonaparte and the Rhetoric of US Empire
Mark F. Ehlers

Before Manifest Destiny: The Contested Expansion of the Early United States
Nicholas G. DiPucchio

Revolutionary Diplomacy: Spanish Connections and the Birth of the United States
Thomas E. Chávez

Declarations of Independence: Indigenous Resilience, Colonial Rivalries, and the Cost of Revolution
Christopher R. Pearl

Dishonored Americans: The Political Death of Loyalists in Revolutionary America
Timothy Compeau

The American Liberty Pole: Popular Politics and the Struggle for Democracy in the Early Republic
Shira Lurie

European Friends of the American Revolution
Andrew J. O'Shaughnessy, John A. Ragosta, and Marie-Jeanne Rossignol, editors

The Tory's Wife: A Woman and Her Family in Revolutionary America
Cynthia A. Kierner

Writing Early America: From Empire to Revolution
Trevor Burnard

Spain and the American Revolution: New Approaches and Perspectives
Gabriel Paquette and Gonzalo M. Quintero Saravia, editors

The American Revolution and the Habsburg Monarchy
Jonathan Singerton

Navigating Neutrality: Early American Governance in the Turbulent Atlantic
Sandra Moats

Ireland and America: Empire, Revolution, and Sovereignty
Patrick Griffin and Francis D. Cogliano, editors